ARCHITECTURE 1970-1980
A DECADE OF CHANGE

ARCHITECTURE 1970-1980

A DECADE OF CHANGE

EDITED BY JEANNE M. DAVERN

DESIGNED BY JAN V. WHITE

ARCHITECTURAL RECORD BOOKS

McGRAW-HILL BOOK COMPANY

New York St. Louis San Francisco Auckland Bogotá Hamburg Johannesburg London Madrid Mexico Montreal New Delhi Panama Paris São Paulo Singapore Sydney Tokyo Toronto

ARCHITECTURAL RECORD BOOKS

Affordable Houses Designed by Architects
Apartments, Townhouses and Condominiums, 2/e
The Architectural Record Book of Vacation Houses, 2/e
Buildings for Commerce and Industry
Buildings for the Arts
Energy-Efficient Buildings
Engineering for Architecture
Great Houses for View Sites, Beach Sites, Sites in the Woods, Meadow
Sites, Small Sites, Sloping Sites, Steep Sites and Flat Sites
Hospitals and Health Care Facilities, 2/e
Houses Architects Design for Themselves
Houses of the West
Institutional Buildings: Architecture for the Controlled Environment
Interior Spaces Designed by Architects
Office Building Design, 2/e
Places for People: Hotels, Motels, Restaurants, Bars, Clubs, Community
Recreation Facilities, Camps, Parks, Plazas, and Playgrounds
Public, Municipal and Community Buildings
Religious Buildings
Recycling Buildings: Renovations, Remodelings, Restorations and Reuses
Techniques of Successful Practice, 2/e
A Treasury of Contemporary Houses

ARCHITECTURAL RECORD SERIES BOOKS

Ayers: *Specifications for Architecture, Engineering and Construction*
Feldman: *Building Design for Maintainability*
Heery: *Time, Cost and Architecture*
Hopf: *Designer's Guide to OSHA*
Portman and Barnett: *The Architect as Developer*
Redstone: *The New Downtowns*

Library of Congress Cataloging in Publication Data

Main entry under title:

Architecture 1970–1980: A decade of change

"Architectural record books."
Includes index.
1. Architecture—Environmental aspects.
2. Architecture—Human factors.   I. Davern, Jeanne M.
II. Architectural record.
NA2542.35.A73   724.9'1   80-11465
ISBN   0-07-002352-2

The editors for this book were *Jeremy Robinson, Patricia Markert* and *Carol Frances.*
The production supervisors were *Elizabeth Dineen* and *Sally Fliess.*
The book was designed by *Jan V. White* with *Anna-Maria Egger.*
It was set in Optima by The Clarinda Company.
Printed and bound by Halliday Lithograph Corporation.
234567890 HDHD 8987654321

Color separations pp IV–V
© 1978 by the AIA Journal,
all rights reserved; used
courtesy of the AIA Journal.
color separations p. 150
courtesy of Bethlehem
Steel.

CONTENTS

1972

1973

1974

1975

1976

1977

1978

1979

PHOTO CREDITS

In 1979, the year I. M. Pei received the Gold Medal of The American Institute of Architects, his John F. Kennedy Library on the Dorchester campus of the University of Massachusetts was completed, 15 years after he was selected by the Kennedy family to design the Library for a site on the Charles River in the heart of Cambridge. Opposition from a coalition of citizen groups to locating such a magnet for tourists as the Library was expected to be on the Cambridge site—and thus, these groups argued, increasing traffic congestion and air pollution—had caused the Library site to be changed to the present site offered by the University of Massachusetts.

If the dream of a citizens' group called the Fargo-Moorhead Heritage and Cultural Bridge Task Force came true, a "cultural bridge" designed by architect Michael Graves (in association with the Fargo firm of Foss Engelstad Foss) would span the Red River of the North and link the cities of Fargo, North Dakota and Moorhead, Minnesota. After a nationwide search, the Task Force commissioned Graves to design their project—a concert hall and television station on the Fargo side, an art museum on the bridge itself and a history museum on the Moorhead side. What Graves has done, critic William Marlin has suggested, "is like a Parisian river quai across a prairie sky" (or "a covered bridge, a bit of old New England showing up"). A contract between the cities of Fargo and Moorhead to build two bridges, one the site of the cultural bridge, one adjacent to a residential area, provoked neighborhood protest expressed in court action and, in Fargo, political and business community opposition to the expenditure of public funds on the project. The original Task Force disbanded, and the building of the bridge itself awaited the outcome of the neighborhood protest. In Moorhead, citizens organized as the Heritage Interpretative Task Force continued to support the history museum which is their side of the scheme.

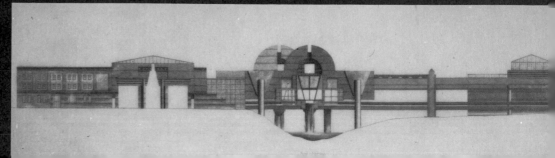

PREFACE

Architecture in the Real World

This is a book about architecture as it was *built* in the 1970s, and about the circumstances in which it was done. It derives largely, though not entirely, from the content of ARCHITECTURAL RECORD in the 1970s. Of some 1500 buildings published from the beginning of the decade through 1979, 132 have been selected for the book (it includes 18 others). They have been selected not as the "best" buildings of the decade, but as significant examples of the diversity of architectural response to a widening range of human problems and concerns as they were being expressed—often vociferously—by an environmentally awakened public.

The book was conceived by the editors of the REC-ORD, who made an initial selection of material to be considered, then invited this former managing editor of the RECORD to take her own trip through the 12,000 or so editorial pages of the decade, make the final selection of buildings to be included and put them into a book which would tell the story of architecture in the 1970s as it was reflected in the pages of the RECORD.

The book derives from the content of the RECORD as both information base and illustration source; and it incorporates excerpts of RECORD articles in an editorial framework intended to let the architecture speak for itself as much as possible. (I have done what I could to help it along.) While the RECORD is the source of information about the buildings selected from its pages, commentary not otherwise attributed is my own.

As a visual clue to the chronology of the architecture shown, the book is organized in ten chapters, one for each publication year of the decade. (This is, of course, a very special kind of "chronology," since the buildings published in any year have been completed at varying intervals before publication, and designed at even more varying intervals.) The final chapter (1979) is the only one in the book for which the material has been selected from current work in architects' offices rather than from the pages of the RECORD, and it consists largely of work in progress rather than completed buildings, offering some clues, perhaps, to architecture in the 1980s. Photographs on the introductory pages of each chapter are sometimes from the RECORD, sometimes not; they are

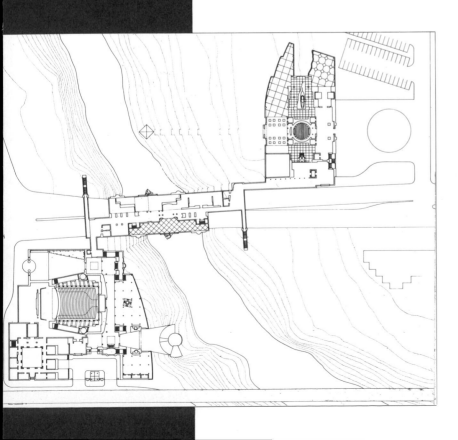

intended as symbols of certain kinds of serious effort that could be discerned in their years.

Editors of the RECORD whose original research, critical judgment in the initial selection of buildings for publication in the magazine, and articles—anonymously excerpted or otherwise used as information base—are represented in the book are: Walter F. Wagner Jr., AIA, Herbert L. Smith Jr. AIA, Robert E. Fischer, Mildred F. Schmertz FAIA, Grace M. Anderson, Barclay F. Gordon, Charles K. Hoyt AIA, William Marlin and Janet Nairn. Former members of the RECORD staff whose RECORD contributions were thus drawn upon are: Gerald Allen, the late William B. Foxhall, Charles E. Hamlin, Robert E. Jensen, Donald-David Logan, Jim Morgan and Elisabeth Kendall Thompson FAIA.

Text and captions for the last two chapters of the book were written by ARCHITECTURAL RECORD Executive Editor Mildred F. Schmertz (Chapter IX, 1978) and Editor Walter F. Wagner, Jr. (Chapter X, 1979).

Architecture is a universe of many worlds. Not only architects but architectural schools, architectural registration boards, architectural consultants, general contractors, developers, producers and suppliers of building materials, clients (public and private), critics and historians: All of these have long been worlds within in the universe of architecture. In the 1970s, it now seems clear, a new world was discovered within that universe: the world of the general public.

When the seventies began, environmental protection was newly established as an area of official national concern, and the potential of the National Environmental Policy Act of 1969 (NEPA) had yet to be tested as an instrument of public policy. Unexpectedly to many, NEPA and the landmark Historic Preservation Act of 1966 were to become cornerstones of effective citizen environmental action throughout the decade.

The first "Earth Day," April 22, 1970, effectively established the public tone of the seventies. The concept of the planet Earth as a "fragile spaceship," with finite resources which must be husbanded and cherished, became probably the most influential public image of the decade. Made vivid in the public mind by the memory of the great photographs of a tiny, visibly finite Earth from the Apollo spaceships of the sixties, it generated a new constituency for conservation. Environmental integrity became, suddenly, everybody's concern. It was the new cause of the young and the new touchstone of politicians.

Another "day," July 4, 1976, the U.S. Bicentennial, generated a great nationwide celebration of American history as community history which had much to do with making preservation a people's cause rather than an elitist cause. In thousands of communities across the country, "heritage" projects cited as part of the national celebration by the U.S. Bicentennial Commission focused public attention on local history and the local heritage from the past, on the part each community and its citizens had played in the history of the nation. The two-year Bicentennial celebration, for which many communities spent years preparing, both stimulated and revealed the degree to which Americans of all ages valued their links with the past.

Many of the great domestic issues of the seventies were to derive from the determination of citizens to bring their environment—from the neighborhood to the planet—under their own control, and from the policies developed in response to that determination by local, state and Federal governments. And the grass-roots political skills honed in the neighborhood battles against urban renewal bulldozers in the sixties gave citizen groups banded together for the environmental causes of the seventies a profound, often decisive, role in the public decision-making process.

As the techniques of the consumer movement began increasingly to be applied to the cause of a more humane environment, architects found themselves increasingly responsible not just to their clients but to the general public for just about every aspect of their buildings — how they should look, where they should be built, and even whether they should be built at all. Architects were increasingly responsible to the public because their clients were. The governments, corporations and institutions which had succeeded the popes, princes and potentates of old as the modern patrons of architecture were subject to a rapidly proliferating variety of public reviews designed to ensure grass-roots citizen participation in the decision-making process.

So architectural concerns became increasingly tied to public concerns and public attitudes. In a sense, the new age of architecture prophesied in the twenties began to be realized in the seventies. Architecture was on the way to becoming a truly social art at last — but people, not machines, were the catalyst.

In this process, the public media came to play an ever more crucial role for which they were ill-prepared. Only a handful have architecture critics; and most cover architecture as fashion or not at all. They are not prepared to deal with architecture as public purpose.

The history and theory of architecture do not exist apart from the world of architecture, they are at the heart of it: worlds within worlds rather than worlds apart. But historians, and most critics, do live in worlds apart from the doing of architecture. They live at the distance they believe will let them discern significant patterns and deduce significant directions. Distancing can enhance vision or distort it; selecting the distance is a consummate art. Whether historians or critics have enhanced or distorted the vision of their contemporaries is often discovered only by a later generation; for their own generation they are, nonetheless, the source of most public awareness of architecture.

Architects doing architecture are always at ground zero. They must respond to now and future needs as they are perceived *now* and in the circumstances that exist *now*. No time for distancing. And unlike painters and sculptors expressing their own visions of reality, architects must apply their creative abilities to expressing the will of a client, for that client's very specific, sometimes conflicting purposes, in the context of complex, often conflicting regulations now devised to pro-

tect not only the public interest, but the more recently asserted right of the public to be part of the process.

To use its own involvement in its own best interests, the public will need to understand far better than it yet does how architecture happens, and especially who is responsible for what in the evolution of the built environment. The stylistic questions which so absorb critics will never be the significant questions for the public. A new breed of investigative architectural reporter is needed, to identify the questions that *should* concern the public and to help search out the answers. Knowledge is needed to illuminate public debate and to inform public action.

Senator Daniel Patrick Moynihan once observed that there is in our time a tendency to yearn for "simplifiers," to shield ourselves from the almost overwhelming complexity of the issues that confront us. What in fact we need, he asserted, is "complexifiers," who can help us to recognize complexity so that we can also recognize the need to deal with its implications in a comprehensive way. Architecture, and the cause of environmental quality, have long suffered from the public inclination to demand simple solutions to complex problems. If the public is to have an effective role in the design of its own environment, it will have to equip itself in many new ways to recognize and work with the complexities of the design process.

As the content of this book attests, architecture has come a long way from its absorption, during the long adolescence of modern architecture, with the single building and the privileged client. The humanistic concerns of so many architects over so many years are more and more being realized in completed buildings; and work in progress holds still further promise. It may be that the next great breakthroughs will have to come from the public sector.

Jeanne M. Davern

Plattsburgh, New York
January 1980

People responding to architecture were to become a more and more familiar sight in the 1970s, as more and more buildings were deliberately designed for public benefit and enjoyment as well as private use and specific function. Here, the roof gardens of the Oakland Museum (pages 12–13) are used, as the architects intended, like a public park. Architects: Kevin Roche John Dinkeloo and Associates.

1970

The facades of office towers had a sculptural look, finding new possibilities of elegance in concrete, or returning to the solidity of granite, and flaring at the base . . . or rippling with bay windows inspired by local tradition, or expressing structure and function by manipulating solids and voids .

Architecture for a new campus alluded to a Victorian heritage both in its use of materials and in details .

Rhythmic facades of a university library derived from disposition of many program elements within the discipline of a design theory based on rotating squares, while rhythms of a dormitory facade derived from disposing L-shaped rooms to create deep recesses between every two rooms, and by angling windows at the corners.

Expo '70 combined technology and tradition to create a lively and evocative site at Osaka for the first world's fair ever held in Asia .

New architectural possibilities for civic design were revealed by a museum built largely underground, with terraced gardens above, to create a new city park .

A sense of community and of domestic scale were sought both in public housing and in private apartments . . . a milestone rehabilitation effort recycled a block of old laboratories and warehouses in Greenwich Village as apartments for artists and their families; and a housing design for Buffalo's waterfront both derived from its topographical context and transformed it .

Design of a new headquarters building for The American Institute of Architects on its landmark site two blocks from the White House in Washington, D.C., was at last approved by the Fine Arts Commission. The approved design, which was to be completed in 1973 (pages 102 – 103), was the work of architects selected by committee in the conventional way after two designs by the winners of a national architectural competition had been rejected by the Commission. The competition-winning design by Mitchell/Giurgola Associates, and a later design by the same firm, would have been 1960s landmarks a hundred years from now. The design by The Architects Collaborative which was approved and built was conceived as a "background" building to frame the historic Octagon House and garden.

The facades of office towers had a sculptural look, finding new possibilities of elegance in concrete, or returning to the solidity of granite, and flaring at the base...

MacMillan-Bloedel Building
Vancouver, British Columbia
Architects: Erickson/Massey and
Francis Donaldson

Poured-in-place concrete made handsome and economical bearing walls for 27-story towers linked by a central structural core of identical height. The size of the openings was carefully calculated to let the wall act as a wall and to permit the use of one sheet of glass, unbroken by mullion or muntin, in each opening. The architect sought the effect "of glass jammed into the concrete directly to bring out the extreme contradiction of character" of the materials. "All detail was avoided," Arthur Erickson said, "to achieve an uncompromising junction between glass and concrete—void and solid."

First National Bank of Chicago, Chicago, Illinois
Architects: C. F. Murphy Associates and
Perkins & Will

A skeletal building that acknowledged its steel structure and its parts was compatible with Chicago's past, but, at 60 stories, it became the tallest building in the Loop, just about twice the height of the older buildings around it; and, along with the completed John Hancock Tower and the Sears Roebuck Building (then in design), it represented a new scale for the city. The sloped design responded to the requirement of providing variable floor areas decreasing in size toward the top.

The office towers shown here suggest the range of architectural interest, continuing as one stream of esthetic exploration throughout the seventies, in developing modes of expression which enrich the facades of buildings. In these buildings, architecture *became* sculpture, as in Ronchamp, Le Corbusier's first sculptural building, which so stunned the architectural world in 1955. There was not yet any such forthright effort to *decorate* facades, nor to borrow details from the Orders, as had begun to appear by the end of the decade. Allusions to earlier styles appeared only as contextual references, as in the windows of the Bank of America, or (perhaps) in the scale and form of the towers of the Knights of Columbus building. The kind of effort represented by these buildings sought to enrich architectural vocabulary while remaining faithful to such basic precepts of modern architecture as clear articulation of function and structure and clear expression of materials. Office towers published in 1970 had, of course, been designed in the sixties— and considering how the design process can be prolonged by the decision-making processes of clients, not always even in the *late* sixties. The glass and metal curtain wall had become the architectural victim of its own success, the darling of speculative builders who valued it as a quick and easy way to get a "modern" building almost out of a catalog, with minimum architectural intervention. A glass and metal curtain wall too often came to mean cheap and ugly. Dating roughly from Lever House (1952) to the Seagram Building (1958), the glass and metal curtain wall had

...or rippling with bay windows inspired by local tradition, or expressing structure and function by manipulating solids and voids

Bank of America World Headquarters
San Francisco, California
Architects: Wurster Bernardi
& Emmons
and Skidmore Owings & Merrill
Consulting Architect: Pietro Belluschi

Dark red polished granite clad a 53-story tower faceted by bay windows and articulated at the top. Early decisions by the architects that the tower should be dark in color and that it should not be "an austere rectangular box" were primary generators of the design. The dark color was intended to diminish the apparent bulk of a very large building and to keep the windows from appearing as "holes" in the facade. The bay window has long been a strong element in San Francisco's cityscape, and the tower's undulating walls offered citizens an easily recognizable link with their architectural heritage.

Knights of Columbus Building
New Haven, Connecticut
Architects: Kevin Roche
John Dinkeloo and Associates

A tower designed to articulate its functions and express its structure and materials with exquisite clarity was also intended to acknowledge its setting, both as an entrance to the city, at the main exit from the Connecticut Turnpike for downtown New Haven, and as a new member of New Haven's rather motley clan of tall structures. They range from smokestacks to Gothic towers, and jut up here and there from a generally low-scaled urban fabric. Circular concrete shafts at the four corners of the 23-story tower carry all services and support the steel and glass structure of the office floors. Elevators are in a central core. Two decisions were basic: that the building be tall and thin, and express its steel structure.

been the focus of serious and intensive architectural exploration. But as the mundane versions proliferated, and as architects mastered the techniques and discovered the limitations of the glass and metal curtain wall, many began to rebel against "designing out of a catalog" and turned increasingly to materials and methods which let them "control the whole building," not just the way the pieces were put together. The impulse toward individuality which had been characteristic of American architecture at least since the Industrial Revo-lution had triumphed over the purist dogmas of the International Style. The next architectural interest in a "pure" esthetic would derive— again characteristically in American architecture—from technological developments which, by the mid-seventies, made it possible to build sheer glass towers detailed so their structure seemed almost to disappear.

Architecture for a new campus alluded
to a Victorian heritage both in
its use of material and in its details

New campus for Skidmore College
Saratoga Springs, New York
Architects: Ford Powell & Carson
Planning Consultant: S.B. Zisman

The architectural character of the new Skidmore
campus was established by popular demand—
students, faculty, and administration, all invited
to participate in the planning process, wanted the
new campus to have something of the architectural flavor of the Victorian era buildings they
were leaving behind. The special brick which
faces all the new buildings, and many details,
adapted or simply borrowed, were a response to
this client requirement and to the general context
of the community.

A college president who sees architecture as a
cultural resource, Skidmore's Joseph Pala-
mountain, and a Texas architect for whom local
and regional cultural traditions have always
been a prime architectural resource, O'Neil
Ford, led a collaborative effort which produced a new campus in the spirit of the old,
but designed to be adaptable to changing uses
and responsive to environmental circumstances. Skidmore is a private women's college
in the small upstate New York town of Saratoga Springs, whose turn-of-the-century hey-

day as summer resort for the nobility of thoroughbred racing was recalled for later generations in Edna Ferber's *Saratoga Trunk*. It is still the capital of thoroughbred racing every August, but is now also the year-round home of the New York State Center for the Performing Arts. The old Skidmore campus was a collection of more than 80 buildings near the center of town, mainly converted mansions, studios, summer hotels, and carriage houses dating from the grand old days, and it was inadequate to house a college that wanted to utilize the latest in educational equipment and which needed space for expansion. Renovation had seemed the only option until the college was presented with a 1000-acre site, Woodlawn Park, once a private estate and more recently a public park. The plan for the new campus concentrated all the new buildings in what is essentially one complex of buildings, designed to be linked by a system of covered walkways and arcades (a stormy weather boon with extra benefits where heavy winter snows are common). The rest of the site, rich in a variety of natural areas, was left for recreation and refuge. "Blending one century with another," as the March 1970 article put it, 19th-century bay windows were adapted from those common to the townhouses of the old campus, squared off and rendered with modern attention to detail. Elsewhere, the oculus as window form appears unchanged, while the gently arched wide span windows of stately industrial buildings are transformed into sheltering arcades.

Rhythmic facade of a university library derived from disposition of many program elements within the discipline of a design theory based on rotating squares, while...

Core and Research Laboratory Library
Northwestern University, Miller Campus
Evanston, Illinois
Architects: Skidmore Owings & Merrill

A total reassessment of the functions of a university library as a "user-directed structure" was the basis for a design which broke from the tower-and-podium solution so frequently adopted for

major campus libraries in the sixties. Walter A. Netsch, SOM partner in charge of design, used the geometries of his then-developing Field Theory to articulate programmatic forms in a way that maximized "edge," as Netsch himself put it, "to give daylight to as many individual readers as possible, and to give this immense library an overall reader scale as collection and as object in the environment."

When they built on existing campuses, architects were working to relate new buildings to their older neighbors so that they became parts of a whole, not discrete "objects." The enormous burst of college building activity in the sixties, continuing as the seventies began, offered rich opportunities for exploring urbanistic relationships, which, by the time the seventies were drawing to a close, were being translated into urbanistic architecture in many U.S. towns and cities. A major concern was breaking down the scale of new buildings, whose programs fre-

quently required them to be very much larger than their older neighbors, so that new did not overwhelm old by sheer size. Buildings like the two on these pages were organizing functional spaces inside so they could become visible as exterior components of facades designed to be seen as the sum of a number of parts rather than as monolithic walls. At Northwestern, the new library required net interior space of 329,941 square feet to accommodate a "core library" of 50,000 volumes and a research collection of 1.2 million volumes. "Netsch

sought a design solution," the RECORD reported, "which would minimize the apparent bulk of this huge structure to bring it into scale with the older Deering library to which it is attached and with other adjacent campus buildings." Netsch had described his basic solution as follows: "Sheltering and enclosing a broad plaza are three levels of three research towers, the octagonal entrance lantern' and Deering Library. Beneath the plaza, a single area of over 90,000 square feet has been devoted to cataloguing, reference, bibliography, periodicals,

...rhythms of a dormitory facade derived from disposing L-shaped rooms to create deep recesses between every two rooms, and by angling windows at the corners

Residence Hall, University of New Hampshire
Durham, New Hampshire
Architects: Ulrich Franzen and Associates

Concern with how students would use this building prompted the architect to propose reducing ground-level common areas called for in the original program and spending the savings on larger student rooms served by a communal study-

lounge for each 12 rooms. Larger room size allowed a plan for double rooms which gave each occupant a nook, with window, desk and bed, for some sense of privacy. Study-lounges were placed in different locations on each floor to suggest an identity for each. Relocating study-lounges from floor to floor also made it possible occasionally to express them as "bridges" over the deep recessions of the facade.

technical services, data processing, receiving new materials and administration. This space forms the main level and acts as a transitional base, physically as it connects to Deering Library, and esthetically as it connects to the main north-south campus walk. . . . The first level above the plaza contains those special group reader environments that logically participate on the plaza—the core library, the reserve collection, an assembly room, the poetry and audio-visual spaces and the student and coffee lounges. Reached by a separate stair

from the entry lantern, each of these spaces can function independently of other library activities."

Social organization and shaping of interior spaces give Franzen's dormitory its visual character and its domestic scale. It is organized as three separate but repetitive units, one high-rise and two low-rise, suggesting the general and flexible ways the coed dormitory for 450 students can separate men and women. The fat L-shape of the double rooms made it possible not only to provide a private nook for each

student, but to create the deep facade recessions. Windows in the recesses look straight out, but windows along the outside facade are turned at an angle, both slightly changing the outlook from within and creating striking visual forms on the exterior. On a restricted budget, the structure was kept as simple as possible; concrete frame with evenly spaced columns, and beams and slabs poured integrally on site. Exterior cavity walls are red brick with block backup.

United States Pavilion
Architects: Lewis Davis, Samuel Brody and Alan Schwartzman

A single-walled, air-supported structure designed for the space within was made of translucent vinyl-coated fiberglass and had a saucer-shaped floor lined with *Mylar* so it became "a shimmering silver sea, in which the exhibits appeared to float." Pavilion and exhibition were conceived from the beginning as a single entity by an exhibition design team whose principals were, besides the architects, graphic designers Ivan Chermayeff, Thomas H. Geismar, and Rudoph De Harak. David Geiger and Horst Berger were structural engineers; M. Paul Friedberg Associates were the landscape architects. It was Expo's most popular spot.

Expo '70 combined technology and tradition to create a lively and evocative site at Osaka for the first World's Fair ever held in Asia

Takara Beautilon Pavilion
Architect: Noriaki Kurokawa

Stainless steel capsules inserted in an endlessly expansible system of clusters of steel pipe, strengthened at corners by steel webs, were an example of Japanese avantgarde experimentation with the idea of capsules as a future home for man.

Sumitomo Pavilion
Architect: Sachio Otani

Nine elevated, steel-framed discs contained exhibits or provided views of the Pair. The discs and their supports were considered by their architect to be prototypes for the city of the future.

Canadian Pavilion
Architects: Erickson/Massey

Four A-frame structures were framed in wood, sheathed in mirror, and dressed with five giant revolving parasols of multicolored plastic (designed by painter Gordon Smith).

A world's fair is always a major architectural occasion, inviting the kind of innovation and symbolism in design that too frequently are inhibited by the constraints of the real world. Intimations for the future of the human habitat are always sought and often result from the creative competition among the world's designers which a world's fair sets up. The first world's fair ever held in Asia was "alive with the vitality, energy and humor of the Japanese people, the strength of their artistic traditions and the apparent durability of their faith in

technology," the RECORD reported. "As such, Expo '70 is a triumph for Japan's architects and artists, who turn out to be very good indeed at doing fairs, because they are skilled in the creation of the physical symbols which make a fair." And it was noted that a strong inspiration for the designers of this Fair, including those from the West, was Japan's rich decorative arts tradition. A spectacular example was to be seen in the Canadian pavilion (above), where designers created the apotheosis of the Japanese parasol in five rings ("spinners") of multicolored transparent plastic which slowly revolved at the center of a mirror-sheathed pavilion. The site of the Fair was a broad plain adjacent to the major industrial center of Osaka. The master plan by architect Kenzo Tange created a "living city" for a daytime population of 400,000. Running north-south across the site was a Theme Pavilion (not shown) conceived as "the ordering and harmonizing spine or trunk" of this city, with a multilevel circulation system that included a monorail and moving sidewalks connecting to a cluster of Japanese pavilions on one side and international pavilions on the other. Envisioned by Tange as the core of a real city that might eventually grow up on the Expo site, the Theme Pavilion was covered by a steel space frame, protected by an inflated plastic roof, and supported by six widely spaced columns. Beneath the space frame, "Festival Plaza" served as a great central agora for Expo, in "one of the most powerful and compelling spaces ever created." But the hit of the Fair was the U.S. Pavilion, designed as exhibit.

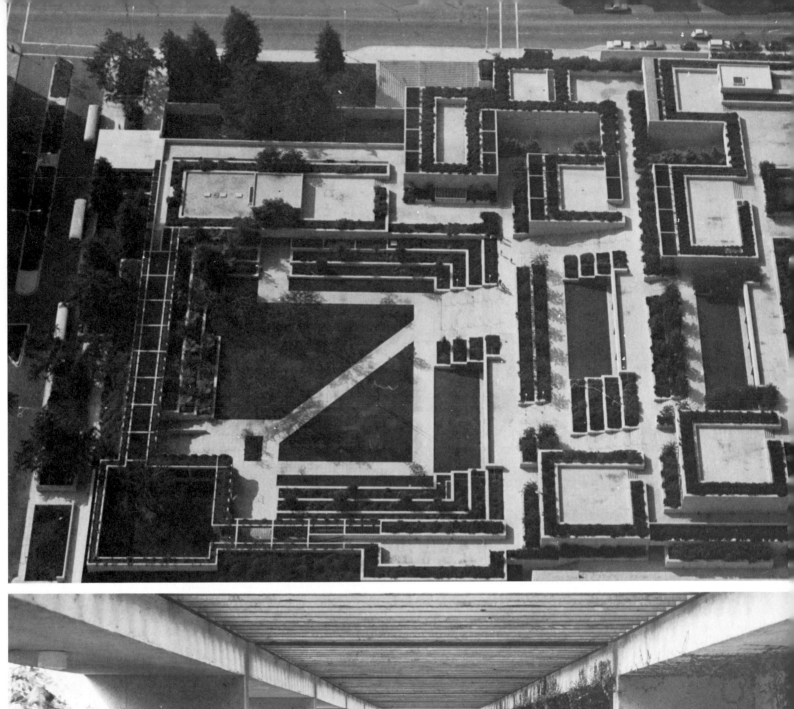

New architectural possibilities for civic design
were revealed by this museum, built largely underground,
with terraced gardens above, to create a new city park

Oakland Museum
Oakland, California
Architects: Kevin Roche
John Dinkeloo and Associates.
Landscape Architect: Dan Kiley

What the city of Oakland asked for was three new buildings on a four-block site to house the collections of the city's existing museums of art, his-tory, and natural science. What it got was a complex of three interrelated museums tucked under terraces and opening onto gardens so that the site became a green oasis in a city starved for parks. The way this happened is an object lesson in the design of civic architecture, and an example of how architects can help clients get what they really need.

The architectural process began with an inten-sive study of the whole Oakland area, not be-cause the client had requested the study, but because the architects felt they needed it as a basis for design. "If the city is to have a sense of order," Roche said, "a building must be part of an overall composition." But the city had no overall plan: a 1915 city plan by city planner Werner Hageman proposing a park system had never been carried out; and a 1947 master plan had long been obsolete. The Roche study produced a new plan for the city, derived in part from the Hageman plan, and inspired the concept of a design for the museum which would let it double as green space, with the possibility of becoming one element of a new greenway system. Architect Kevin Roche was convinced from the beginning, the RECORD reported, that the collections of Oakland's three museums belonged in one place: "After a careful analysis of Oakland's actual and po-tential urban design structure, Roche also de-cided that an urban park was urgently needed on the site as the first link in a chain of integrat-ed work and leisure facilities designed to give order and coherence to the city. Since Roche believes museums and parks belong together, the solution then became obvious to him—a three-part underground terraced structure with a park on top." This concept, and the design process from which it derived, were a vintage example of the urbanistic approach to archi-tecture which became a major thrust of the seventies. Architects were helping clients to see their buildings as part of urban fabric, to want civic architecture.

By the end of the sixties, housing built for rental had come to comprise nearly half the new housing units built each year in the U.S.—a big change from the post-World War II years when single-family houses built for owner occupancy comprised 80 to 90 per cent of all new housing construction. In 1970, the 15th annual RECORD HOUSES inaugurated a special section on "Apartments of the Year" to recognize the growing importance of apartments as a housing type and to encourage quality in their design. Two of the eight low-rise multi-

family housing complexes selected for that issue are shown on these pages—one a public housing project near Detroit, the other a cluster of condominium apartments for a ski and summer resort high in the Rockies. They exemplify in housing the tendency, already noted in other building types, to break down the scale of buildings into humanly recognizable parts, as well as the additional concern in the design of housing—frequently visible by the early seventies—with planning sites for a sense of neighborhood or community. Multi-family

housing was becoming another testing ground for the developing urbanistic thrust of architecture in the 1970s.

And, as the public housing project for the elderly shown here suggests, public housing was in the process of becoming something other than the project stereotype—one or more identical brick buildings standing isolated on a site adorned only by "keep off the grass" signs (often more visible than the grass). The small number of units in this project, the domestic scale of the buildings, the cedar-shingled exte-

A sense of community and of domestic scale were sought both in public housing and in private apartments...

Public Housing for the Elderly
Wayne, Michigan
Architects: William Kessler and Associates

These buildings were one of three groups built on contiguous sites to provide 36 nearly identical one-bedroom apartments. Most of the units were to be ground-level, but a few split-level units were wanted: and the architect used this difference to create variety in roof heights by intermingling the one- and two-story units. He further enlivened the visual character by siting units in an informal, staggered plan.

Snowmass Villas
Snowmass at Aspen, Colorado
Architects: Ian MacKinlay and Henrik Bull

A system of "opposing" roofs gave this 28-unit condominium project its visual character and solved a variety of functional problems. Roof planes were "opposed" to let heavy snows slide off without buildup at valleys or chimneys, and to avoid snow "creep" and dripping as well as overload. The roof plan also served to protect entrances and decks. Angled planes allow decks to receive sun in winter, shade in summer.

riors, the amenity of sitting terraces for each unit, and the character of the site planning and landscaping, create the atmosphere of a well-planned private residential area, which had begun to be not only an acceptable but a necessary objective for public housing. For many years, a public housing project which outwitted budgetary and bureaucratic hurdles to achieve some degree of individuality and amenity was in danger of official or taxpayer criticism as "extravagant" (within a stringent budget, but "you could do it cheaper"). Major

shifts in public attitudes began to occur in the mid-sixties, stimulated both by increasing problems with management of large-scale projects and by increasingly vociferous community objection to construction of such projects, with their growing history of crime and vandalism, in the midst of residential neighborhoods. One result was the concept of much smaller public housing projects conceived as parts of a neighborhood rather than as enclaves set apart. Another was that housing authorities began to see architecture as an ally in making

their projects acceptable to the communities in which they were built. The fear of having public housing look too good had been superseded by the fear of having it look like public housing. So at least some architects in some places were being invited—at last—to make public housing look like a nice place to live. In the private sector, the condominium concept was creating apartment complexes where once enormous resort hotels might have been built. Snowmass became a little village on its meadow site.

...a milestone rehabilitation effort recycled a block
of old laboratories and warehouses in Greenwich Village
into apartments for artists and their families; and a
housing design for Buffalo's waterfront both derived
from its topographical context and transformed it

Buffalo Waterfront Development
Buffalo, New York
Architect: Paul Rudolph

Buildings were designed to follow the configuration of existing piers, which were to be recycled
as a marina. Rudolph described his solution as
essentially "an undulating wall forming a bowl of
space defined by land, water and cliffs."

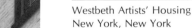

Ezra Stoller © Esto

Westbeth Artists' Housing
New York, New York
Architects: Richard Meier and Associates

The central air court of the former Bell Telephone
Company laboratories, which had been roofed
over and used by Bell as a truck loading area,
became the unifying spatial feature of the reno-
vated complex, connecting at ground-level with
three of the peripheral streets and with a new on-
site park. With the roof removed, this area could
become a courtyard open to the sky, and provide
a focal point for both residential units and
ground-floor commercial spaces. Balconies projecting into the central court were designed to
meet a code requirement for a second means of
egress from apartments.

As it became clear in the early sixties that the
urban renewal process was proving to be a
good deal less than adequate to the task of re-
newing communities and stimulating provision
of suitable housing for those who needed it,
new approaches were sought in both public
and private sectors. The $10-million Westbeth
project was made possible by a combination of
private initiative and public financing which
derived from a new Federal subsidy program—
221(d)3—established in 1968 to encourage
nonprofit sponsorship of middle-income housing. The J. D. Kaplan Fund and the National
Endowment for the Arts identified the site as
suitable for a large-scale living and working
complex for artists, then provided seed money
grants and interim financing of $750,000 to
launch the rehabilitation process as a nonprofit
venture eligible for 221(d)3 funding. The process and the result were described in the RECORD
as "a clue to improving our cities" and "a gen-
erative experiment in both the financing and
physical reclamation problems which occur in
rehabilitating an existing structure for residential use." At a time when the creative potential
of rehabilitation for community revitalization
was only beginning to be understood, Westbeth became an architectural landmark.
Rudolph's housing for the Buffalo waterfront
(finished units shown on page 64) was commissioned by the New York State Urban
Development Corporation, one of a cluster of
innovative state construction authorities
created by New York State in the sixties.
Financing problems developed in the state's
budget crisis, but frontiers had been opened.

A museum especially designed to educate the young to their heritage seemed to succeed in its intent of presenting museum-going and getting acquainted with history as among the pleasures of life rather than as formidable duties. Ohio Historical Museum, Columbus, Ohio; Ireland Associates, Architects.

In Chicago, the long battle to preserve Louis Sullivan's Stock Exchange was finally lost, and the building came down. In Philadelphia, Mitchell/Giurgola's design for a new 21-story Penn Mutual Building incorporated the four-story facade of an existing 19th-century Egyptian Revival building (John Haviland, Architect) into the new building by making it part of the lobby entrance. The site is across Washington Square from Independence Hall.

1971

The Miesian esthetic was very much alive, in the work of gifted disciples, and in one last great work by the master himself.

Another modern master used sun and shadow to modulate the rhythms of a precast concrete facade . . . and old ideas were combined with new to create a modern "bazaar" for shopping.

Modern architecture appropriate to its purpose, and civil in scale, massing and materials, took its place among buildings of earlier eras.

New opportunities for architecture were created by new kinds of clients, none more notable than New York's State University Construction Fund.

Out of fashion with critics, monuments continued to be designed for human purposes that transcended social or functional goals—memorials like the LBJ Library . . . a government center shaped by clear expression of spatial organization to read both as monument and as neighbor to older buildings on a small-town street . . . a civic and cultural center shaped by citizen participation in the design process, and by climate and regional traditions . . . a public museum designed as one with its two-acre site to create an oasis on a busy campus, a research and educational facility made into a community resource . . . a cathedral, the first to base its design on the new liturgy of the Catholic Church, that, like cathedrals of old, made a strong structural concept into symbol as well as structure, "an engineering form as an expression of the modern age" . . . a library for a Benedictine monastery, Aalto's second building in the U.S., that on one side celebrated the Abbey and its site far above a quiet valley, and on the other appeared among its monastic neighbors at smaller scale, only its top level visible.

Preservation and conservation were still generally thought of as separate causes, and neither was yet much related in the public mind to the economics or politics of an age of shrinking resources, but architects were increasingly involved in restoration of historic buildings, like Adler & Sullivan's Auditorium Theater in Chicago . . . in combining old and new to meet today's needs, as in the State Bar Association complex in Albany, New York . . . and in recycling of old buildings for new uses, historic character preserved by a combination of restoration and renovation, like the Old Patent Office in Washington, D.C., which was made into two museums .

The Miesian esthetic was very much alive, in the work of gifted disciples, and in one last great work by the master himself

McCormick-Place-on-the-Lake
Chicago, Illinois
Architects: C. F. Murphy Associates

A convention center initially inspired by a Mies concept which was never realized was rebuilt in an even more Miesian image after it was destroyed by fire in 1967. A great steel truss roof covered two glass-enclosed buildings set on a platform and separated by a pedestrian and vehicular mall. One building contained a 302,000-square-foot exhibition area, the other a 4451-seat theater flanked by restaurants and meeting rooms.

Toronto Dominion Centre, Toronto, Ontario
Consultant: Ludwig Mies van der Rohe
Architects and Engineers: John B. Parkin Associates and Bregman & Hamman

Twin towers whose elegant detailing closely resembled the Seagram Building provided 3.1 million square feet of office space (Seagram had 850,000) and put Toronto Dominion Bank's headquarters branch (22,500 square feet) in a separate single-story clear-span building. A shopping concourse was put one level below the plaza and above the parking area.

Mies van der Rohe, who died in 1969 at 83, devoted his architectural life to refining an esthetic derived from the concept of architecture as structure, created as a process of design and construction. His works of the fifties and sixties, as the RECORD observed in an article discussing the Toronto Dominion Centre, "differ from one another in only the subtlest ways. Proportions, spatial relationships, the color and texture of chosen materials vary slightly from project to project as architecture's most conservative genius painstakingly adjusted

them, partially in response to programmatic content, but essentially because he believed these elements to be endlessly perfectible in an absolute sense. Mies' Toronto Dominion Centre, the last great work in which he took an active part, is a structural and architectural development of ideas which have matured over four decades, and which were finally crystallized in New York City's Seagram Building (1955–58) and Berlin's New National Gallery (1962–68)." The heritage for architecture from the Miesian tradition would continue, as

suggested by a presentation of current work of C. F. Murphy Associates, including the rebuilt convention center, with one of Mies' most gifted former associates, Gene Summers, as partner in charge of design. "As buildings change in kind, and as technology develops, the work of good architects within the Miesian tradition will change," the RECORD noted, "for that tradition is not a fixed esthetic, but a design process. . . . But they are in no hurry. Like Mies, they refuse to invent a new architecture every Monday morning."

Another modern master used sun and shadow to modulate the rhythms of a precast facade…

IBM Office, Laboratory and Manufacturing Facility
Boca Raton, Florida
Architects: Marcel Breuer and Robert Gatje

Twin office structures flank one of three lakes on a 500-acre site, linked to each other and to manufacturing and materials distribution facilities by a ground-level circulation spine. Laboratories curve around a smaller lake at some remove from other activity. Precast panels 35 feet high and stiffened with sun screens are carried by tree columns to form an aracade at the building's periphery. Powerful visual rhythms are set in motion by sun and shadow on the strongly sculptural repetitive elements of a facade nearly 800 feet long—a virtuoso example of Breuer's characteristically urbane use of concrete.

While the mature work of the masters of modern architecture like Mies, Breuer, and (pages 40–41) Aalto continued to develop concepts each had evolved for himself over the decades, new generations of architects schooled in the precepts of modern architecture were applying these precepts in their own ways. In the U.S., they were strongly influenced by pluralistic cultural traditions, wide diversity of climate, and pragmatic attitudes toward problem-solving that had survived the frontier days to become (and remain) a significant national char-

acteristic. The European masters who emigrated to the U.S. in the thirties and became (or trained) the influential architectural educators of the forties and fifties taught modern architecture in terms of principles, but in his own work each developed a recognizable esthetic which he progessively refined and adhered to throughout his architectural life. So Breuer, working on through the seventies with one or another of his much younger partners, was adapting to new programs and new circumstances of site and climate esthetic concepts

long familiar in his work. Regarding the IBM facility in Boca Raton the RECORD noted, "The precast panels and the sculptured tree columns are among his signatures. The 'Y' plan, with its potential for growth in three directions, can be traced in slightly varying form from UNESCO (or earlier) through the IBM facility in La Gaude, France (1961) to the new headquarters for HUD in Washington, D.C. (1969)." Suave and elegant manipulation of precast concrete components, and conscious anticipation of the play of sun and shadow in creating the visual

...and old ideas were combined with new to create a modern bazaar for shopping

The Bazaar at Village Green
Heritage Village
Southbury, Connecticut
Architects: Callister & Payne

A 19th-century system of heavy timber construction created an interior in the 20th-century Miesian tradition of "universal space" for a shopping ambience that recalled the ancient concept of a bazaar. The interior was enriched and enlivened by its functional use and users. Varied merchandise and signage of some 20 small shops on four levels (provided by a split-level ground floor and two mezzanines) of a 420-foot-long building, and shoppers moving through it, filled the space with vibrant color, form, and activity. Shops were grouped by specialty in five sections identified by boldly lettered cubes hung from rafters; maps showed locations within sections.

rhythms of facades were equally familiar characteristics of Breuer's work.

An architect of another generation, Warren Callister, created in Heritage Village Bazaar a "universal space" (Mies) and let it become "what it wanted to be" (as still another master, the late Louis Kahn, would have it) as a contemporary version of an ancient bazaar. There were intimations, at least, of that new guru of the sixties and seventies, Robert Venturi (Complexity and Contradiction in Architecture), in an ambience of which it could be said:

"One of the most elusive charms of the building is the pleasant sense of confusion, of being overwhelmed with choice of things to see, samples to nibble, and crannies to explore." With this building, Callister was adding to a retirement community for which he had been the architect from its inception. Heritage Village had been notable for an architectural character derived from adapting familiar New England forms and materials in contemporary terms, and the exterior of the Bazaar was in the same spirit. Within, the exposed heavy timber

structure, right out of the 19th century, was frankly intended to invoke memories of the past. As the environmental conservation and historic preservation movements began to build on their landmark legislative charters won in the sixties, and as the consumer movement began to equip more and more segments of the public to express their convictions effectively, architecture which related perceptively to its surroundings, whether rural or urban, was more and more encouraged by clients more and more subject to public review.

Ezra Stoller © ESTO

Modern architecture appropriate to its purpose, and civil in scale, massing and materials, took its place among buildings of earlier eras

Athletics Facility, The Phillips Exeter Academy
Exeter, New Hampshire
Architects: Kallmann & McKinnell

Unlike most, this athletic facility was not expressed as a volume or a series of volumes, but as a structural system and a forceful circulation network. A multilevel central spine with a continuous skylight provides separate circulation for athletes and visitors, as well as views of all the activities—swimming, skating, basketball, squash and gymnastics—which are continually going

on. The roof of the spine is framed with precast concrete struts which act as counterforces to steel trusses supporting the roofs of gym, pool, and rinks. The exterior truss system, which rests on concrete girders supported by paired columns on opposite sides of the spine, makes possible interiors free of visual distraction. Outside, columns of weathering steel are held away from walls, to avoid staining them. A ramped entrance for use by students and faculty faces the campus; a separate entrance for public use faces the town.

Kittredge Dormitories, St. Paul's School
Concord, New Hampshire
Architect: Edward Larrabee Barnes

A community of students, faculty, and administrators was created by a design concept which put three one-story dormitories and three three-story townhouses on either side of a one-level circulation spine—two dormitories and a townhouse on one side offset one dormitory and two townhouses on the other, so views are preserved for all. Upper-level apartments are reached from the circulation spine by enclosed stairs for each townhouse; with all circulation cut off above the first floor, apartments have maximum privacy. The complex is sheathed in red brick and roofed with copper batten like its Georgian and Victorian neighbors, and the modest scale of its individual elements is another neighborly quality. Spaces between elements were made into brick-paved landscaped courtyards defined by low brick walls.

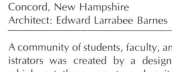

Ezra Stoller © ESTO

Two of the oldest and most prestigious prep schools in the country added modern buildings strictly contemporary in expression to their rural New England campuses. Both were buildings which interpreted their functions at many levels, and which derived their architectural character from expressing these interpretations in elevation as well as plan. Kallmann & McKinnell's athletics facility for Exeter not only provided the physical spaces required for specified activities, but celebrated them by putting them on continuous view for all who

entered the building. "Most gyms conceal their separate functions behind closed doors along endless undifferentiated passages," the RECORD observed, "but at Exeter, the activities are revealed." The structural system which is so dramatically expressed on the exterior was developed out of close collaboration from the earliest stages of design between the structural engineer, William LeMessurier, and the architects. As Barnes interpreted the program at St. Paul's, a dormitory to house 60 lower-school students, housemaster, assistant housemaster,

bachelor teachers, and a matron, became three one-story dormitory units with roofs sloping down to eight feet at the eave-line and three three-story townhouses containing apartments for staff and faculty. Each dormitory unit provides private sleeping cubicles — a lower-school tradition at St. Paul's — for 20 boys, arranged in a tight pattern around the perimeter, and a communal central space, carpeted and skylit, which can be used "for impromptu Indian wrestling and other forms of controlled mayhem." Having designed low-scaled units

with pitched roofs for the youngsters and townhouse units with flat roofs for the adults, Barnes had two kinds of elements of recognizably domestic scale and character to work with. He arranged them along a one-level circulation spine to maximize views to a wooded millpond setting, to develop spaces between for landscaped courts and to create an urbanistic whole that read as a group of residential buildings related in scale to their older neighbors. Dormitories were designed to be a community of students, faculty, and staff.

New opportunities for architecture were created by new kinds of clients, none more notable than New York's State University Construction Fund

Dormitory-Dining Hall Group
State University of New York at Stony Brook
Long Island, New York
Architects: Gruzen and Partners

Two clusters of dormitories partially enclosed wooded courtyards and shared a dining hall. The irregular contours of the buildings and the way a procession of tall narrow elements came down to a paved "street" created the casually urbanistic quality of a small village.

Lecture Hall Center
State University of New York at Stony Brook
Long Island, New York
Architect: William Kessler

Hexagonal modules containing one to three lecture halls were clustered around a hexagonal center hall used for display as well as circulation. Subdivisions of the module, also hexagonal, provided room sizes ranging from 60 to 480 seats, all equipped with multimedia capability.

Agronomy Building
State University of New York College of Agriculture at Cornell University
Ithaca, New York
Architects: Ulrich Franzen and Associates

Cornell is a private university noted for the beauty of its campus, but like many private universities with state university tenants, it had allowed the state schools on its campus (agriculture and home economics) to develop as separate and architecturally very unequal components of the university scene. When Ulrich Franzen was commissioned by the State University Construction Fund to design the Agronomy Building, he was determined to use the opportunity to give the state section of the campus its own symbolic identity. A highly rational disposition of functional elements was the basis for the formal evolution of a strong and dignified building that could appropriately assert the State University presence.

Examples shown here (pages 26–29) are among the many commissioned in what must have been the biggest 10-year university expansion program in the history of the world. It was the responsibility of New York's State University Construction Fund (SUCF), a public benefit corporation proposed by the late Nelson A. Rockefeller, then Governor of New York, and created by the New York State Legislature in 1962. Its mission was to organize and manage the design and construction programs required to accommodate a threefold increase

in full-time students on some 37 campuses of the State University of New York in the decade ending in 1972. During that decade, a $4.5-billion budget, together with its almost total reliance on design by contract with private professionals, made SUCF one of the nation's largest public clients for architecture. It also became a pioneering force in the evolution of effective techniques for organization and management of the design and construction process on a very large scale to produce architecture of very high quality on schedule and with-

in budgets. A 24-page RECORD article, "An Analysis of Excellence," revealed the wide variety of architectural problems the SUCF program encompassed, as well as the quality and diversity of the architecture it was stimulating. "Some of the campuses, designed from scratch, were small enough to be the work of a single architectural firm, who were thus able to create and implement an overall cohesiveness, consistency and order for site and buildings." Other campuses like Stony Brook had become so large that SUCF broke them down into sys-

tems of more comprehensible parts. "SUCF conceives such projects as a series of campuses, designed by different firms within a huge interconnecting circulation network." On still other campuses (as at Fredonia, pages 28–29), "the SUCF planning teams found Department of Public Works-type buildings sited, hit-or-miss fashion, on any convenient piece of ground. Thus the architects' task was to bind these buildings together by the strategic placement of new structures to create—for the first time—a sense of community or place." The

SUCF program also contributed to conceptual development of various building types, perhaps especially through the communications and lecture hall centers which became principal core elements on many campuses (as at Stony Brook). The need for this relatively new college building type was growing from the increasing sophistication of audiovisual equipment and its increasing importance as a teaching and learning tool. Though it avoided the traps of bureaucratic planning and design, SUCF owed its management effectiveness to a

small but strongly professional staff headed by the late Anthony G. Adinolfi, and to a small Board of Trustees well qualified to monitor this particular program. Adinolfi was an educator turned administrator who had been brought from Detroit to head the Planning Division of SUCF after achieving a national reputation for his management of a major school expansion program which was also notable for architectural quality. As key associates, Adinolfi selected two architects who had been on the staff of the university, Frank J. Matzke and Grover

Tarbox. Adinolfi reported directly to a three-man Board of Trustees appointed by the Governor and headed by Clifton Phelan, then president of the New York Telephone Company and a trustee of the State University. Other members of the Board were James W. Gaynor, then the state's housing commissioner and chairman of its Housing Finance Agency, which was the state agency charged with issuing the bonds to finance self-liquidating projects of the university (except student housing); and architect George A. Dudley, then director of the state Office of Regional Development and chairman of the state Council on Architecture.

In the first stages of the program, construction phases were handled in a construction division parallel with Adinolfi's planning division. In 1968, after experience demonstrated that design and construction of each project comprised a single continuous process as far as management considerations of the Fund were concerned, a general reorganization brought the planning and construction divisions together under the single leadership of Adinolfi as general manager, with Matzke and Tarbox becoming deputy general managers. The management tools developed by SUCF to support the decision-making processes of the architects it commissioned included information resources of many kinds (eventually computerized), among them a research program directed by architect Roger Hallenbeck. Publications ranged from guides on campus planning and design of facilities for accessibility to the handicapped to a series on problems of specifica-

Administration Tower and Reed Library
State University of New York at Fredonia
Fredonia, New York
Architects: I. M. Pei
and Partners

New buildings at an old state college in upstate New York created a sense of community and identity for a flat, featureless campus of nondescript red brick buildings built over the years and sited apparently at random. Buildings shown here are the heart of a new academic core designed by the Pei firm which deliberately established for the campus a new order, a new architectural vocabulary, and a new scale. The new order is based on three principal elements, each with a clearly defined functional significance and each with a formal and spatial significance as well—a V-shaped circulation spine composed of principal interior circulation spaces and exterior terraces, steps and paths; the broad-stepped terraces which are part of the circulation system but intended also to create natural frontages for classroom buildings which may be added in the future; and a circular ring road designed to link all major activity zones of the campus, including the new core. All the new buildings are cast-in-place concrete, and their form and architectural vocabulary were further affected by the integration of the spine into all buildings which are used in common by the students (student union, lecture hall center, and fine arts center as well as Administration Tower and Reed Library). In the new architectural hierarchy of the campus, the mundane buildings are background.

tions and cost management. The philosophy of the Fund as client was to encourage maximum involvement of its architects in the decision-making process, from programming and planning stages to design and construction, with Fund management and staff contributing information resources and critical evaluations of the work at every stage, and continually monitoring budgets. Unlike public agencies dependent on the stop-and-go financing so often characteristic of construction programs funded by the Congress or state legislatures, the Fund had not only the authority to plan and schedule its own program but—within the limits of its $4.5-billion legislative authorization—timely access to construction funds through the bonding processes of a state agency headed by one of its trustees and made responsible by the enabling legislation for funding the program. "The Fund differs from most other public planning and design agencies," the RECORD concluded, "in that it does more than develop plans, it develops plans that can be carried out—and proceeds to do so—on time and within budget. As a client, it gives its architects a chance to do a good job, it comprehends good work yet is able to play a constructive critical role; and most importantly, it sees each project through to completion with as many architectural and environmental values intact as possible. The impact of SUCF's continuing accomplishment could become national, to the good fortune of this country, if other state and Federal agencies were to use the Fund as a model in their own efforts to organize themselves to build facilities of every kind."

Out of fashion with critics, monuments continued to be designed for human purposes that transcended social or functional goals — memorials like the LBJ library...

Lyndon Baines Johnson Library and East Campus
Library and Research Center
University of Texas, Austin, Texas
Associated Architects: Skidmore Owings & Merrill
and Brooks Barr Graeber & White

Two great parallel walls, 200 feet long, 65 feet high, and 90 feet apart, define the main mass of the LBJ Library itself. The walls taper up from a base thickness of eight feet. Tapering delineates the vertical cantilevered thrust of the closely spaced columns within the walls. At three quarters of the height of the walls, the surface splays out to receive and distribute the weight of girders supporting the cantilevered top story and spanning the space between the walls.

Ezra Stoller © ESTO

To honor the first Texan ever to become President of the U.S., the state of Texas provided a 30-acre site in a section of the U.T. campus at some remove from its densely developed central areas. It was a site selected for a monument, and the great travertine building which houses the Presidential archives and museum and (in the cornice) an office floor was designed as a monument. Texas would have expected nothing less; and this monument seems, in fact, very much attuned to Texas, not only in scale and color but in the vigor and serene assurance of its formal expression. A RECORD article with the forthright title "In Praise of a Monument to Lyndon B. Johnson" took issue with some then fashionable critical attitudes about "architectural monuments": "For some critics," Mildred F. Schmertz observed, "even the words 'monument' or 'monumental' are pejorative, summoning images of millions of dollars diverted from pressing human needs and squandered instead on stone and marble to celebrate the dubious, not to say iniquitous, deeds of an establishment villain. This line of reasoning, while it helps Lyndon Johnson's political enemies score points, should not be allowed to pass for architectural criticism. For one thing, amounts of money diverted from human needs to construct monuments are a pittance compared to the flow of public and private funds to other areas of doubtful social utility. Further, how can we be sure that there is no longer a human need for monuments? Man has built them since prehistory, and people have been going to look at them ever since."

...a government center shaped by clear expression of spatial organization to read both as monument and as neighbor to older buildings on a small-town street...

Orange County Government Center
Goshen, New York
Architect: Paul Rudolph

A complex but superbly organized spatial order, clearly expressed inside and outside the building, responded to a complex program calling for many specific kinds of interior spaces. Rudolph's solution divided the building into three parts, one for adult and one for juvenile courts and one for government assembly and licensing facilities, each clearly articulated but closely grouped around a central court conceived as the building's focal point. Put on the highest rise on the site, the court gives the complex its monumental character.

At first glance, it looked "improvised, random, almost capricious," the RECORD said. "Monumental, as befits a building from which law and order is dispensed, it is at the same time oddly picturesque in a rugged, earnest way. It disdains elegance. Most of Rudolph's buildings of recent years can be described in this way, yet all of them, including this one, are in fact not improvised at all. Typically, this latest major building is close in spirit and form to the works of Le Corbusier's last years, and reveals an understanding of the buildings of Frank

Lloyd Wright which far exceeds that of Wright's more literal-minded disciples. Like all of Rudolph's buildings, it is based upon a carefully worked out system of intersecting and parallel surfaces and planes. Rudolph is under no compulsion to achieve the appearance of structural clarity, which he considers a naive aim and a pitiful remnant of 20th-century architecture's still lingering 'commitment to an enfeebling, narrow interpretation of functionalism.' This courthouse has clarity of another kind. It is superbly organized within a complex

spatial order. . . . The interior spaces thrust upward, diagonally and horizontally. The enclosed volume of one room often penetrates the adjacent room, giving what Rudolph calls a 'sense of implied space,' which he attributes to Mies." For acoustical privacy, Rudolph enclosed his volumes not with Mies' freestanding partitions, but with continuous solid walls on either side of their major axis, and a glass wall opposite entry or storage wall on their minor axis. Outside, these volumes were expressed as an assembly of small-scaled units.

...a civic and cultural center
shaped by citizen participation
in the design process, and by
climate and cultural traditions...

City Hall, Scottsdale Civic Center
Scottsdale, Arizona
Architects: Gonzales Associates

Exterior walls were angled to create
several "corner" locations on the interior perimeter to house various city
agencies around a central lobby space
which serves as council chamber. This
city hall is a building without interior
partitions: everything and every process is open to public observation, reflecting community conviction that citizens should participate in the processes of their government and that the
building which houses them should
make it easy to do so. Structure is
mortar-washed, load-bearing masonry,
slabs and beams prestressed concrete.

The city hall was one of the first two buildings
in Scottsdale's projected civic and cultural
center. A 20-acre site had been assembled by
the city in what had become, during a meteor-
ic 10-year increase in Scottsdale's population
(12,000 to nearly 70,000), a semi-blighted section of town. Construction of the city hall and a
library (not shown), with their surrounding
park, were having the intended effect of stimulating private development in the area; and the
master plan called for future development to
provide facilities for such cultural activities as

music, drama, and arts and crafts. The RECORD,
in featuring the city hall and the library, found
two points of special interest: "first, that citizen
participation can be of a very high order in the
design process, and when it is, can be an important factor in achieving fine architecture;
and second, that regional design influences, far
from stultifying the creative process, can—in
the right hands—lead to entirely individual
and contemporary design of a singularly appropriate kind. Scottsdale's city hall and library
belong to, and in, the Southwest desert; but

their architecture is also extraordinarily suited
to the dynamic sophistication and the open,
casual way of life of Arizona's third largest
city." A remarkable procedure—the Scottsdale
Town Enrichment Program (STEP)—involved
some 400 residents, representing every section
of the city, in providing direction for planning
the center, and architect Bennie Gonzales reported that the buildings were a direct transla-
tion of STEP's beliefs. The heart of the concept
was use of the central lobby in each building
as a community focus. In the city hall, the

council chamber occupied this space; in the library, the periodical lounge. In both buildings, the space was sunk four feet below entrance level, with a low balustrade (for leaning onlookers and overflow audience) surrounding it, and skylighting above through faceted colored glass. Departments to which the public needed ready access were on the main floor.

...a public museum designed as
one with its two-acre site to create
an oasis for a busy campus,
a research and exhibition facility
made into a community resource...

Florida State Museum
University of Florida
Gainesville, Florida
Architect: William Morgan

North and east sides of the building are set into a natural hillside; their elevations are treated as simple but powerful earth forms crowned in concrete and interrupted only once, for an entrance on the north side with a projecting canopy. Glass walls facing the court are protected by wide, canted overhangs that double as parapets for terraces above. Broad, shallow steps link all levels of the courtyard and provide exterior access to all levels of the building.

Using earth forms to shape a dramatic setting for display of artifacts from Florida's ecological history, Morgan made this public building, on its two-acre site, an oasis of community amenity on a campus that like so many old campuses had more than its share of "object" buildings. The site was a natural hillside on the northeast fringe of the Florida campus. Surrounding buildings, part of a biological research complex, defined the site but "posed no problem of architectural etiquette," the REC-ORD reported. The museum's functional rela-

tionships were clearly defined both in plan and in elevation. The lowest two levels contain research and storage space for the departments of natural and social sciences. Offices line the wall facing the courtyard. Small laboratories link the offices with storage ranges buried in the berm. These simple juxtapositions made it possible to concentrate three kinds of staff space for maximum convenience and flexibility. Loading docks at both levels lead to spaces where newly acquired materials can be cleaned, sorted, fumigated, and catalogued

before being put on display or into research collections. The upper level, in addition to a reception area, contains guides' offices and a large multimedia exhibition hall for the display of a collection that includes brightly colored Indian potlatch and totems as well as the skeleton of a prehistoric mammoth recovered, not long before the museum was built, from under 40 feet of water in a swamp near Tallahassee. At the south end of the exhibition hall, a bridge leads to the top of an earth pyramid and on down into the courtyards, "where the earth

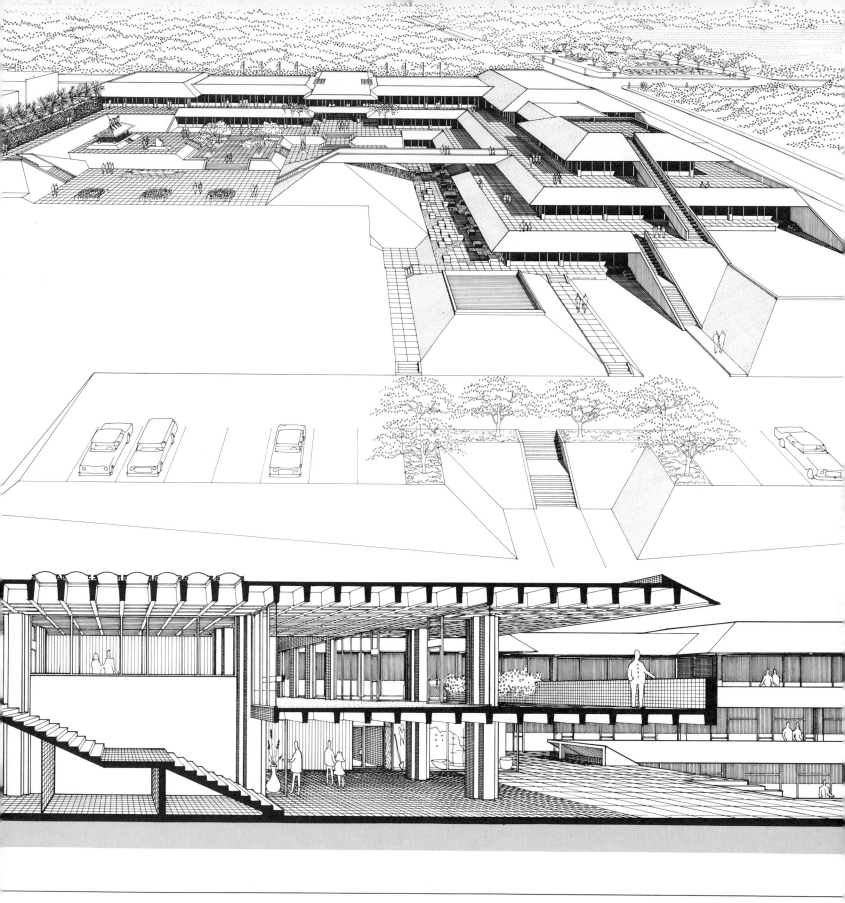

form motif reaches its climax. This two-acre sequence of staged platforms provides more than a splendid and appropriate setting for ecological display. It also serves as connective tissue with adjoining but functionally dissociated portions of the campus. The museum's planned future expansion to the north will continue this process of unification."

Saint Mary's Cathedral
San Francisco, California
Architects: McSweeney Ryan & Lee.
Consulting Architect: Pietro Belluschi
Consulting Engineer, Design:
Pier Luigi Nervi

Belluschi's concept, a 190-foot cupola created by two great hyperbolic paraboloids, had a structure developed by Nervi. Cost had cut the intended height of the cupola by a third; but the concept remained intact: interior surfaces enriched by the triangular panels so familiar in Nervi's work; narrow stained glass windows designed by Gyorgy Kepes at the edge joints of the paraboloids; Richard Lippold's shimmering baldachino suspended from the cupola. Massive piers support 140-foot arches that define the "square within a square" from which the cupola rises.

...a cathedral, the first to base its design on the new liturgy of the Catholic Church, that like cathedrals of old made a strong structural concept into symbol as well as structure, "an engineering form as an expression of the modern age"...

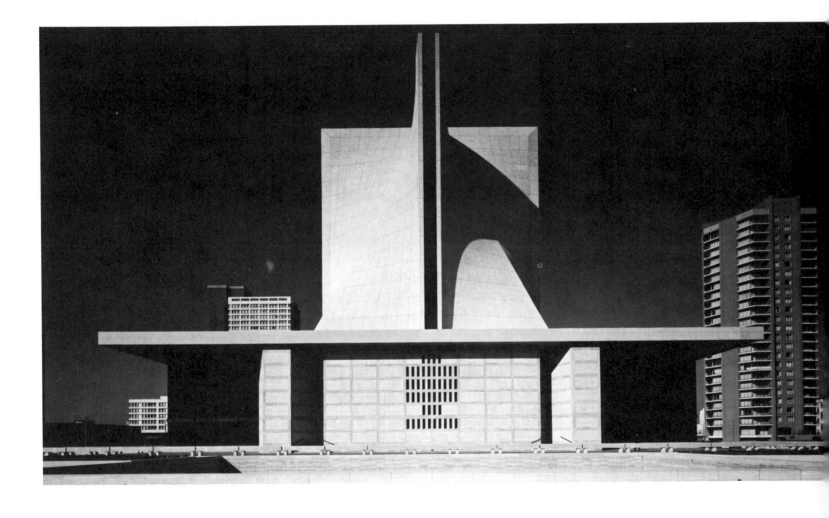

"The essence of contemporary architecture," in Belluschi's words written to the Archbishop, "is not the avoidance of style, or the creating of a new one, but an insistence on integrity of thought." Belluschi's philosophy in approaching the design of the cathedral was described in the RECORD: "His conviction was strong that a cathedral for today, if it was to 'endure as a symbol of our faith and of our seriousness as builders,' must consist of elemental forms, handled with 'the kind of simplicity that becomes both structure and symbol, to be looked at and remembered.' He became convinced that 'there was a need for a strong structural concept—an engineering form as an expression of the modern age, comparable in scale and size to the cathedrals of the past, a form that could only be done now.'" The new cathedral, sheathed in travertine, replaced a red brick Victorian Gothic building of 1887, which burned to the ground in 1962. It stands on Cathedral Hill, the highest point in the city's Western Addition Redevelopment Area. The principal entrance, on the north, is approached across a forecourt 200 feet wide and 150 feet deep, from which the full sweep of the cupola can be seen. In what Belluschi felt was a necessary compromise, the cupola was set on a base. The idea of a pure form resting on the ground, and large enough to provide the required seating for 2500 people, would have meant a building too large, overwhelming in the city and on the skyline. (Kenzo Tange's cathedral in Tokyo, which does use a warped surface "dome" without base, is a much smaller building.)

Finland's Alvar Aalto, another of the first-generation masters of modern architecture who worked on into the seventies, in 1971 completed his second building in the U.S. There was not to be another before his death in 1976, at the age of 78. His first U.S. building, Baker House at Massachusetts Institute of Technology, had been built 24 years earlier. Aalto was much admired by his American colleagues—he received the Gold Medal of the American Institute of Architects in 1962—but he was an infrequent visitor to the U.S. His professional life was centered in Finland, and his work in Finland and Europe. In 1963, the monks of Mount Angel Abbey sent a letter to Aalto in Helsinki: "We need you," they told him. "We have a magnificent monastic site. We don't want to spoil it. . . . Give us a building that will fill our needs in a beautiful and intelligent way." The result was this building—"unmistakable Aalto," said the RECORD. "In the Aalto manner, there are recognizable trademarks: the visually simple handling of complex relationships; forms, like the fan-shaped plan of the library's reading room and stacks, and the curved skylight that floods this three-story space by day; details, like the parabolic roof wells which are light sources by day and by night; the use of natural wood in small-sectioned strips; and the white interior surfaces. But most characteristic of all is the complete individuality of the solution based on the uniqueness of the building's requirements and of its site. The site is remarkable and beautiful, an epitome of the ideal monastic situation. It is a wooded knoll (not unlike some of Finland's

...a library for a Benedictine monastery, Aalto's second building in the U.S., that on one side celebrated the Abbey and its site far above a quiet valley, and on the other appeared among its monastic neighbors at smaller scale, only its top level visible

Mount Angel Abbey Library
Saint Benedict, Oregon
Architect: Alvar Aalto

Important buildings of the Abbey, which includes a college and a seminary, are located on the crest of the knoll, and the library is entered from this level. Unlike the other buildings (designed in pseudo-romanesque), only the library's top floor is visible from the campus; the other two floors descend the hill into which the building fits. Approached from the campus, the library seems unpretentious and small-scaled, and its buff-colored brick recognizes the color of neighboring stone buildings. On its opposite, public, side, the building is monumental, a symbol of the Abbey.

low wooded hills) rising several hundred feet above the farming fields of a peaceful valley, looking over the Willamette River Valley to Mounts Hood, Adams, St. Helens, and Rainier and, on the horizon, to the Coast Range on one side and the Cascade Range on the other. The monastery is, in effect, removed from the world, but with, and in full view of, the world. The site fits the Benedictine program of teaching and study, but its location within a few miles of Oregon's capital city, Salem, and within 50 miles of Portland, makes it accessi-

ble to a variety of cultural interests for which the Abbey hopes to become a focus. . . . It was the site, and the monks' appreciation of their responsibility for its sensitive development, along with the Benedictines' emphasis on a contemporary approach to the world, that led the monks to Aalto. His understanding of nature, and his emphasis on man, exemplified in his statement of some years ago that 'true architecture—the real thing—is only to be found when man stands at the center,' was the basis on which they wrote him in 1963, and in

1964 approved his appointment as architect for the library.'' But not until 1967 were funds available for construction. Execution of the project, with Aalto in Helsinki, was accomplished by appointment of DeMars & Wells of Berkeley, California, as executive architects, responsible for carrying out Aalto's concept, for developing working drawings and for representing Aalto at Mount Angel during construction. American designer Erik Vartiainen represented Aalto in Berkeley during preparation of final drawings.

Preservation and conservation were still generally thought of as separate causes, and neither was yet much related in the public mind to the economics or politics of an age of shrinking resources, but architects were increasingly involved in restoration of historic buildings, like Adler & Sullivan's Auditorium Theater in Chicago...

The Auditorium Theater
Chicago, Illinois
Architects: Adler & Sullivan and (restoration)
Harry Weese and Associates

The aim in restoration was to bring the theater back to its original form through repair and reconstruction wherever possible, replacing only what was missing or beyond repair. Major costs were for plaster repair, paint, and a new electrical system. The stage floor was replaced, and new stage lighting, new ropes for scenery placement, new dressing rooms, and new plumbing were provided. Chairs in the original design were made, and the red carpet Sullivan had designed was duplicated, as were the long carbon filament bulbs that made the "Golden Arches" scintillate.

A special RECORD issue on "New Life for Old Buildings" revealed not only growing architectural involvement but significant architectural accomplishment in the restoration and renovation of existing buildings. Twenty examples presented in the issue (of which three are shown here, pages 42-47), were organized in four categories, reflecting the diversity of architectural activity in the field—restoration of historic buildings and places, renovation with a major new addition, rehabilitation of buildings for the same use, and rehabilitation of build-

ings for a different use. Seventy-seven per cent of firms responding to a survey by the RECORD's Research Department had been involved in renovation of some kind within the previous two years, and 35 per cent expected more of their work to be in renovation within the next two years. But more significant than the indications of an increasing volume of activity were the indications from the quality of the work presented in the issue that serious architects were finding in renovation a serious creative architectural challenge. Renovation (or remod-

eling, or "alterations and additions," as the F.W. Dodge Division of McGraw-Hill still calls it) had long been an aspect of architectural practice that was considered suitable for young architects just getting started, or as fill-in activity when real work (i.e., *new* work) was scarce, or as a necessary additional service to important clients (between new buildings). It was not where the energies of the most gifted architects were focused, and it was not generally thought to demand major creative effort. Restoration was the province of a few architect

specialists who were thought of more as architectural historians than as architects. But many forces were combining as the seventies began to change the role of renovation in architectural practice. The most visible was the historic preservation movement, since the passage of the landmark Historic Preservation Act of 1966 no longer the province of "little old ladies in tennis shoes" and of organizations financed through private philanthropy alone, but a *public* cause financed by *public* funds which — however inadequate they were (and are) —

were distributed in response to the views of a far broader constituency. States were required to set up their own preservation machinery to be eligible for Federal preservation funds; and a shift toward more populist evaluations of what was worth saving was the natural result as evaluations began to be made on behalf of public rather than private interests. The still-separate environmental movement, which got its own landmark legislation in the National Environmental Protection Act of 1969 (NEPA), was beginning to have an unexpectedly strong

impact on what could and could not be built. Not only was there a NEPA requirement for an Environmental Impact Statement (EIS) to evaluate public cost and benefit of any proposed Federal construction project that might have substantial impact on the environment, but there were air and water quality standards which — it soon developed — a private construction project might be held to threaten. Framers of the legislation were mainly concerned with the ecological impact of air and water pollution and with any threats to the

...in combining old and new
to meet today's needs
while preserving the character
of historic neighborhoods
as community heritage, as in
the State Bar Association
complex in Albany, New York...

New York State Bar Center
Albany, New York
Architects: James Stewart Polshek
and Associates

The front halves of three row houses, part of a
19th century residential enclave only two blocks
from the state capitol, were linked across a new
courtyard to a tripartite addition larger in total
volume than the space preserved, but so shaped
and so fragmented that its visible volumes are
smaller in scale than the old houses. The three
parallel elements of the addition, set parallel to
the row of houses, recede in plan so that the element nearest the houses is only as long as the
width of the widest house, while the farthest element is twice as long. Exterior mass was also reduced by utilizing the downward slope of the site
behind the houses to get major interior work
spaces under the courtyard at ground level. Main
entrance to the Center is through the middle row
house, but a major secondary entrance has been
created through the courtyard.

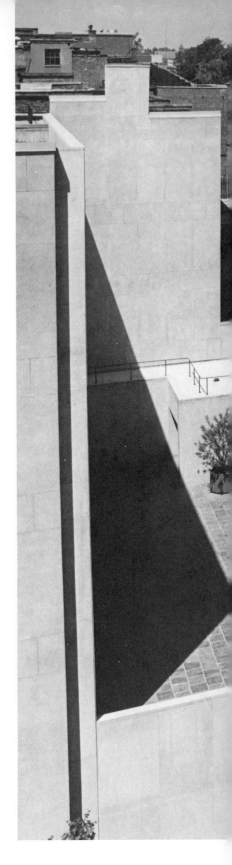

ecological health of the environment of im-
proper (generally thought of as industrial) intrusions on the natural habitats of wildlife, especially scarce or dwindling species. The EIS
was a "sleeper" clause, little debated when it
passed the Congress, that was to become a critical force in the future development of the nation, delaying, even when it did not eventually
stop, hundreds — perhaps by now thousands —
of construction projects. While the NEPA legislation applied to Federal construction, its impact was vastly broadened by legislative ac-

tions in a number of states extending its provi-
sions to both public and private construction.
Preservationists as well as environmentalists
found a powerful ally in NEPA, and a powerful
tool in the EIS requirement, so the demolition
of older buildings — whether or not of particular distinction either historic or architectural —
as well as potential threats to air, water, wildlife or its sustaining habitat, or even any
change in an existing natural landscape, became potential roadblocks to new construction. And the class-action suit, so effectively

used as a technique for citizen action by the
consumer movement in the sixties, became the
device for a new kind of citizen action, a challenge on environmental grounds of any construction project dissenting citizens saw as an
environmental threat and could organize and
finance themselves to take to court. The very
possibility of delay in a time of rapidly escalating construction costs was enough to make
clients think twice before going ahead with
new construction if there was any organized
public objection to it (or the prospect of any).

And "alterations and additions" became a more attractive alternative to clients faced with the possibility of class-action lawsuits if they opted for new construction. As preservation became more and more a public cause, restoration of historic buildings also began to emerge as a route to public esteem, for public as well as private clients. And more and more often — as with the New York State Bar Association complex — it was to become the price for building at all on a site occupied or partly occupied by old buildings. Though blackouts, brownouts,

and a steady rise in fuel costs were beginning — even before the Arab oil embargo of October 1973 — to make all citizens uneasily conscious that the days of cheap and abundant energy might be numbered, there was not yet any public inclination to do anything about it, so renovation of sound older buildings was not yet linked in the public mind with energy conservation, which would be, before the seventies were over, a very powerful incentive for renovation. (Among the most sophisticated building clients, energy consciousness *was* already a factor.)

For architects, the gathering forces that created the need for new kinds of approaches to renovation were also creating a new frontier in architectural practice. In 1971, preservation still was regarded more as a cause than as a new demand for architectural services. The lead article in the RECORD's special issue said of the architect's role in preservation: "He must be persuasive with unconvinced clients, seek out funding for local preservation, and act as a synthesizer, when necessary, of historic and modern architecture." As so many examples in

...and in "recycling" old buildings for new uses, historic character preserved through a combination of restoration and renovation, like the old Patent Office in Washington, D.C., which was made into two museums

National Collection of Fine Arts
Portrait Gallery
The Smithsonian Institution
Washington, D.C.
Architects: William P. Elior,
Ithiel Twon, Robert Mills,
Thomas U. Walter, and (restoration)
Faulkner Stenhouse Fryer & Faulkner

Four architects of note had contributed over a 27-year period to the Greek Revival design of the old Patent Office. The exterior character had survived; but interiors rebuilt in 1877, after fire destroyed two wings, reflected newer tastes, as indicated in the photograph of the library, with its three tiers of stacks and reading areas. Rebuilt wings had roofs supported by iron trusses and vaults instead of the masonry vaults and wood roofs used by Robert Mills, which had survived in the unburned wings. There were great halls for display of patent models; in one of them, 28 freestanding square marble columns and four pilasters support a series of groined vaults 300 feet long.

the first two chapters of this book show, architects were already absorbed in the problems of effectively relating old and new. All the pressures which were escalating the demand for preservation (whether restoration or renovation) were creating more occasions for dealing with such problems, and a new dimension was developing: "The important work in preservation now," Robert E. Jensen wrote, "is developing new uses for older buildings or districts. Much of our old architecture may be destroyed if it cannot be made productive. The new uses

that must be created may allow an old building to be accurately restored to some former period in its history, or it may not. It is acceptable if the old facade can be retained while the interior is entirely remodeled, or if a substantial new addition can be made that is compatible with the old work and revitalizes it." In the same issue, the late William B. Foxhall suggested the direction in which preservation was, in fact, rapidly heading: "Reasonably, the notion of preserving a building of 'architectural significance' for a useful contemporary purpose

might extend the definition of 'architectural significance' to many well-designed buildings in addition to those of historically notable facade or technically interesting structure and materials. The preservation of any sound building for economically feasible contemporary use might be considered a sound architectural objective. The difference between such broad objectives and strict preservationism would be, of course, in the wider extent of acceptable remodeling and in the increased degree of architectural freedom from

the requirement to 'preserve' the appearance
and identity of the existing structure.'' The architectural response to issues raised by preservation and renovation was to become a critical
influence on the urbanistic trend of modern
architecture.

1972

A new geometry by Walter A. Netsch, based upon an intricate system of intersecting diagonals, was juxtaposed with the classic form of a landmark dome when Skidmore Owings & Merrill remodeled the interiors of the Engineering Library at the Massachusetts Institute of Technology. The dome, which had long crowned the library's reading room, was designed in 1916 by Welles Bosworth as part of his scheme for M.I.T.'s neo-classic East Campus.

A museum in Portland, Oregon, completed a 40-year development program by one architect, and a Denver museum was designed to challenge the imagination . . . a landmark art gallery was "restored to its gilded past," and a new university art gallery made dynamic architecture of an innovative museum concept . . . and skylit cycloid vaults of a Fort Worth museum permitted uninterrupted floor areas and created memorable interior spaces .

A house designed for a family with six children revealed many levels of architectural purpose .

A building designed as "fragment" took its place in the natural order around it, not "complete" within itself, but a continuation of "events" of which it was seen as a part.

Architecture celebrated function and exalted the specific to evoke a new urban vision .

Quiet architecture and a master plan melded old and new to create a strong overall form for a nondescript campus and give it a more urban character .

Another new public client created by New York State was generating rental housing of high quality on downtown and suburban sites for moderate-as well as low-income tenants.

Urban architecture was emerging as a resource for public agencies and private developers as they learned to deal with the assertion of neighborhood control over neighborhoods.

Pietro Belluschi, who received the Gold Medal of The American Institute of Architects in 1972, was the architect of the Equitable Building and the Zion Lutheran Church, both in Portland, Oregon, both completed in 1948. His oldest and newest work in a 40-year development program for the Portland Art Museum is shown on page 50 (his cathedral in San Francisco, pages 38–39).

A museum in Portland, Oregon completed a 40-year development program by one architect, and a Denver museum was designed to challenge the imagination...

Mall and Sculpture Court and Art School
Portland Art Museum
Portland, Oregon
Architect: Pietro Belluschi

The landscaped pedestrian mall and sculpture court through which the Art School is entered replaced a street vacated by the city at the museum's request and created a connection with the city's "Park Blocks." Both natural and artificial lighting were important elements in the design of the new Art School building, which consisted of three floors of studios, an auditorium located to serve the museum as well as the school, an exhibit gallery and administrative offices. The school, mall and sculpture court were the final phase of the museum's development plan.

Denver Art Museum
Denver, Colorado
Architects: James Sudler Associates
and Gio Ponti

A building designed to be provocative and "entirely unrelated to anything in Denver's past or present" had the overall height of a 10-story building, but since its floor-to-floor height was 17.6 feet, it actually contained seven floors. Though no openings were needed—the museum director wanted only artificial light on displays—windows of various sizes and shapes were used in a pattern designed to suggest, but not describe, the interior spaces. The site is small, and would not have permitted the typical horizontal solution; but since no skylights were wanted, the eleven galleries could be stacked, two to a typical floor. Exterior walls were faced with a special gray glass tile.

Though most often built with private rather than public funds, the museum is one of the most public of building types. It is an expression of community aspirations as well as a major educational resource for the whole community, a link with a cultural heritage all can share. So the museum is seldom expected to be a background building, and the architecture of museums in any era tends to call upon the most gifted architects for their most serious efforts to design buildings which are symbolically appropriate as well as functionally effective. The museums and art galleries shown (pages 50–55) were all such buildings, and in their visual diversity they reflected an increasing receptiveness of institutional clients and even of the public to widely varying and "different" modes of architectural expression. At the Portland Art Museum, Belluschi built from beginning to end of a 40-year development program with the "eloquent simplicity" which has been his hallmark. The Denver Art Museum got a "spirited and unconventional" building from an unusual collaboration between a young Denver architectural firm, James Sudler Associates, and the venerable Italian architect (and editor of *Domus*), the late Gio Ponti. In Washington, D.C., a 19th-century building which had been the first example in the U.S. of the French Second Empire style was restored (next page) by two architectural firms working in sequence—John Carl Warnecke and Associates and Hugh Newell Jacobsen and Associates—and "recycled" to its original use as an art gallery by the Smithsonian, which then named its new art gallery for the original

...a landmark art gallery was "restored to its gilded past" and a new university art gallery made dynamic architecture of an innovative museum concept...

architect, James Renwick. The University of California at Berkeley held a national design competition to select an architect for its new art gallery, "a lively work of architecture" which was at once "bold and innovative" and evocative of both Frank Lloyd Wright and Alvar Aalto. And in Fort Worth, Texas, which had been extending to the cultural realm its always spirited competition with Dallas, the new Kimbell Art Museum (pages 54–55) was designed by Louis I. Kahn, 1971 recipient of the Gold Medal of The American Institute of Architects,

an architect who in the last years of his life had become perhaps the most significant influence on the course of modern architecture after the first-generation "masters."

When he designed the first wing of the Portland Art Museum, completed in 1932, Pietro Belluschi was a young architect not many years in the United States from Italy, only a few years in practice in Portland, and unknown outside the Northwest. In 1972, when the art school and its entrance mall and sculpture court were published, Belluschi was at the

apex of a distinguished career as practitioner, teacher, consultant and critic which was about to be recognized with the Gold Medal of The American Institute of Architects (presented in Houston in May 1972). In all those years, a steadfast philosophy had guided him in all his work. So Elisabeth Kendall Thompson could say of the Portland Art Museum, "In the 40 years since the first building was completed, the original design decisions have proved themselves, rooted as they were in the museum's requirements, and not in the style of the

Renwick Gallery
The Smithsonian Institution
Washington, D.C.
Architects: James Renwick and (restoration)
John Carl Warnecke and Associates and
Hugh Newell Jacobsen and Associates

A restoration in two stages recycled a national
capital landmark to the use for which it was
originally designed. Exterior ornamentation
largely destroyed by weathering was reconstructed from Renwick drawings and Matthew
Brady photographs. Interiors were restored
"in the spirit of Renwick's time."

The University Art Museum
University of California
Berkeley, California
Architects: Mario J. Ciampi and Associates,
in design partnership of Mario Ciampi,
Richard L. Jorasch and Ronald E. Wagner

A rugged concrete exterior is offset at the
entrance by grassy mounds and a large black
Calder stabile. Inside, ramps take off on either
side of a central court and lead up or down
through a great volume of skylit space to different levels of the exhibit areas and galleries
which radiate from the court.

moment. The solution was then, and it has
continued to be in all of Belluschi's work, in
the 'functional demand,' to use his terse and
descriptive phrase, of the building itself. His
early work remains as fresh, as real, as clear in
purpose as when he produced it 30 and 40
years ago, not because he designed a style, but
precisely because he did not."

The design collaboration on the Denver
museum came about, the RECORD reported,
because "the museum's board, mindful of its
need to get popular support for the museum

(which had never had a proper building) and to
raise funds for the project, wanted to add the
prestige of an international name to that of its
local architectural firm, James Sudler Associates. Sudler chose Ponti, partly because he
greatly admired the Pirelli Building, partly
because of Ponti's long and wide architectural
experience." They had not previously known
each other. "Neither difference in language
nor in generation interfered with the collaboration. In four intensive visits to the Ponti studio
in Milan, Sudler and Joel Cronenwett, his part-

ner, absorbed the Ponti philosophy and fused it
with the program requirements and the museo-
logical theories of Otto Karl Bach, the museum's vital director for 27 years."

The two-stage restoration that created the
new Renwick Gallery of the Smithsonian Institution was, in fact, a *fourth* "recycling" of a
national capitol landmark. Begun in 1859 for
the Corcoran Gallery of Art, the building was
seized before it could open by the Union Quar-
termaster Corps for use as a Civil War cloth-
ing warehouse, and did not open as an art

...and skylit cycloid vaults
of a Fort Worth museum permitted
uninterrupted floor areas and
created memorable interior spaces

Kimbell Art Museum
Fort Worth, Texas
Architect: Louis I. Kahn. Associated Architect:
Preston M. Geren

Site of the museum was a nine-and-a-half-acre park. The main entrance fronts on a landscaped plaza and is flanked by two cycloids which face reflecting pools. The plaza opens into the upper level of the museum, which provides 30,000 square feet of gallery space as well as reception area, auditorium, research library and bookstore. Patios and sculpture courts are spaced throughout the building. Natural light, diffused through special filters to protect the art, is admitted through three-foot-wide slits that run the length of each of the vaults. Structure is primarily concrete, vaults are post-tensioned. Finishes include travertine, stainless steel, wood and lead.

gallery until 1871. After the Corcoran moved to its present quarters, the U.S. Court of Claims moved in (1899) and out (1964). A feasibility study of the restoration and rehabilitation of Lafayette Square done by the Warnecke firm at the request of President John F. Kennedy urged that the old Court of Claims building be restored to its original function as an art gallery. President Lyndon B. Johnson approved its transfer to the Smithsonian for that purpose, and restoration began. The Warnecke firm restored the exterior and made the basic interior

renovations, removing Court of Claims partitions, strengthening the structure in critical areas, and replacing the plumbing, wiring, heating and ventilating systems. More than 90 per cent of the original ornament had been obliterated by over a century of weathering. Hand-carved models were made from blowups of Renwick's drawings and contemporary photographs by Matthew Brady, and latex molds were made from these. The new exterior ornamentation is a cast composite, containing crushed particles of the previously removed

stonework, which blends extremely well with the older portions of the building. The Jacobsen firm got the commission to further restore the interiors. Between the time architect James Renwick finished his design of the original Corcoran and its completion as a museum, Renwick "had gone out of fashion as an architect. While he was responsible for shaping the noble interior spaces of the gallery, he had little subsequent influence on the interior finishes or the selection of furnishings. But even without the Renwick touch, the 19th-century

interiors of the Corcoran represented the epitome of the taste of the time. Architect Hugh Jacobsen's task was not to reproduce these interiors, but to evoke them, which he has done with great skill."

The University Art Museum at Berkeley "will inevitably be compared with the Guggenheim [Frank Lloyd Wright's Guggenheim Museum in New York City]," the RECORD asserted, "because of its great court and its use of ramps. Unlike the Guggenheim, however, it clearly recognizes the function of a museum building and the challenge it faces in the works of art it is designed to shelter. Its very special virtue is that in meeting the rigorous demands of that function, it does not lose sight of its own role as an expression of the art of architecture. Dynamic as the building is, it neither detracts nor distracts from the viewing of the objects on display. One of the reasons for this is that the ramps—the obvious but not the only way of reaching the galleries—lead visitors directly into the galleries: visitors are within an exhibit area before they can proceed further. Another reason is that the galleries, radiating from the court [in a favorite Aalto plan configuration] like parts of a giant fan, are each 60 feet deep and are therefore fully adequate places for the display and contemplation of paintings, sculpture and other art objects. A third and more subtle reason is the great flexibility which the building affords not only as a place in which a variety of objects in a variety of sizes and types can be displayed, but also as a place through which people move, creating dynamic spaces."

This house alone might have sufficed to refute those critics who, for a time after the social upheavals of the sixties, were ready to mourn the demise of "the house as architecture." But as other houses in this book will also attest, and as the RECORD's annual Mid-May issue, RECORD HOUSES, continues to demonstrate year after year, houses remain a supreme challenge in the evolution of an architecture that both satisfies ordinary human needs and transcends them. "This house near New York for a family with six children," James D. Morgan wrote, "is

worth study on four levels: First, as it responds to the work and thought of Le Corbusier. Second, as it conveys the special delight of architectural sculpture. Third, as a thoughtful solution of the client's program on a specific site. Fourth, as a series of details which solve house-building problems economically and well. Richard Meier believes that every architect working today has been affected by Le Corbusier. In his own work, and particularly this house, he cites Le Corbusier's interest in structural clarity, in the relationship of the hori-

zontal plane to its columnar support and the ensuing visual framework. He cites the bold expression of vertical circulation patterns, such as the ramp, and their incorporation as major design elements. Finally, he cites the play of light and shadow upon form. Here, as in his earlier houses, Meier has carefully balanced interior daylight level with the exterior light. Thus, even in the daytime (when many glass buildings become solid mirrored volumes), there is a transparency that is reminiscent of Corbu's tropical buildings—those at Chandi-

A house designed for
a family with six children
revealed many levels
of architectural purpose

House near New York
Architects: Richard Meier
and Associates

Ramps in an acrylic-glazed gallery
were the most compelling architectural feature of this house. The gallery
was designed to be the vertical circulation spine of the house. The ramps
connect all four levels, although there
is also a winding metal stair connecting the two-story living room pavilion
with the third-level bedrooms. The
entry leads immediately to the ramp,
which ascends to the living room. The
second leg of the ramp lands above the
entry, and then goes on to the master
bedroom. There its terminus is celebrated by a cylindrical two-story space
topped with a flat skylight. Ramps are
framed with 2 x 12's and floored in
dark-stained oak.

Ezra Stoller © ESTO

garh, or the mill owners' building at Ahmeda-
bad. In other words, in a climate that requires
tightly controlled and completely enclosed
buildings, Meier has achieved the apparent
openness of an unenclosed building. The illu-
minated building at twilight conveys the quality well, but transparency in daylight is the true
test. With admirable bravura, the architect has
used ramps to connect four levels and has
underlined their presence with quasi-industrial
detailing such as the welded pipe railings and
the arched metal glazing structure. The juxta-

position of the arched glass wall and the two
glass walls of the living room produces a visual
depth that eludes most designers. It is this transparency, of course, that makes the house truly
sculptural in contemporary terms. Set as
an object in the meadow, the scale of the
house is deceiving. The linear quality is
largely achieved by the connected pool
house/playroom at the second level. The total
length on that level is almost 160 feet, though
the house itself is 85 feet long. Thus, using a
swimming pool and other structures, Meier has

maximized the thrust of the form into the site.
In spite of its steel frame, this is a wood house
which owes as much to American house-
building techniques as it does to formal European traditions. The 4-foot, 6-inch-wide ramp
is wood framed and, like most of the floors, is
of dark-stained oak boards. This material,
played against white walls inside and out, adds
an appropriate warmth.''

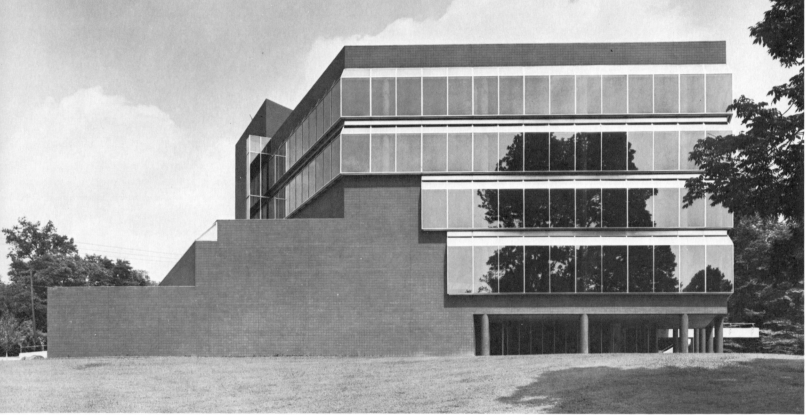

The work of Mitchell/Giurgola Associates, as both partners attest, is the work of a firm, not of any one designer. Robert E. Jensen discussed in the RECORD the firm's approach to architecture and related it to the design of the MDRT Foundation building: "Romaldo Giurgola is an influential theorist in American architecture, but neither he nor his partner, Ehrman Mitchell, dictate design. Rather, design is accomplished in a dialogue between groups; associates are given major design problems, and their solutions are used. Giurgola, however, is the origi-nator of ideas about architecture. Giurgola does not believe that any single building today can be complete within itself; he does not be-lieve it can be finite, with a beginning and an end, or create any kind of private world. Rath-er, he conceives of buildings as fragments, as part of, and related to, an order in nature, or part of a larger social context that is best seen today in the cities. Giurgola may thus think of his work as part of an itinerary of events, com-menting on or clarifying his perceptions of the physical, social or political context of a build-ing, but never believing that he may include all these ideas in the formal metaphors that be-come the architecture. In fact, it is impossible to include them all; our culture is too complex. Giurgola says that the realization of this com-plexity, and the gradual rejection of the holistic classicizing ideas of Mies, or even parts of the theoretical basis of Le Corbusier's work, are a major event in modern architecture's evolution to maturity. A projection of the fragment idea can be seen in MDRT Foundation Hall. In eith-er plan or elevation, additions to the building

A building designed as "fragment" took its place in the natural order around it, not "complete" within itself, but a continuation of "events" of which it was seen as a part

MDRT Foundation Hall
American College of Life Underwriters (ACLU)
Bryn Mawr, Pennsylvania
Architects: Mitchell/Giurgola Associates

An adult learning research facility on the 45-acre campus of ACLU was "modeled from the simplest geometric solids of rectangle and trapezoid, but the designers have carved out acute-angled pieces from these root forms, twisted them in perspective, and made their surfaces gleaming and precise." The main pedestrian entrance of a six-level building was located off the central court (above); from there the ground slopes sharply downward, so that the back of the building (south side) is one story below the front. Ground level and basement contain studios for film-making, radio and television.

are possible without harm to the esthetic whole. The long columns, the irregular silhouette, the lack of symmetry in the voids and in the rhythms of the walls in relation to the windows are a projection (frankly man-made) of the elegant natural context around MDRT Hall. The building is in this way a continuation of the events around it, a part or 'fragment' of the events. The strong diagonal walls in plan are themselves a representation of 'fragment.' Diagonals cut through the established rectilinearity of Mitchell/Giurgola's plans as if to cut off any 'completeness' before it begins; they are perhaps the central formal device of the architecture. Diagonals also create changing vistas and interesting shifts in proportion as people walk through a building, and are useful in directing traffic patterns; Giurgola mentions both these purposes when suggesting that the firm's use of diagonals is not capricious. At the same time, Giurgola says the 'fragment' idea cannot be allowed to dissipate into everything around it. . . . He continues to believe in the fundamental basis of modern architecture—in our cultural conception of technology and scientific rationality as remaining the most powerful generating force for modern architecture. He says they still allow a first critical place to 'begin.' But he believes that technology is not capable of developing forms adequate to the substance of human aspirations—technology solves needs; architecture comes from hope."

Architecture celebrated function and
exalted the specific
to evoke a new urban vision

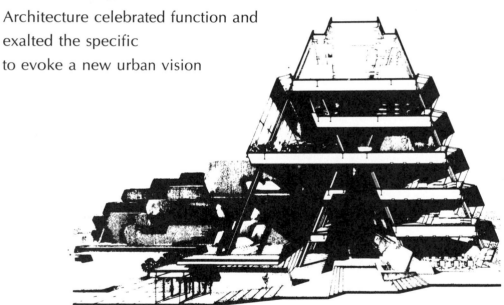

Corporate Headquarters and Research Facility
Burroughs-Wellcome Company
Research Triangle Park
Durham County, North Carolina
Architect: Paul Rudolph

The building was conceived as a man-made extension of the ridge on which it is built, stepped up and back to terraces created at the apex of the ridge. The plan disposed administrative, research and service facilities in three blocks, each designed to be infinitely expansible, in the form of a fat "S" around an entry court and a service court. A three-story-high lobby (page 62) is not only a reception area but a communications focal point for the building; some three-fourths of the offices are grouped around it. Structure is a truncated A-frame; diagonal supporting members are linked at the roof by a system of horizontal beams. Mechanical systems, housed in both vertical and diagonal shafts, converge at a common location in the penthouse.

The architecture of Paul Rudolph, like the architecture of Frank Lloyd Wright, has always been the reverse of abstract. It transcends the ordinary without the crutch of elegance and derives exuberance, not confusion, from complexity. Since at least the late fifties, it has been consistently exploring issues of size and scale related to human beings and their diverse environments, as well as the potential of evolving technology for helping to resolve those issues. This building on a 66-acre rural site, for a client who wanted an architecturally distinctive building, was completed in 1972 and the photographs and drawing shown were published in that year; but the design concept was described, and related to the body of Rudolph's work, in an earlier article by Mildred F. Schmertz when the building was just under construction. "This building," Miss Schmertz wrote, "may be considered a summation of the characteristics by which Rudolph's architecture may be identified. The site has been a key consideration, and the building is essentially topographical; single stories are clearly articulated to define scale; specific elements are elaborated within a clear and regular structural system; the plan is infinitely expansible in each of its three major blocks; and great attention has been paid to the flow of interior space as well as to the handling of reflected light. The building, though it doesn't actually consist of totally prefabricated modules inserted within a structural system, almost looks as though it does, and thus it prefigures and helps lay the groundwork for future technological development."

In Rudolph's own words, quoted in the REC-ORD: "From a spatial viewpoint, the interior is given a new dimension with its sloping walls, giving an impression not unlike a growing tree—angles, light, shadow, flexibility. The building will impart a sense of being a living organism, rather than a box-like form. The laboratories will have an individuality and a uniqueness quite unlike other laboratories because they will have higher ceilings lit by skylights at each end. The functions of the building are celebrated architecturally. There is contrast between those things that cannot be changed (mechanical shafts, columns, etc.) and the parts that can be changed—for example, the laboratories and other work areas which must be essentially flexible. Permanent interior structural components are being finished the same as the building's exterior—in rough textured sprayed aggregate within a plastic binder. The flexible components are being finished in a variety of surfaces—paneling, painted drywall, etc. In a sense, the building can be read according to the materials."

Quiet architecture and a master plan melded old and new, creating a strong over-all form for a nondescript campus and giving it a more urban character

State University of New York at Potsdam
Potsdam, New York
Architects: Edward Larrabee Barnes and Associates

Open gateways placed at all four corners of the central court were designed to create a symbolic as well as a functional entry to the academic core. The court was defined by new classroom buildings, all the same height, with the same court facade, linking the old colonial buildings together. The vast scale of the court was modified by placing the library at its center, a position both functionally and symbolically appropriate. Library and gate towers are the same height. The gates express the essence of the new design vocabulary of the campus.

Another campus expansion commissioned by New York's State University Construction Fund inspired an architectural approach quite opposite to that at Fredonia (pages 28–29), although the basic problem may seem quite similar. Potsdam was another old, small, upstate New York college with a mixture of undistinguished non-architecture built over many years and haphazardly sited on a very large rural campus. "Barnes might have found it tempting to turn his back on such a campus and start a new building group elsewhere on

the generous site," the RECORD observed. "He decided, however, to weave these random, hit-or-miss Department of Public Works-type buildings with the threads of new buildings into a strong new fabric. The new buildings were to have a kind of quiet unity which would mute the clash between them and their pseudo-colonial neighbors. Attempting this sort of solution with landmark buildings of esthetic merit is, of course, acceptable practice — and considerably easier than the task Barnes set himself with the existing structures at Potsdam.

He may be the first contemporary architect of note to deal seriously with the problem of enhancing the appearance, without remodeling the fronts, of existing structures of no esthetic quality whatsoever. Barnes compares the new Potsdam campus to medieval walled university towns in Italy, which emphasize concepts of ordered space. He believes that the concentration, rhythm and intensity of urban forms provide a more appropriate academic setting than the rural-type campus, diffused and sprawling, so cherished in the U.S."

Buffalo Waterfront Housing—
Area B, Phase I
Urban Development
Corporation
Buffalo, New York
Architect: Paul Rudolph

Relatively simple sloped-roof dwellings were transformed by the addition of balconies, patios and a special extended niche in each bedroom. Balcony walls and ground-floor patio enclosures, and the vertical end walls that connect them, are independent of the parts of the building that enclose interior space. Bedroom niches jut out from end walls of each double group of apartments and step down one floor at a time. Patios are 18 by 16 feet. Top-level apartments have high and pitched ceilings.

Another new public client created by New York State was generating rental housing of high quality on downtown and suburban sites for moderate as well as low-income tenants

New York State's Urban Development Corporation (UDC) was established in 1968 as a catalyst for community revitalization, with a legislative mandate to build housing for low- and moderate-income tenants in urban centers where housing was needed. It was equipped with powers extraordinary for a state construction agency: it could issue its own bonds to finance its construction programs; it could condemn property and buy and sell land; and it could override local building codes on its own projects. By the fall of 1972, it had 63 projects under construction in 23 New York communities. Its first completed projects revealed a high level of architectural quality; but there were already signs of political and economic problems that would culminate, in 1975, in financial crisis, default and reorganization. "There are major confrontations ahead," the RECORD predicted in 1972, "as UDC attempts to build for the first time in the suburbs, thereby creating substantial local animosity. Another problem is developing. UDC depends on Federal housing funds (Section 236) for some of its work. If the 236 program is reduced or eliminated [as, in 1973, it was, by then President Richard Nixon], the UDC may have to do the same with some of its goals. Edward Logue [then head of UDC], writing in the most recent annual report, makes clear the UDC's need for Federal interest subsidy programs." As for the completed projects, "they show that UDC has produced extraordinary results, in an architectural sense, in a very short time. These buildings are certainly better planned, are more handsome, and are more innovative technical-

Ely Park Housing, Stage One
Urban Development Corporation
Binghamton, New York
Architect: The Architects
Collaborative

Four-level units are clustered in groups of 15 to 30 dwelling units on this suburban site, each group sharing a grassy area in front and a parking area in back. A modular design concept which would have given each unit its own fenced lawn or patio was superseded, for reasons of cost and logistics, by a system of factory-made panels. The panels are plywood siding vertically grooved with cedar, on standard 2 × 4 stud construction.

ly than the vast majority of agency-built or agency-financed housing in the country.

"The Buffalo Waterfront Project is potentially the most dramatic project the UDC has undertaken, and its first housing is now completed and mostly occupied. We must say 'potentially,' because a large part of the project remains to be built. But the 142 units now finished follow almost exactly the original vision [page 17], as do the additional 472 units now under construction. The completed new housing is being rented to moderate-income tenants (70 per cent), low-income tenants (20 per cent) and low-income elderly (10 per cent), the standard 'mix' in UDC projects. There are 28 one-bedroom, 102 two-bedroom and 12 three-bedroom apartments. There are community laundry rooms, but no other community facilities. Phase II will be mostly efficiency through two-bedroom units, concentrating on tenancy for the elderly. Phase III will add three- and four-bedroom units, a park, some commercial development with parking, and a K-6 school, not financed by UDC. The Binghamton project has been judiciously inserted in a beautifully wooded area, on a hilly site that gives some apartments sweeping views of the valley below. The architects envisioned this project as a group of single-family residences next to each other, row house style, to keep the largest portion of the site in common woods, but with each house having its privately fenced lawn or patio. Though the modular concept was lost, and with it the private lawns and patios, Ely Park still has an idyllic feeling. Over 200 two- to four-bedroom duplexes are completed."

Urban architecture was emerging as a resource for public agencies and private developers as they learned to deal with the assertion of neighborhood control over neighborhoods

Riverbend Housing
HRH Construction Corporation, for Riverbend Housing Corporation
New York, New York
Architects: Davis, Brody and Associates

High-rise apartment blocks containing 625 units were conceived as row houses in the sky, each with its own "stoop," in the spirit of the neighborhood from which its residents were to come. Duplex apartments are entered from exterior circulation galleries which occur at every other level. Each duplex has a terrace enclosed with a low wall and up a few steps from gallery level, creating a transitional private space between the public space and each resident's front door. Though the site is split by an elevated highway, buildings are linked by walkways at various levels and raised for views of the river.

A fundamental change in the context of architecture occurred when citizens discovered how to insert themselves into the political decision-making process from the grass roots. In the wake of the urban disorders of the late sixties, official attention from the White House to state house and city hall focused on "the urban crisis," and on devising measures for revitalizing the nation's cities, not only to rebuild already devastated areas, but to halt further decay in declining neighborhoods. And for the first time in the history of a national effort to deal with urban decline stretching back to the Housing Act of 1949, politicians were now forced to work from the neighborhood up rather than from city hall down. Residents of neighborhoods where housing or other construction was to be done were not only insisting on being part of the planning process, but were learning how to make their voices heard. The "needs" of the user (resident of housing, office or factory worker, teacher or student, preacher or worshipper) and the "needs" of the client (i.e., whoever pays for the building) are always to some degree in conflict, and effective resolution of such conflicts has always been for architects one of the most critical factors in the design process. Their efforts to create buildings which are humane environments for users, not to mention humane additions to cityscape or landscape, are always modified by the constraints of the so-called "real world"—that is, the complex of institutional forces, from banks and lending institutions to public agencies, developers and building committees, where the decisions that in

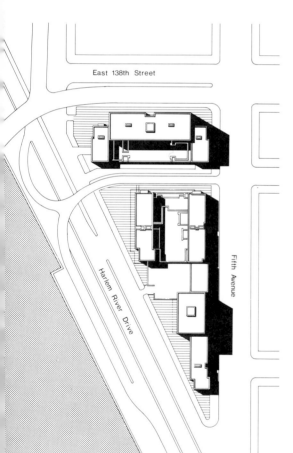

East 138th Street

Harlem River Drive

Fifth Avenue

large part dictate the architectural result are made. So the emergence of "citizen participation" in the planning process had to a significant degree the effect of bulwarking architects in their efforts to recognize user and community needs, because it forced clients, public and private, to take such needs into account—or risk delay or cancellation of projects.

Riverbend was a precursor that showed what urban architecture might become. ("We thought that architecture might make life more pleasurable for people," architect Lewis Davis

says.) It was a middle-income cooperative financed under New York State's Mitchell-Lama limited profit housing law, and it turned a derelict site at 138th Street between Fifth Avenue and the Harlem River into a special place to live—special in the sense of being what the people who were going to live there thought *they* would like to live in. The concept evolved in the closest collaboration among members of the cooperative, a group of long-time neighborhood residents; the architects; the developer, Richard Ravitch of HRH; and the city's

housing agency, then headed by the late Samuel Ratensky, an architect and veteran city housing official who had long crusaded for quality in the city's housing. Riverbend could not have happened without the diverse talents and inordinate dedication of a very special group of people; but it represented a kind of effort that the times were calling for, and would soon *demand,* all across the country.

1973

An abbey church built mostly underground made a striking but unpretentious entrance to a monastery, its triangulated roof planes creating a lofty sanctuary with sky views.

A single building on a prairie site launched a new university.

One side of a rural school expressed its plan, while the others were designed as signs or symbols of something more — or less, depending to a large degree on the eye of the observer.

An urban school planned and built on modern principles, of modern materials, became part of a historic street, its elements scaled to relate easily to well-preserved row houses around it.

Design of a new Federal Reserve Bank solved the client's problems by putting operations above and below grade, and opened the site to public use with a 2.5-acre site at ground level.

A commercial bank headquarters linked a small-city downtown and its riverfront by providing a public plaza and a riverside promenade in its own back yard.

A parallelogram generated "a building designed primarily as a drive-through billboard".

An automated drive-in bank in Pedregal, Mexico's first, celebrated the auto age with a canopy which was intended to symbolize moving auto pistons.

The house as architecture was offering as always an index to the range of architectural trends, revealing diversity and a common inclination to defer to the landscape and recall from the past, high style or vernacular.

A Michigan house filled a natural bowl and echoed the landscape's sweep from water's edge to treetops.

A Long Island beach house with its own guest house celebrated complexity and contradiction and evoked the vernacular in some of its finishes and details.

A developer vacation house at California's Sea Ranch was adventuresome inside and rural vernacular outside, and another California house in old farmhouse tradition was surrounded by porches; but these were designed to merge outdoors with indoors when wall panels were folded up against porch ceilings.

Urban housing was "scattered" on smaller sites in response to citizen opposition to vast renewal projects requiring demolition of whole neighborhoods.

On another "scattered" site, the conceptual focus was on community, the design of buildings sited, massed and detailed to create outdoor spaces that could become a new nucleus for the neighborhood.

An extraordinary approach to city rejuvenation, urban renewal financed by private enterprise, was made possible in Kansas City by a corporate client convinced that architectural quality counts and willing to wait for profits.

A tower-and-podium scheme capitalized on a rocky site to create a building that celebrated the emergence of the hotel as architecture.

Spectacular architecture became a human and commercial success in a series of hotels designed by an architect who was also a developer.

A humanist's critique of a new building found symbolism that reached deep into the human psyche and related to images common to the mythology of primitive cultures.

In the 11-year process of planning and building a headquarters, AIA as client held to principles it had long advocated, while it confronted from a very different perspective many of the issues that challenged architects in the 1970s.

An abbey church built mostly underground
made a striking but unpretentious entrance
to a monastery, its triangulated roof planes
creating a lofty sanctuary with sky views

St. Benedict's Abbey Church
Benet Lake, Wisconsin
Architect: Stanley Tigerman

A 68-foot-square concrete box was concealed by an 8-foot-wide sloping earth berm. The roof was made of 10 laminated beechwood trusses, with sloping planes created by leaving out the top horizontal chord of the perimeter trusses. Vertical planes on the perimeter were sheathed in metal, the others in solar bronze glass to become clerestories for the main sanctuary. Seats for 300 laymen and choir stalls for a maximum of 36 monks were arranged to create two major axes forming a cross which was expressed in the roof truss system as well as in plan. Access to and from the monastery is by means of a double ramp and connecting corridor, through an exposed concrete link containing the hollow cylinder in which the bell is hung.

For some years before he designed this church, Stanley Tigerman had been exploring a range of urbanistic problems not only in his architecture but in his painting and sculpture. He had produced such visionary architecture as "Instant City," a proposal for a grouping of self-contained housing and office pyramids which would span expressways; and "Urban Matrix," which proposed inverse pyramids to create habitation on water. His painting and sculpture were continually both prefiguring and developing his urban concepts, and so was his architecture. In designing St. Benedict's Church, he was exploring on a beautiful rural site some of the principles of scale and context evolving out of his urbanistic studies. The church was required not only to serve the monastery as a chapel, but to be physically connected to it; and the relationships of the church to the monastery and to the rolling landscape of its site were critical design determinants. The result was both strange (in the sense of unfamiliar) and powerful, probably Tigerman's most significant effort in a direction he was soon to abandon. "The exterior of St. Benedict's Abbey Church in Benet Lake, Wisconsin refocuses the eye and challenges one's preconceptions about how a church should look," the RECORD observed. "In essence the structure appears to be a roof and a base with no building in between—rather like one of sculptor-painter Rene Magritte's somber images of hats perched on shoulders instead of heads. There is something curiously dissatisfying in the lack of transition between the terne-coated stainless steel roof and the sodded grass

berms which surround the chapel. The only unity between roof and berms is a common geometry of triangular and trapezoidal planes. The building appears scaleless, due in part to the fact that the doors are hidden in deep reveals and other elements which clarify scale are invisible or absent. Such first thoughts are soon followed, however, by the realization that Tigerman was purposefully attempting to create exterior forms of indefinite scale which are at the same time modest and unpretentious. The triangular-shaped vertical walls and

sloping roof planes were carefully sized to diminish the scale of the four-story Tudor-style monastery to which the church is attached. The interior of the church is as simple and direct in its juxtaposition of functional elements and its use and joining of materials as is the exterior. The ceiling is sharply defined from the walls by the straightforward use of beechwood trusses and interior decking, as well as the solar glass. Even the carpet has its own clearly articulated edge. The principal structural materials are all exposed, and no veneers or facings

have been used. Since the bulk of the building has been constructed below ground, heat loss or gain is minimized, and energy is conserved.''

A single building on a vast prairie site launched a new university

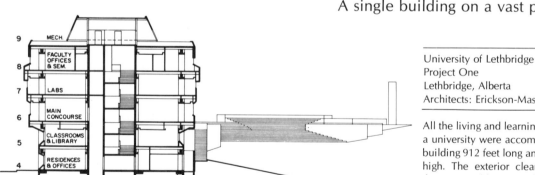

University of Lethbridge
Project One
Lethbridge, Alberta
Architects: Erickson-Massey

All the living and learning functions of a university were accommodated in a building 912 feet long and nine stories high. The exterior clearly expressed the variety of functions that take place inside. The broad bands of concrete and glass on the upper levels vary in depth as the overall function of each floor varies—sixth floor, main concourse, large windows; seventh floor, laboratories, only a narrow band of glass set high on the wall and slanting outward so that it counts as slightly more than a line; eighth floor, faculty offices. On lower floors, the structural supports break the continuity of the glass and diminish scale.

An old railway bridge that stretches its flat length across the nearby Oldman River "like a horizon line," fitting its supports into the banks and bed of the river, strongly influenced Arthur Erickson in the design of this building. Struck by the way the bridge used the terrain it had to cross, Erickson fitted his building into a series of large and small gullies so that its roof stretches 912 feet across its prairie site "like a horizon line." The prairie landscape is "a distillation of all the elements of earth and sky," in Erickson's words, and "objects caught between earth and sky appear trivial unless they emerge intrinsically from one or the other, or unless they reflect in generosity of size the prairie scale."

This first building for the University of Lethbridge, the RECORD reported, "has a superb location overlooking the valley of the Oldman River and the undulations of its site, using the contours to its advantage and for its own purposes, so that its height varies while its roofline remains constant, a flat plane that hardly rises above the line of the horizon. The best overall view of the building is from the east, from Lethbridge, and it is the only view of it that can be had on the nine-mile drive from city to campus. The road climbs from the river valley to the high prairie and then turns down toward the coulees (a western word for gullies) for a sudden and dramatic change in scale which is reflected in the siting of the building. Gradually the roof comes into view as you near the campus, but not until you stand on the brink of the coulee is the whole immensity of the building visible and comprehensible. It is a breath-

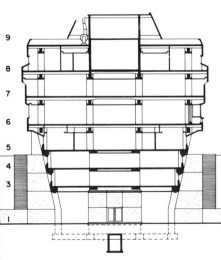

taking moment, for this is a very large building—912 feet long, nine stories high—and it stands, for the moment at least, in the midst of a barren landscape. In such a setting, the building had to be bold; and, because of its program, it could not be other than large. Even when development takes place around it—the university itself will grow, and the city expects to grow to the west of the campus—its 'generosity of size,' to borrow the Erickson phrase, will be right for its site. Within this one building are contained all the elements that make

up a university: student residences, classrooms, laboratories, offices for administration, faculty and student activities, library, bookstore, dining room, snack bar—everything except Fine Arts and Physical Education, which have their own building (Project 1A, Robins Mitchell Watson, Architects).

So complete an integration of residential and learning spaces in one structure is rare if not unique, but here it represents an architectural response to academic goals set up in 1967 by the Univeristy Planning Committee. Those

goals called for 'flexibility and openness to innovation; encouragement to the highest degree of interaction between students and faculty; fostering the spirit of free inquiry and the critical interpretation of ideas.' The essential character of the university was that it was to be a place where, as its first president, Sam Smith, said, 'Everything can happen at once,' and where there would be 'a chance to make the whole person.' "

One side of a building expressed its plan, while the others
were designed as signs or symbols of something more—
or less, depending to a large degree on the eye of the observer

Mt. Healthy Elementary School
Columbus, Indiana
Architects: Hardy Holzman Pfeiffer
Associates

A building triangular in plan was designed to have two sides that look like
an avant-garde version of the red brick
schoolhouse with a flag out front and a
third that expresses the complexity of a
multi-level plan. "These architects,"
the RECORD observed, "see no reason
why all sides of a building should look
like the same building. Nostalgia is
popular, and so the architects have
used rusticated limestone lintels and
sills for the windows on the two
straight sides. Like those commonplace structures which Robert Venturi
has made us see—modest sheds hidden behind huge signs which proclaim
their symbolic function—the Mt.
Healthy school has two facades which
appear to be detached from the building and proclaim what the building is
not and yet somehow is. The saw-
toothed facade has an unrepentant
modern factory look—no nostalgia
facing southeast. Lighter brick expresses the pivoting upper levels of the educational 'clusters' within."

This open-plan school for team teaching was
built in a rural area where most of the pupils
came from farm homes, for a conservative
board of education which had resisted the
open-plan concept for 20 years. The architects
developed an innovative plan based on multi-
level "clusters" of grade levels and arranged in
a triangle with two sides straight and one saw-
toothed. On the saw-toothed side, you could
read the plan in elevation; on the others you
could deduce what meaning your experience
and imagination permitted. The lofty interior

spaces with exposed structural and mechanical systems painted in vivid colors were characteristic of the work of Hardy Holzman Pfeiffer, which has been strongly influenced by
concepts of the late Louis I. Kahn; but exterior
facades conceived as cryptic "signs"—the
game codified by Robert Venturi—were not.
Intensive investigation of functional requirements and the new architectural possibilities
they might suggest has also been strongly characteristic of the work of HHP, and the RECORD
considered their approach to planning for

open education both innovative and promising. "From the start," the RECORD reported,
"the architects wished to avoid the creation of
over-scaled spaces. To this end, they developed
three multi-level clusters of 180 students
each—a primary cluster (kindergarten through
second grade), an upper primary cluster (third
and fourth grades) and an intermediate cluster
(fifth and sixth grades). Within each cluster are
six articulated spaces accommodating 30 students each. The plan was generated by pivoting the superimposed layers of each cluster in

a manner which produces four half-levels or two two-story buildings. Within the clusters are well-scaled one-story and two-story spaces creating a variety of interior enclosures. At the same time, each cluster is a place with which a child can identify and to which he or she belongs. Essentially, the clusters are simple rectangular boxes (mostly without lids) skewed within a standard skeleton grid. And essentially, the clusters are one building, the services and general spaces are another, while the corridor spine divides them. The corridor is not defined by open volumes or walls, but all elements open on it—principal's office, administration space, library, reading carrels, coat rooms, toilets, teacher preparation rooms, combined lunch and large group instruction room, gymnasium and art and music areas. While the building's spatial geometries are too intricate to be easily grasped by anyone moving about and through it, the structural frame and the elements which furnish the interior spaces have sufficient clarity to act as visual clues to aid a child in orientation. The architects' color coding of the structural and mechanical systems helps, as do the varying carpet patterns. In addition, each cluster has its own supergraphic designation "A," "B," "C." Excluding skylights, interior height is 24 feet 6 inches, and no partitions go to the roof except those which surround mechanical equipment, kitchen and gym. For acoustical reasons, and because the children spend a lot of time on the floor, carpet has been used wherever possible. Sound is also modified by a background hum in the mechanical system.

An urban school planned and built on modern principles, of modern materials, was designed as part of a historic street, its elements scaled to relate easily to well-preserved row houses around it

William Kent Elementary School
Boston, Massachusetts
Architects:Earl R. Flansburgh
and Associates

Large, long-span, relatively scaleless elements were grouped in an almost windowless stepped block on the western side of a 2.7-acre sloping site in the center of Boston's historic Charlestown district. Against this static mass, the classroom spaces were manipulated into a lively pattern of setbacks that generated design interest while responding to the scale of the street and the surrounding row houses. The main entrance, at the juncture between the two major groups of elements, became a tall and dramatic space kept human in scale by its vigorous expression of levels, with a canted skylight as its climax.

Another school intended mainly for unstructured classes was designed to relate to a dense urban site in a straightforward way that any observer could comprehend. The school is not only in a historic district but (as the RECORD noted) it "stands on the flank of Bunker Hill — about a three-iron shot from the monument itself — in the center of the historic Charlestown district of Boston. Covering 2.2 acres of its 2.7-acre site, it is surrounded by well-preserved frame row houses and is highly visible from the approaches and span of the Mystic River

Bridge. Because of its conspicuous location and the historic associations of its site, the school had to relate visually to its 19th-century neighbors in matters of cornice height, setback and scale." But, as the RECORD also remarked, "the school has very different genes. It is a contemporary steel frame structure, shaped by noticeably different principles of planning and design and embodying decidedly 20th-century notions of how the young should be educated." The neighborhood proprieties were observed by careful proportioning and concern

for scale in the design of the component spaces as well as in the overall massing of the building. "From the downhill side [photo page 68]," as the RECORD pointed out, "the school could easily have become massive and inhospitable. Instead, because the designers were sensitive, it is a carefully composed series of ascending levels that culminate in a gently dominant central stair tower."

Entry and vertical circulation were put in a dramatically skylighted four-story volume. Exterior brick is carried inside for continuity, and

the stair landings, framed out using exposed steel, are fitted with double height pipe railings for the protection of youngsters. The same pipe railing is used for handrail, augmented by a lower wood rail for the use of younger children. Flansburgh originally conceived the space as part of a public circulation route throughout the community. These plans were later dropped at the request of the school board, "but the tall space with its vigorous expression of levels retains," in the RECORD's view, "much of the strength of the first conception. In spite of its apparent height, the viewer is not 'shrunk,' the eye is drawn rhythmically upward, pausing for a moment at each level, and easily finding release through a canted skylight over the entrance to the teachers' fifth-floor lounge. For a school, it is a surprisingly powerful spatial composition. But for so steeply contoured a site, it seems especially appropriate to express the elements of vertical circulation with force and conviction."

Design of a new Federal Reserve Bank
solved the client's problems by
putting operations above and below
grade and opened the site to public use
with a 2.5-acre plaza at ground level

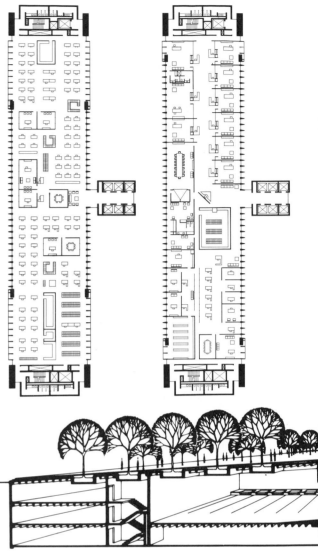

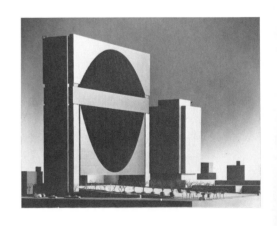

Like the Oakland Museum (pages 12–13), Ulrich Franzen's Binghamton bank (pages 80-81) and still other buildings in later chapters, this building responded to urban issues beyond its client's program, and made the design of an ordinary building type the occasion for an extraordinary contribution to its community. Banks of the Federal Reserve System were never known for their avant-garde architecture, nor for their sensitivity to public (as against financial community) opinion. But, like other once-conservative clients, they began in the

1970s to think of modern architecture as a tool for the creation of a contemporary image, and of prestige architecture as a source of public esteem. The original Federal Reserve Bank of Minneapolis, as the RECORD reported, was built in the early 1920s and was a windowless, forbidding structure. The architect, Cass Gilbert, described it as "a strongbox for the currency of the Northwest." The president of the Bank in 1973 was said to echo Gilbert's concern for security while adding a new twist: "The responsibility of the Bank to serve the financial

community and the public requires openness and accessibility." The new Federal Reserve Bank of Minneapolis served, then, to explore some significant issues of urban design, an uncommon but heartening contribution of the banking community to civic architecture. (Citicorp Center, pages 216–219, would make another.) Supporting a large office building by spanning an entire city block with catenary arches "has the potential," the RECORD pointed out, "of spanning throughways and occupying other types of air rights space, and could be a

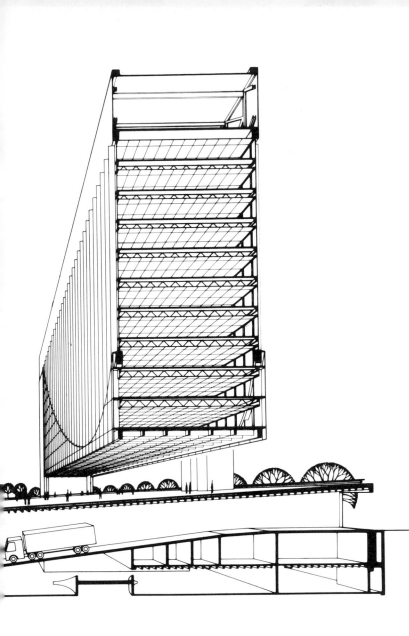

Federal Reserve Bank
of Minneapolis
Minneapolis, Minnesota
Architects: Gunnar Birkerts
and Associates

The building spans 330 feet to provide office floors with clear spans of 275 feet. Security operations which require protected facilities were put below grade. The plaza slopes gently upward to a height of 20 feet above the building's entrance level. Administrative and clerical operations were housed in an office block suspended from two concrete towers. Catenaries 60 feet apart, one on either side of the building, support the major facades, rigid frames, which in turn support the concrete slab floors. The tendency of supporting towers at either end to topple inward is checked by two 28-foot trusses at the top of the building; the space between contains mechanical equipment. Catenary members are echoed in the curtain wall—below the curve, the glass stands forward; above, it stands behind.

model for future high-density, multilayered design.'' Its architect had just that in mind. ''The 330-foot span which supports this bank office tower,'' the RECORD declared while the building was under construction, ''is more than an amazing structural *tour de force*. While he acknowledges the excitement his structural gymnastics will generate, Birkerts denies that he was merely trying to be the first architect to integrate a suspension bridge with a multistory office building. He supports his structural concept with a convincing program-matic rationale which points out that, because the high security portions of the bank are under the plaza and call for a complex system of truck access and turn-arounds, as well as other specialized spaces, it was difficult to work out a conventional system of column spacing to support the office tower above. Birkerts has conceived this building as having three layers, each of which he has strongly articulated. In addition to the office block and the vast underground areas, there is the site itself, a full city block of 108,000 square feet, which, except for access ramps, the two great pylons and the elevator core, will be uninterrupted by permanent structures. In a sense, Birkerts' scheme gives this open space back to the city. The office block can be said to occupy the bank's own air rights. Birkerts hopes that this building will become a prototype for large-scale interconnected urban structures which will conserve open space in two ways: by spanning it far above the ground plane, and by relegating all support facilities to subterranean levels.'' [See also photograph inside front cover.]

A commercial bank headquarters linked a small-city downtown and its riverfront by providing a public plaza and a riverside promenade in its own back yard

Ezra Stoller © ESTO

Not only the Federal Reserve but commercial banks were turning to architecture for help in the increasingly important process of creating and maintaining an environmentally positive image in the public mind. An architect like Ulrich Franzen, long concerned with "place" and "context" as prime generators of architectural concepts, could now be permitted, even encouraged, to serve the client better by serving the community as well. An extra dimension of architectural service was beginning to be in demand. In his design of this bank headquar-

ters for an urban renewal site, Franzen was able to create a major link between downtown Binghamton and its riverfront by providing a public plaza and riverside promenade as the setting for the back of his building. Those amenities, one supposes, could only increase pedestrian traffic to, through and around the bank, so that client and community would both profit. "Circulation is an important key in the intelligent development of this handsome riverfront site," the RECORD observed in describing the design concept. "Franzen has con-

centrated much of his attention on creating an inviting pedestrian scale and environment. Parking and drive-in banking services are provided below plaza level, with access confined to one end of the site. Pedestrian approaches from all directions form part of the generous plaza ambulatory. The main banking room is located in a double-height space overlooked by an executive mezzanine that provides the scheme's only vertical spatial tie. The two upper floors are rental space. The strong horizontal emphasis of the design is intended to

First-City National Bank Building
Binghamton, New York
Architects: Ulrich Franzen and Associates

Similar functions and similar structural requirements were organized to create two groups of elements: garage and terrace levels and office floors. Raising the main banking room above street level made basement parking and drive-in teller service visible from the street, and simplified both pedestrian and vehicular traffic flow. The building has two main entrances, both on the street side—one up a gently sloping ramp, the other up broad steps beside the banking room. Lobby elevators serve floors above and garage below.

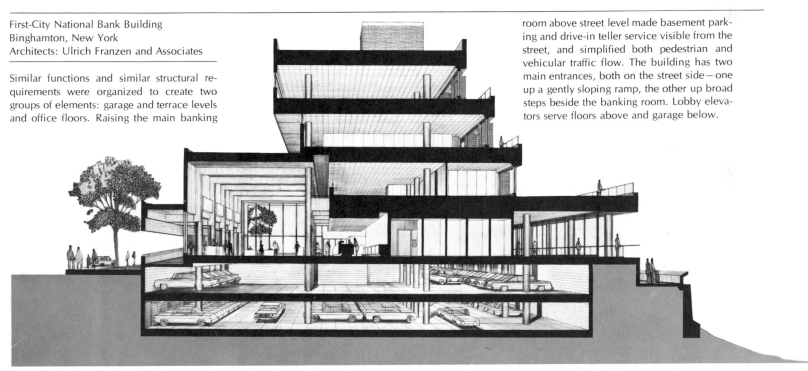

bring the building into empathy with its low-rise surroundings. The visual alternation between window wall and parapet forcefully stripes the long elevations. Solid end walls, buttressed by enclosed stair towers, close the composition decisively.'' When the building was completed, the RECORD discussed it in terms of civic architecture: ''The combination of handsome, buff-colored brick exterior, elegantly appointed interiors, and landscaped public terraces with connecting walks make this new headquarters building a significant and

sensitively conceived addition to the city. The strong horizontality of the building agrees with the scale and tone of the city, and relates pleasantly to the river along whose banks the building is disposed. That such a site with such a river frontage was available in the downtown business district made its attractions more compelling than its disadvantages, including a less-than-desirable amount of foot traffic on the street side of the building. To overcome this problem, the building is designed as a welcoming environment, inside and out, for

both customer and employee. The main banking floor is raised half a floor above street level to make it a very visible 'destination' for pedestrian and vehicular traffic. There are four entrances to the building, one of which is a ramp. The executive floor above the banking room opens onto a wide terrace; below are a public terrace and a path along the river.''

A parallelogram generated
"a building designed primarily
as a drive-through billboard"

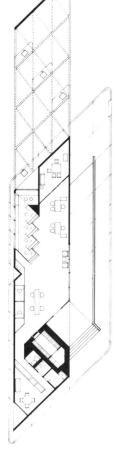

Park Road Branch
North Carolina National Bank
Charlotte, North Carolina
Architects: Wolf Associates

The steeply sloping site was on a main
artery between two major shopping
centers and several large office buildings. Diagonal movement across the
site—and thus the shape of the building itself—was derived from placing
the main entrance at the lower south-
eastern corner and the exit, as well as a
secondary entrance, at the upper
northeastern corner. This configuration also served to preserve trees at the
northeastern corner of the site. A large
parking lot at the front of the building
provided parking for employees and
for customers with business inside.

Not only architects but clients as well were seeing architecture in terms of sign or symbol, and this phenomenon was not limited to big cities and big buildings. Small buildings and workaday building types are where architecture begins for most people and also for most architects—so when *their* clients want buildings that not only function but communicate something more, it signals a major change in the circumstances in which architecture is being done, and offers architects major new opportunities for creative design. The awakened

public concern with environmental quality, and the developing public determination to be in control of it (pages 42–47), were the broad new context in which clients were operating.

Beyond those considerations, some rather spectacular examples of commercial profits from public response to spectacular commercial architecture seem likely to have been a significant influence on attitudes of other commercial clients. It was in hotels, of all places, that commercial exploitation of architecture as experience began. As remarked in

the preface of another ARCHITECTURAL RECORD book, *Places for People* (McGraw-Hill, 1976), "The idea that you could design a hotel so that people got a kick out of their surroundings, and that it could be good business to do it, probably got its commercial start in the brashly fantastic hotels designed for the fantasy world of Miami Beach in the fifties by architect Morris Lapidus. Architect Minoru Yamasaki's Century Plaza in Los Angeles adapted the concept to more worldly tastes, and the spectacular series of hotels by architect John Portman that began

An automated drive-in bank in Pedregal, Mexico's first, celebrated the auto age with a canopy symbolizing moving auto pistons

with the Atlanta Regency Hyatt (1965) has effectively institutionalized the idea that the hotel you stay at may be one of the things you come to see—and experience." The commercial success of these hotels was as spectacular as their architecture, a result that was quickly communicated in the traveling world of business executives. Some of the architectural consequences for other building types were awful; but for architects of talent and conscience, a new freedom—not to be mundane—had been established.

Branch, Banco Nacional de Mexico
Mexico City, D.F.
Architect: Jesus Enriquez Vega

Architecture flavored by fantasy was turning up far from Miami Beach. This branch bank was built for the residential community of the famed Gardens of the Pedregal, south of Mexico City. The canopy designed by the architect to shelter the auto-teller stations was a series of cylindrical aluminum drums symbolically expressing automobile pistons in motion. Each drum is topped by a tinted acrylic dome controlling the light level over TV receivers below.

Ezra Stoller © ESTO

Ezra Stoller © ESTO

The house as architecture was offering as always an index to the range of architectural trends, revealing diversity and a common inclination to defer to the landscape and recall from the past, high styles or vernacular

House on eastern Long Island
East Hampton, New York
Architects: Gwathmey Siegel Architects

Recollections of the thirties were unmistakable in this very large house, which was deftly planned and massed, in a thoroughly 1970s way, to diminish its apparent bulk and maximize views of a serenely beautiful rural landscape. The front of the house (above) is relatively closed and dramatizes the automobile approach. The back (top) is largely glass and has a number of outdoor viewing decks to take advantage of a panorama of pond and ocean. The real spaciousness of the house is visually extended by the big window wall and the viewing deck, and, vertically, by the ramp which links all levels of the house and the long skylight above it.

"The lean, powerful elegance of this sizable house," the RECORD remarked, "synthesizes some of today's design directions—and with great aplomb. The house is very much in the stylistic vein of Gwathmey Siegel's work, and demonstrates a continuing growth in assurance and maturity. The house sits like a big, artfully asymmetrical sculpture on a gently sloping five-acre site. It is bounded on the south by a pond, with views of the ocean beyond. To take full advantage of these vistas, the living-dining areas are elevated, European fashion, to the second floor. The ground floor level is zoned by an entry which separates car and service areas from bedrooms for the family's three children and their adjoining indoor and outdoor play spaces. On varying levels above the main living spaces are ranged the master bedroom suite, a study, guest accommodations and a roof terrace; all are connected by a ramp and by stairs. Thus each activity area of the house has its own 'zone' and full privacy. The structure has a regular column grid of white-painted steel which supports the basically rectangular roof. The rest of the structure is wood frame, clad inside and out with tongue and groove cedar siding treated with a bleaching oil to obtain a soft gray color. All cabinet work is treated as a 'secondary building system' and is also surfaced in white. The basic rectangle of the house is relieved by what the architects describe as 'variations in erosions, transparencies and extensions related to views and indoor-outdoor, public and private, activities.' The resulting interplay of geometric voids and solids, great stairs and elevated pipe-rail ter-

races, strongly recalls the 'International Style' of the 1930s. It is an approach to design which works well in such a big-scaled house as this without seeming pretentious or overbearing. But the house is very much of today, especially in its amenities—including a very well-handled and integrated automobile approach and carport; there is even a dumbwaiter to transport groceries to the second-level kitchen. Landscaping and interior design for the house were also done by the architects and contribute enormously to the visual cohesiveness and unity of the place. Daylighting has been as carefully considered as artificial light; clerestories and skylights add balance and drama, and operable canvas awnings shade the big living area window wall. All interiors are furnished in a generously scaled, low-key, comfortable fashion, with bright spots of color for accent against the basic gray of the bleached cedar siding and the white monochrome of the steel structure.''

A Michigan house filled a
natural bowl and echoed
the landscape's sweep from
water's edge to treetops

Beach house in Michigan
Harbor Springs, Michigan
Architects: William Kessler
and Associates

A house made of cedar shingles
and field-stone had its living,
dining and kitchen areas at
ground level on the shore side;
the master bedroom on the top
level also faced the shore. The
site is surrounded by thickets of
pine, spruce and birch trees.

A Long Island beach house
with its own guest house evoked
the vernacular in some of
its finishes and details

House on eastern Long Island
Long Island, New York
Architects: Robert A.M. Stern
and John S. Hagmann

A house with a program like
those of great country houses of
yore (servants' rooms and a
separate guest house) was designed with all the conscious
complexity of a Robert Venturi
disciple.

The complex order of this house reflected unusual and rather intricate client requirements
and an architectural response of considerable
savoir faire. "From the first approach by car the
way is, literally, circuitous," as the RECORD put
it. "It presents sequential views of clusters and
great gatherings of trees, of the sea, and finally
of the front door of the main house (left in photo above). The more public rooms of the house
are spaces peculiarly configured and assembled, sometimes high, sometimes low, sometimes opening to the sea, sometimes turning

away to the patio and pool behind. Long diagonal vistas are provided through all this complexity, anchoring axes that give the inhabitants some of the sense of the whole from any
one part. The complex order of the house is
thus revealed by these swathes cut through the
inside. Faint memories of old beach houses on
the Atlantic are evoked on the outside by the
cedar shingles and on the inside by the old-
fashioned, consciously clumsy brick fireplace.
Memories are evoked, too, by the surfaces of the
walls and ceilings, made from narrow tongue

and groove boards with half-round beadings at
their joints that used to be used for wainscot-
ing, or for porch ceilings. With these elements
of recall, with its light and airy spaces, and
with its handsome contemporary furnishings
and bright colors, the house is a complicated
potpourri of old and new, allying itself exclu-
sively with neither, but with the needs and
dreams of its owners."

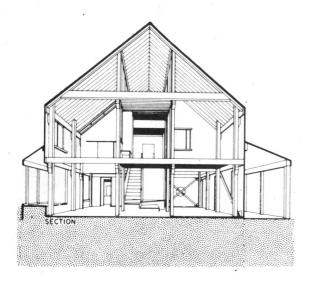

SECTION

Vacation House
The Sea Ranch, California
Architects: William Turnbull and
Charles Moore of MLTW/
Moore-Turnbull

The "Binker Barn," so named for the
developer's salesman who came up
with the idea, was repeatable in several different versions, of which this was
one. The basic shape was a heavy-
framed box, with a kitchen and living
areas on the first floor, two bedrooms
and a bath above and, higher still, lofts
for sleeping or simply for retreat. The
lean-to could be a carport, a garage or
a third bedroom. A separate garage
could be added.

"This ingenious vacation house," the RECORD reported, "has been built well over a dozen times at the Sea Ranch in California. The basic notion is simplicity itself: a barn-like space with a plan that can be flipped and with an appended lean-to whose function is variable. The working out of the notion, though, assures that simplicity does not lead to dullness. The ground floor plan is circuitous, so that the apparent size of the space is increased because the eye can never see all of it at once. The Z-shaped plan of the second floor allows sun-

light to fall into the living areas from skylights in the roof, casting patterns that change with the hours and with the seasons. It also provides upward vistas from below, and the pleasure of moving from a low space, like the dining area, to one that is dramatically higher. One can also move outside the enclosing walls of the house to lounge in a bay window, or right up to the peak of the roof to doze or sleep in one of the lofts there. What begins, then, as a simple space ends up providing an admirable array of different places to be and things to do.

The feeling of the interior is relaxed with simple details: rough-sawn boards are left unfinished and heavy framing members are fully exposed. Outside, this way of building produces an effect that is downright modest, recalling simple rural structures."

A developer vacation house
at California's Sea Ranch
was adventuresome inside and
rural vernacular outside,
and another California house
in old farmhouse tradition
was surrounded by porches,
but these were designed to
merge outdoors and indoors
when wall panels were folded
up against porch ceilings

W. Hamilton Budge House
Healdsburg, California
Architects: MLTW/Charles Moore and
William Turnbull

A house for summers and weekends
evoked the California farmhouses of
the surrounding countryside with its
gabled or hip-roofed rectangles surrounded by porches to protect the
house from summer sun. In this house,
walls adjoining the screened porches
on three sides are made of plywood
panels which fold up against the porch
ceiling (as in the photograph of the
kitchen, at right) thus merging indoors
and out.

Photos © Morley Baer

"A house with rooms which open up to make a giant screen porch, a pavilion among the trees," as the RECORD described it, "was built for weekends and summers in a beautiful oak forest above a pond 70 miles north of San Francisco. In these hills, the summer, when the house is most used, is six months long and almost cloudless; rain is virtually unknown, the days are hot and still, and in the evening cool breezes blow. In that nostalgic world of endless summer days, the architects made a very simple house, like the classical farm-

houses of California. These houses of memory were generally gabled or hip-roofed rectangles surrounded by porches which kept off the hot summer sun. In this version, the walls themselves are made so they fold up against the porch ceiling to merge indoors and out. In each corner lies a room, two bedrooms in opposite corners and in the alternate spaces a kitchen and a living room. The living room corner breaks the system; its walls of fixed glass and sliding doors reach to the edge of the house and give it space and outlook even in

winter, when the counterbalancing walls in the other rooms are shut against wind and cold. The living room has for those days and nights a fireplace. The middle of the house, unlike a California farmhouse (but like a California barn) is open to the peak of the redwood roof, and skylights dramatize the center of the house."

Urban housing was "scattered" on smaller sites
in response to citizen opposition to vast renewal projects
which required demolition of whole neighborhoods

"Twin Parks Southwest took its shape from the conjunction within the last decade of several important housing and planning concepts whose time had finally come," the RECORD reported. "By 1967, it was clear that the days of large-scale urban renewal were over in New York City. Neighborhood citizens' groups had learned to prevent, by intense opposition, the dislocation of people demd the disruption of community life which the renewal practices of the fifties and early sixties had engendered. The Urban Design Group, a team of in-house

consultants to the New York City Planning Commission, began to devise a new approach. This team then consisted of Jaquelin Robertson, Richard Weinstein, Myles Weintraub and Jonathan Barnett. With Pasanella's collaboration, they began to work with various community groups in the Bronx to select appropriate sites for 'vest pocket' renewal. The sites selected are irregular in shape and varied in topography, unlike the vast sites formerly leveled for urban renewal. These sites demanded a new kind of housing design." The floor-

through, split-level scheme developed by Pasanella for Twin Parks Southwest separated living and sleeping areas by a half level, and served two and a half floors with one elevator stop and one corridor space, thus saving 60 per cent of the public corridor space for redistribution into apartments. The practicality of the split-level dwelling unit in terms of the difficulties it gave contractors with no experience in this type of construction was challenged after the construction of Twin Parks Southwest; but while it was no surprise that contractors prefer

Twin Parks Southwest
The Bronx, New York
Client: New York State
Urban Development Corporation
Architect: Giovanni Pasanella

An approach to design of multifamily housing which gave precedence, in the architect's words, to "the capsule of space in which each family lives" over "the more technical aspects of the building process" produced a concept based on a typical cross-section rather than a typical apartment plan. The five-level section element incorporated two "floors" of floor-through, split-level apartments which shared corridor space and an elevator stop. Savings in public corridor space over a conventional apartment plan amounted to 60 per cent apartment space gained. Other pluses: cross-ventilation and separation by a half level of living and bedroom areas.

to build the familiar, the UDC cost figures showed that Pasanella's split levels were brought in at the same price per dwelling unit as the single-level apartments in comparable UDC projects, which suggested to the RECORD that "split-level dwelling projects could and should become commonplace."

It was Pasanella's view, the RECORD reported, that even trained architectural eyes had not always seen "the wealth of evidence in New York for the existence of the 'counter-thematic' apartment type." Such antecedents of the ideal housing type, Pasanella had found, "always embody characteristics which are displayed more in the cross-section than in the plan, and typically are less the function of those details that give the building its 'look' than of certain efforts to give the building its proper ambience. These efforts cause some rooms to be 1½ or even 2½ times as high as others, or to relate to each other in particular ways — apartments arranged on several levels as in our own split-level paradigm, or the more common duplex type." The conventional solution, with its high proportion of corridor space to apartment space, makes far less efficient use of elevator stops, fire stair landings and other common elements. Beyond the spatial advantages of the five-level section developed by Pasanella for Twin Parks Southwest, the concept assured more intensive use of corridors, making them safer as well as more conducive of social contact. With elevator stops two and a half floors apart, vertical travel was safer for everybody; apartments could have cross-ventilation and different levels for living and sleeping.

"With this design scheme of hard-edged volumes, containing small-scale private uses and defining large-scale public spaces, Richard Meier has resolved perhaps his most challenging design problem to date," the RECORD said. "Given parts of three adjacent blocks on an irregular site in the Twin Parks section of the Bronx, Meier's problem was to produce badly needed housing for limited income tenants within a low budget, while reinforcing the existing neighborhood and at the same time creating an architecturally decisive entity.

Meier was commissioned by the New York State Urban Development Corporation (UDC) soon after the concept of the Twin Parks projects was developed [page 90] and was subject to the same growing pains as his client. Realizing that an overall, meaningful resolution was not going to be easily accomplished, the architect took initial steps toward problem simplification. Conventional poured concrete construction and traditional apartment layouts were early decisions. This Twin Parks project was one of the first of many selected by devel-

opers from those offered by the public client. It was selected, developer Fred De Mattheis said, because of its straightforward building plans and the high percentage of repetitive, efficient simplex units. Single-loaded corridors, intended to light outdoor spaces and offer easy surveillance, were partially eliminated for budget savings. The brick cladding was chosen in common with several other projects for UDC in Twin Parks. In an effort to compensate for the clearly small, sometimes unworkable, programmed rooms (the client later increased

On another "scattered" site, the conceptual focus was on community,
the design of buildings sited, massed and detailed to create
outdoor spaces that could become a new nucleus for the neighborhood

Twin Parks Northeast
The Bronx, New York
Client: New York State Urban
Development Corporation
Architect: Richard Meier

Overall massing placed the lower buildings of this 523-unit complex so that they and the existing six-story neighbors form public spaces of both intricacy and larger symbolic meaning, a new focus for community life. Higher buildings faced existing city parks (outside the drawing's boundaries), and gave a sense of place to the two major plazas without blocking sunlight. A smaller scale common space was ingeniously cut from one of the few rectangular block intersections by the placement of one of the buildings. The street between the buildings was closed to traffic.

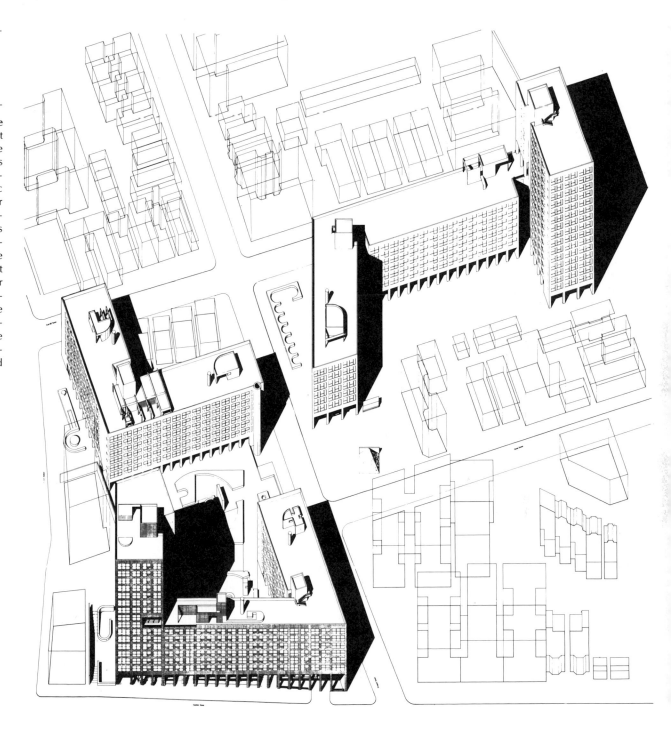

such standards), apartment windows are maximum in size, though this requires some contortions in placement of partitions. Meier avoided a monotonous cadence by grouping windows in large-scale blocks, and the glazing is pushed to the building face to minimize detailing and to emphasize the buildings as masses defining outdoor space. To fulfill the UDC's role of bolstering and (hopefully) turning around slipping neighborhood situations, a tough site in a difficult neighborhood was chosen, and everyone involved knew it. The site is on the bor-

derline between two ethnic neighborhood groups. If any physical effect could turn down the burner, it had to be a major statement of confidence that these groups could live together. Given the site limitations, the housing might have taken the form of infill, but this would have neglected problems of social contact and any natural assets. The architect knew that this stronger solution was required if any psychological dent was to be made. While great effort has been made to relate to existing buildings in scale, orientation and roof lines,

and selected street patterns have been maintained, there is also something new: a neighborhood nucleus. Perhaps the most controversial aspect of the design was the architect's intention that exterior public spaces should be open to the neighborhood. In the large view, the architect has provided an open passage aspect consistent with the public benefit. The general design success here might well be an example of how a building complex can become more of a success than any of its parts might indicate."

An extraordinary approach to city rejuvenation, urban renewal financed by private enterprise, was made possible in Kansas City by a corporate client convinced that architectural quality counts and willing to wait for profits

Crown Center Office Complex
Kansas City, Missouri
Architects: Edward Larrabee
Barnes and Associates. Associated
Architects: Marshall & Brown

This office complex, designed to symbolize and prefigure the quality of the architectural environment to come, was the first building group to be completed at Crown Center, followed by the public plaza and (pages 96-97) the hotel. The five seven-story buildings provide a total of 626,000 square feet and individually range from 90,000 to 157,000 square feet, in floor sizes from 8,600 to 28,000 square feet. Structures are linked on alternate floors, but each has its own entrance. Crown Center as visualized at completion is shown in model photo superimposed on aerial photo (lower left in aerial), which also shows (at top) Kansas City Municipal Airport and downtown towers.

Crown Center was conceived by the Hall family, founders and owners of Hallmark cards, as a private renewal effort for the decaying area surrounding their headquarters, five minutes from downtown Kansas City. A $400 million expenditure was anticipated over a 10-year period for development of 23 square blocks with office buildings, a bank, a shopping center with 65 stores, apartment buildings and townhouses, a 730-room hotel and a motel. No Federal subsidies were to be involved, and the Halls were prepared to wait twice as long

for profits as comparable developments under less extraordinary sponsorship. "Economic studies began in 1958, and land use analysis in 1961," as the RECORD described the process. "The principal land use planners were Victor Gruen and Associates. In 1967, Edward Larrabee Barnes was named coordinating architect and master planner responsible for giving form to the project. Although the Hallmark plant is adjacent to a large park and a major medical center, its prevailing context is a gray area of nondescript older buildings. To create an ur-

ban center within this worn and aging metropolitan fabric called for a bold initial statement—sufficient construction at the beginning to create what Barnes called 'a critical mass.' To develop public interest and bring tenants to Crown Center, Barnes advised the Halls to start construction of a 626,300-square-foot office complex distributed in a five-unit medium-rise structure with continuous horizontal space, and to include in the first phase of construction the terraced lawns and plaza, the hotel, the shopping center and, finally, the housing.

95

A tower-and-podium scheme capitalized on a rocky site to create a building that celebrated the resurgence of the hotel as architecture

Crown Center Hotel
Kansas City, Missouri
Architects: Harry Weese
and Associates.
Associated Architects:
Marshall & Brown

A 730-room hotel was perched on a limestone outcrop on the western edge of the Crown Center site, its elements superbly organized around the rock-face. Part of the rock itself was left exposed inside to help create a spectacular rock garden and waterfall designed to be seen from lobby seating areas. A winding staircase was provided so guests could wander through the garden and into an upstairs cocktail lounge which overlooks it. The view from glassed-in elevators includes a Helen Anselevicius tapestry in a diamond pattern that echoes the 45-degree angle used by Weese as the geometric basis for the hotel design.

''Barnes believes that, generally speaking high-rise buildings belong in the inner urban or downtown core, but that medium-rise is appropriate for what he calls 'the middle ground,' where Crown Center is located. His design for the horizontal office block follows the contours of the site and of the street. His master plan closes and builds over one north-south street to create the terraced lawns and plaza, but allows the other north-south artery to remain. The plaza is set on the level of this street, but a shopping arcade bridges the street itself.

All parking is either rooftop or underground. The V-shaped hotel by Harry Weese and Associates breaks the medium-rise scale Barnes had wanted maintained. Weese tried a number of horizontal schemes, but Western International Hotels was convinced that guests prefer elevator rides and short walks to the longer walks implied by the horizontal concept. The tower-and-podium design Weese then developed is superbly organized around the limestone outcrop of its site, and partly exposes the rockface indoors. The five-story-high podium element

literally backs into the rock. Here are the spaces which typically form the guest room tower base—lobby, shops, ballroom, restaurants, kitchen and service areas, with extensive garage space adjacent and below. The V-shaped 14-story tower begins at the top of the rock, approximately 70 feet above the level of the surrounding streets. What is splendid about the architecture of this hotel is the spatial transition from lobby through indoor rock garden to outdoor garden, swimming pool and roof terraces.''

Spectacular architecture became a human and commercial success in a series of hotels designed by an architect who was also developer

Hyatt Regency San Francisco
San Francisco, California
Architects: John Portman and
Associates

The hotel's north face was sloped back at a 45-degree angle and on the bias, a facade that could properly be called dynamic, with an effect that changed with light and viewpoint. But as spectacle, it was only a prelude to the lobby space within—170 feet high by 170 feet wide by 300 feet long. This 17-story atrium, daylighted by a narrow skylight, is molded and modulated by the planes that enclose it, perpendicular on one side, sharply angled on the other. The focal point for this great space which brought the whole interior into scale was a gigantic sculpture, 40 feet high, 30 feet in diameter, by Charles O. Perry. The great hollow sphere stands on three massive legs in a pool, its curved tubes of gold anodized aluminum making a web of intersecting pentagons.

This 20-story 840-room hotel was one of five buildings programmed for Embarcadero Center, the last parcel to be developed in San Francisco's Golden Gateway Redevelopment Project, Embarcadero Center, for which Portman was architect and a development partner of David Rockefeller and Associates, Trammell Crow and PIC Realty Corporation, was the latest in a series of large-scale projects in which Portman had participated as both architect and developer. When he began with his "one-man renewal program" for Atlanta (as the RECORD described it in 1965), the idea of an architect who was also a developer was not only unusual but, in some quarters of the architectural world, suspect. Could an architect be serious about architecture when he put money into it? John Portman always said (and eventually, in fascinating detail, in his book *The Architect as Developer,* co-authored with Jonathan Barnett and published by McGraw-Hill in 1976) that he put money into architecture so he could have more control over the architectural result. He also believed that architecture which created places for people to experience and enjoy as well as use could expand real estate profits as well as human enjoyment. His hotels, with their great atrium "people spaces," got national attention, both architectural and commercial, from the first (the Atlanta Hyatt Regency, 1965). But in his dual role as architect and developer, Portman was up to something far more significant than the most spectacular hotel could symbolize: an effort to make architecture a creative force in the decision-making processes of real estate development.

A humanist's critique
of a new building found
symbolism that reached
deep into the human psyche
and related to images
common to the mythology
of primitive cultures

State Service Center
Boston, Massachusetts
Architect: Paul Rudolph

This building was presented as "a vision of human space" in a RECORD article by Carl John Black. The State Service Center, in Black's view, was "a hymn to enclosure: the freedom of protection, the sweeping spaces of a defined openness, and the reassurance of massive pylons. All elements are expressive of the sheer power of defined nothingness, but they celebrate a nothingness turned to the full uses of life. The architect's vision is monolithic, but the monolith moves into life, flowing outward, spiraling upward. . . The monolith dissolves into movement as baroque staircases break against gigantic columns and impenetrable walls. It is as though matter had by magic metamorphosis melted into liquid arabesques."

"Paul Rudolph once said, 'Psychological demands are met primarily through the manipulation of space and the use of symbols,'" Mildred F. Schmertz recalled in her introduction to an article by Carl John Black on this building. "Most of today's critics write about space as total abstraction. When architectural writers talk about form and space, they speak in terms of solids and voids, vertical thrusts, intersecting planes, juxtapositions of scale, symmetry and other formal concerns. Unacknowledged are the philosophical, esthetic and psychological concerns which truly inform the work. Carl John Black, a young humanist, critic and teacher, has never had formal training in architecture or the history of architecture. Nevertheless, he sees Rudolph's work as especially rich in symbolic content." Black begins by quoting Rudolph: "'I wanted to hollow out a concavity at the bottom of Beacon Hill, a spiraling space like a conch, in negative relation to the convex dome of the State Capitol on top of the Hill. I wanted it to wrap around a tower which turned and was not only visible in its upward thrust but penetrating visibly below ground.' Rudolph hints at the symbolic content of the Service Center. The image cluster: Water-Serpent-Cave-Shell is a constant in the symbolism of primitive cultures and corresponds to a deep structure of human consciousness. Rudolph improvised his spaces with astonishing consistency around these symbols. A key image is the staircase of the Mental Health Clinic [above]. It recalls the form of the 'wentle-trap' shell, meaning 'winding staircase' in Dutch. In mythology, the conch, spiral and

coiled serpent emerged as images of earth rhythms and life cycles which ruled birth, death, regeneration, health, agriculture, the social order and the dispensation of justice. By contrast to the rationalist space of Bulfinch's domes symmetry, Rudolph's building is a vision of deep-earth symbolism, the life meanings of which lie at the heart of government's humane service to its people. . . . Carl Jung's studies of the psychological process of individuation reveal that the spiral is an archetypal symbol which incorporates the notion of *fixity*

and of *transformation*. On several levels, Rudolph has attempted to integrate these two qualities in the State Service Center. 'Where I've used curves, that denotes a *fixed* element as opposed to something which in time could be changed. The rectilinear room is more flexible.' While the cube has taken over, the curve has all but disappeared from our daily enclosures. Nevertheless, our deepest memory of space—the womb and the cave—has to do with strong ties to the earth. In his design of the State Service Center, Rudolph has attempted to

synthesize 20th-century rectilinear or 'universal' space and 'primordial' curved space with its deeper psychological appeals.''

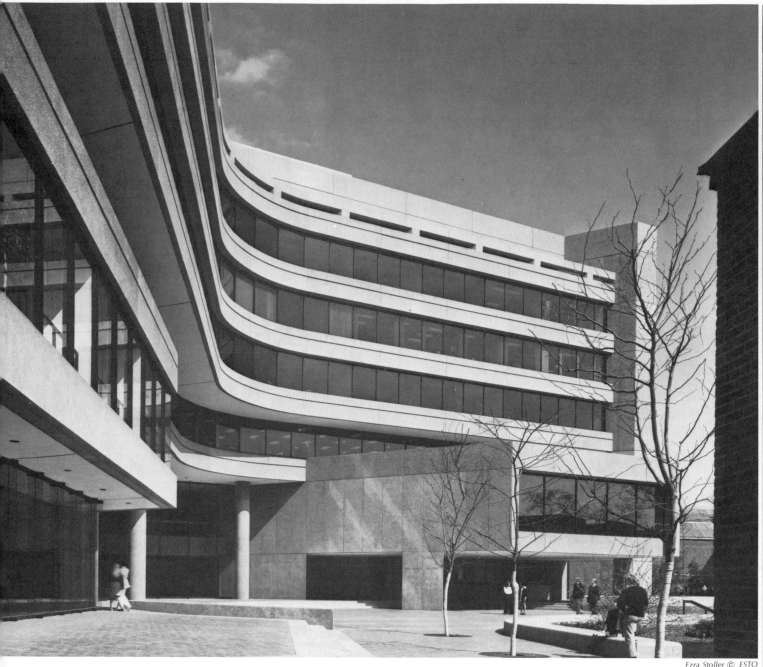

In the 11-year process of planning and building a headquarters, AIA as client held to principles it had long advocated while it confronted from a very different perspective many of the issues that challenged architects in the 1970s

National Headquarters
The American Institute of Architects
Washington, D.C.
Architects: The Architects Collaborative

A seven-story building conceived as a "background building" framed the 175-year-old Octagon and its garden, which occupy a triangular site at the juncture of New York Avenue and 18th Street, N.W. Old and new were linked by a broad, curving plaza which created a pedestrian way open to the public and connecting the intersecting streets. The plaza was paved with brick that matched the old brick of the reconstructed garden paths, and the same brick paving was extended into the ground floor exhibit area of the new building. Views of the Octagon create a visual link between old and new.

Building a new headquarters appropriate both to the needs of a rapidly expanding membership and to its historic setting was an 11-year process which engaged many of the major issues of architecture in the 1970s. It also evoked all of the frustrations and the anguish, the conviction and the fortitude, that are involved in the pursuit of the more exalted purposes of architecture. The AIA began by deciding to preserve the historic Octagon and its garden; it held a competition for design of a new headquarters to share the site in harmony with the landmark; it deferred to a series of rejections by Washington's Fine Arts Commission of the winning design and modifications thereof; it faced the necessity of accepting the resignation of the competition winners; and it selected another firm to design its headquarters. "By living up to its own high standards and practicing what it preaches," the RECORD said, "the architectural profession has not only enhanced the Washington landscape, but it has created the physical framework for projecting a continuously effective image."

1974

New urban design techniques encouraged a trend toward mixed use developments and multiple use buildings that served as connectors with existing neighbors and with transit systems, pedestrian and vehicular .

A mix of conservation and new development, of public and private uses, and of functional building types was designed to create a three-dimensional park on one downtown site .

A raised pedestrian plaza designed to connect with future neighbors was a requirement of another downtown project .

A prophet of urbanism made density and complexity serve his urbanistic goals in a building organized to make connections both with its own environs and with the city and region beyond .

A very large urban housing development designed to reinforce the potential of existing housing adapted planning concepts of the older buildings and invited public use of outdoor spaces .

A police headquarters emerged as civic architecture after an 11-year struggle with the decision-making processes of a big city and its multiple bureaucracies.

A medical center was designed as a piece of a city's master plan, health care facilities developed in layers above a commercial base .

On expansive rural sites, topography and highways influenced architectural concepts as did connections among a variety of uses on dense urban sites.

A vertical solution for one small office building both deferred to the scale of an older neighbor and created an impressive image from the highway .

A building appeared to float over a hilltop between two highways and became its own sign, reflecting the corporate seals from sculptured rods in the mirror glass sheathing of its facade .

A second ceremonial entrance to the city from the subway was created when the first major building in Philadelphia's Market Street East Transportation Mall was completed (page 108). It was one of two such entrances (Penn Center had the first) envisioned in architect-planner Edmund N. Bacon's concept for the redevelopment of the center of the city, first introduced to the citizens of Philadelphia in the 1937 Better Philadelphia Exhibition, of which architect Oscar Stonorov was co-designer. The Market Street East development will complete the realization of the Bacon concept which began with the construction of Penn Center (completed by 1960). When in 1970 he left his post as executive director of the City Planning Commission, Mr. Bacon had spent 21 years designing and monitoring the processes through which his original concept was modified, developed and implemented.

"How do I turn off the solar energy?"

Alan Dunn's last drawing for the RECORD (June 1974) was captioned (by Dunn himself, as always), "How do I turn off the solar energy?" Mr. Dunn's unfailingly keen perception of the foibles and predicaments of architecture, reflected in the drawings he did for the RECORD every month from June 1937 until his death, was exceeded only by his passion for it. "If you love it, it will love you back," he once said of architecture. "I love it."

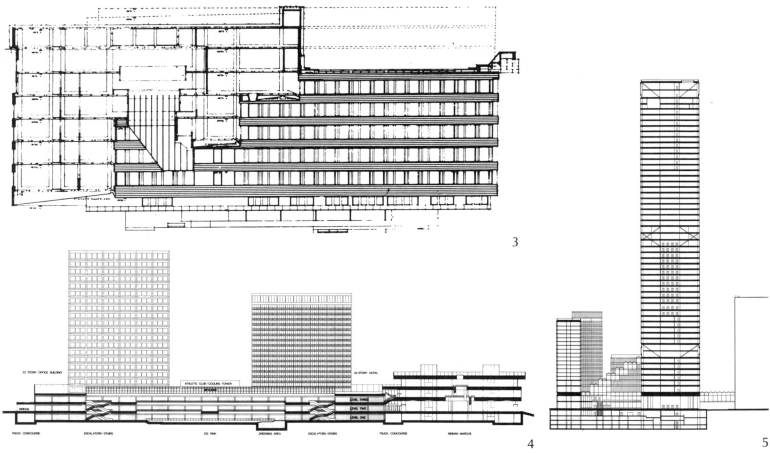

New urban design techniques encouraged a trend toward mixed use developments and multiple use buildings that also served as connectors with existing neighbors and with transit systems, pedestrian and vehicular

Jonathan Barnett, in an article on the future of the office building, noted the trend to mixed uses among other departures from the stereotypical office building; illustrations included both precursors and new work. Frank Lloyd Wright's Larkin Building in Buffalo (1) was an office structure where work was a communal experience, his Price Tower in Bartlesville, Oklahoma (2) combined apartments and offices in the same building. Alvar Aalto's offices for the government pensions agency in Helsinki (3) showed another alternative for office space, "but one in which growth and change were limited." Five new projects that "combined office space with other downtown functions in new relationships" were Galleria Center, Houston (4)—Hellmuth Obata & Kassabaum; IDS Center, Minneapolis (5)—Philip Johnson and John Burgee; and Carleton Center, Johannesburg (6), Olympic Tower, New York City (7), and John Hancock Tower, Chicago (8)—all by Skidmore Owings & Merrill.

"It is time architects took a good look at the way office buildings are designed," Jonathan Barnett declared, in a RECORD article that illustrated many of the urban issues influencing the design of many kinds of buildings by the mid-1970s. Barnett, an architect who was a founding member of New York City's pioneering Urban Design Group, was (and is) also director of the graduate program in urban design at the City College of New York, author of *Urban Design as Public Policy* (McGraw-Hill, 1974), co-author with John Portman of *The Architect as Developer* (McGraw-Hill, 1976), and an urban design consultant. "Mies' original, simplified version of the office building, made more workable by improved artificial lighting and climate control, and more explicit as Mies had a chance to see some examples built, has ended up by becoming a stereotype," Barnett pointed out. "But the Miesian formulation, applied universally, is a drastic oversimplification both of the nature of office work, and of the relationship of such work to the rest of our society. Urban designers and entrepreneurs are discovering that office space should be related to a matrix of shops, restaurants, entertainment, exhibition space and hotel rooms, and that all of these elements, in turn, are more successful if there are residences nearby.

"John Portman, the architect and real estate developer, is one of those who has seen most clearly that downtown requires a variety of uses to stay vital. The Peachtree Center in Atlanta, which Portman designed and to a large extent financed himself, combines the country's second-largest merchandise mart (after

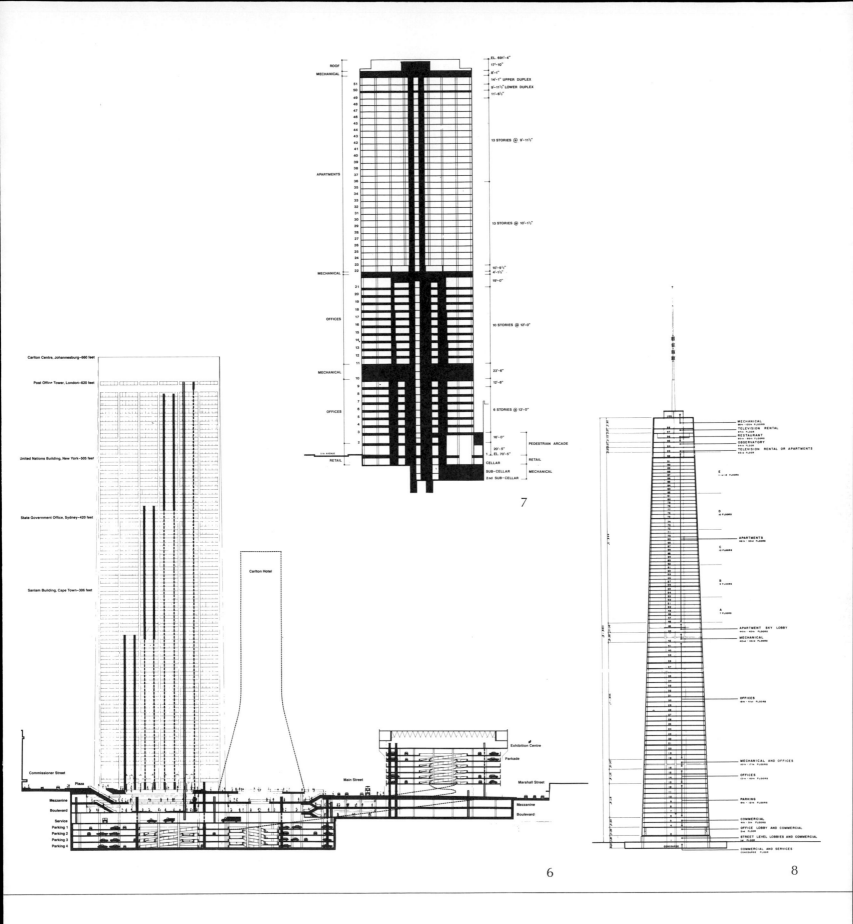

7

6

8

Chicago) with hotel rooms, office space, restaurants and shops. The principal architectural experiences are not the facades of the buildings, but the huge interior court of the hotel, the concourse system with its garden courtyard and the rooftop restaurants. Other urban renewal projects, whether privately funded or government supported, have been planned to include a variety of uses and to introduce some of the amenities of a suburban shopping center into the downtown. Until recently, however, such developments have remained an amalgam of conventional building types. The Galleria complex in Houston, the Carleton Center in Johannesburg, the IDS complex in Minneapolis and Portman's Embarcadero Center in San Francisco and Renaissance Center in Detroit all represent steps in the evolution of a new concept of downtown, with the concourse system becoming the controlling element in the design and the office building a subsidiary part.

"While developers have been discovering that this kind of integrated urban development makes economic sense, cities have been trying to encourage it in order to preserve their competitive position against the newer suburban centers. However, urban development of this nature is contrary to some of the conventional wisdom about the separation of land uses embodied in zoning controls. The special zoning districts created in New York City were needed to preserve a variety of land uses in the central areas of midtown and lower Manhattan. Without special legislation, the legitimate theaters would have been obliterated by office

1234 Market Street East
Philadelphia, Pennsylvania
Architects: Bower & Fradley,
George M. Ewing Company

The first major building in Philadelphia's Market Street East Transportation Mall Center had a lobby that functioned as public space, a link in a three-level pedestrian walkway system leading along a skylit shopping mall and connecting with subway and commuter railway systems. The new building kept its place, but held its own between two landmarks to which it also connected—the 1930 Philadelphia Savings Fund Society Building of Howe and Lescaze, and the much older John Wanamaker department store (of classical derivation). The glass facade was made clear at the base, to denote public spaces, and opaque for office floors above.

buildings; without the Fifth Avenue Special Zoning District, office development might well have killed the effectiveness of Fifth Avenue as a shopping street. The Zoning District mandates or encourages greater complexity of uses: major retail shopping, large covered spaces and apartments, as well as office space. The Fifth Avenue Zoning District in effect requires architects to invent a new building type which combines apartments and offices in a single structure, and which gives over the lower floors to high-intensity retail uses. The

John Hancock Tower in Chicago represented an important step toward this new kind of building, and was one reason why urban designers in New York City felt that it would be practical to specify combined residential and office uses in the Fifth Avenue Special District. The architects [Skidmore Owings & Merrill] of Olympic Tower have elected to conceal the building's complexity behind a facade that is similar to a conventional office building; but the section shows the relationship between apartments, offices, shopping and a major gal-

leria space. Still another interesting example of a building that combines several different downtown uses in one structure is Water Tower Place in Chicago. It is located opposite the Hancock Building at the head of North Michigan Avenue, and it was designed by Loebl Schlossman Bennett & Dart and C.F. Murphy Associates. There are only two floors of offices; the major ingredients are a multistory shopping center, a hotel and apartments.''

Design of connections was becoming as significant as design of the building itself.

100 William Street
New York, New York
Architects: Davis Brody and Associates

A 20-story office building in lower Manhattan contained the first "covered pedestrian space" to be completed under a special zoning ordinance developed by the New York City Planning Commission's Urban Design Group. This interior plaza was lined with spaces for retail shops and restaurants and provided access by escalator to offices above and more shops below. It also provided for future connections to subway concourses. Its diagonal course through the building becomes a shortcut as well as a shopping destination for many who do not work in the building. The new zoning regulations allowed a developer to increase the floor area (thus site coverage) of a building in return for providing public amenities like underground concourses, arcades, loggias, plazas and pedestrian bridges.

A mix of conservation and new development, of public and private uses and of functional building types was designed to create a three-dimensional park on a downtown site

51-61-71 Project
Vancouver, British Columbia
Architects: Arthur Erickson Architects

A three-block-long renewal site was planned as a three-dimensional park, its elements including old and new buildings along with its planting. An old courthouse would be preserved, along with its formal plaza. A low building to house the Provincial Government Services Center would be roofed with gardens. A dramatic glass-walled Law Courts Building would be terraced back to maintain a scale appropriate to that of the old courthouse. The courthouse itself would be converted for use as an art gallery and performing theaters. Outdoor spaces for public activities would be provided, including ice skating in winter and art and craft as well as sculpture shows in summer.

"The 51-61-71 project in downtown Vancouver, British Columbia, is part preservation, part new development," as the RECORD described it. "It includes preservation of the old courthouse and its formal plaza, with conversion of the building to civic/cultural uses, and construction of a new courthouse at the far end of the new three-block-long park which is to be developed on three blocks behind the old building. Each of the three blocks of the park will have quite specific functions—51, for instance, will be essentially a civic-cultural complex; 61 will contain a low building with public roof gardens for the Provincial Government; the new Law Courts Building will be on 71—but the concept of the park as three-dimensional is the governing factor in the design. The buildings are important in themselves, but in the overall plan, they are elements, not dominants. It is the park that becomes the unifying means of relating old and new, open and closed space, high and low building levels. The concept of the complex as a park directly reflects the expressed wishes of Vancouver citizens, who expressed their desire for a place of public gathering, for outdoor events such as art and craft shows, for ice skating in winter and sculpture shows in summer. They also wanted an art gallery and performing theaters. The 'three-dimensional park' provides for all of these, with the art gallery and the performing theaters in the converted old courthouse, and the sculpture court adjoining it. There are many open spaces for gatherings and for shows of various kinds. The Provincial Government Services Center is to be a low building de-

signed as a series of roof gardens. The most dramatic structure in the complex will be the new Law Courts Building, a terraced building with a sloping glass roof through which there are views to the North Shore Mountains. With careful regard for scale, the height of the new building has been kept to that of the old.''

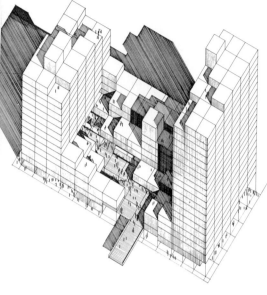

Park Central
Denver, Colorado
Architects: Muchow Associates

Design for future connections between it and its neighbors made one building of this full-block downtown development. A critical "given" was a raised pedestrian plaza to connect by street overpass with the raised pedestrian plazas projected for surrounding blocks, a downtown circulation system proposed in a master plan by architect-planner Marvin Hatami which recalled the "skywalk" system begun in downtown Minneapolis in the mid-sixties. The plaza topped a block-long structure containing three levels of parking. Three office towers were set on the plaza, which is the entrance level for both towers and shops. The basic design module was a 30- by 30-foot structural grid. Curtain walls are black anodized aluminum and bronze glass.

"Dark, disciplined and distinguished, this new business center, built as a speculative development in downtown Denver's renewal area, handsomely achieves the objectives of both developers and architects," the RECORD reported. "It is designed and built within a tight budget, providing varied and stimulating spaces to excite both workers and visitors with a new definition of urban quality. Park Central's location in the Skyline Renewal Area of downtown Denver imposed certain constraints on its design—height limits, for instance, dif-

ferent for each part of the site (8 stories, 14 stories and unlimited), and a raised pedestrian concourse—which influenced the final solution, but not so much, in fact, as the exigencies of the design process itself. The irregular form of the building is no mere design whimsy; it derives from the need for an overall design concept which could, without loss of integrity, adjust to the frequent changes made by the developer-owner in the building program. Because of the lively building profile which evolved—three towers of varying height and

mass rising from a raised plaza on top of a block-long structure—the curtain wall exterior of the building is dark in color, charcoal black anodized aluminum and bronze glass, set flush, in startling contrast to Denver's other tall buildings. To accomplish so elegant a building within a tight budget—total cost for the project was $20.5 million, but the basic building cost came to $13 million—was a notable achievement, obviously strongly affected by the early and close relationship among those most deeply involved: developer (who was also con-

A raised pedestrian plaza designed
to connect with future neighbors
was a requirement of this program

tractor and a part owner), curtain wall manufacturer, engineers and architects. The main entrance to the complex is by way of a unique and unusually lofty loggia leading from the street to the plaza level. The plaza tops a three-level, below-grade garage and is the base for Park Central's three office towers. It serves as both entrance to the tower lobbies and the shops, and as protected open space for pedestrians.

"If a master plan by architect-planner Marvin Hatami and Associates is implemented, the pla-

za will eventually connect by street overpass to other blocks, and the entire area will have a raised pedestrian concourse. At plaza level, the precise detail and the terse design of each element is clear. The 30- by 30-foot structural grid which is the building's design discipline applies both horizontally and vertically; where openness is needed, as for pedestrian access, it is 'carved away'; where additional volume or space is required, it is added to. The result is the lively form and mass of the building."

A prophet of urbanism made density and complexity serve urbanistic goals in a building organized to make connections both with its own environs and with the city and region beyond

Undergraduate Science Center
and Chilled Water Plant
Harvard University
Cambridge, Massachusetts
Architects: Sert, Jackson and Associates

The Science Center consists of five basic elements: the laboratory wing at the rear of the site, the six-tiered classroom wing for the mathematics department, the three-story library, the lecture hall and the one-story administrative wing. Lower elements face Harvard Yard across a new park created by depressing Cambridge Street. The steel and cable space frame supports the roof of the fan-shaped lecture hall. Two skylit interior passages at right angles to each other create a T-shaped pedestrian spine, one leg heading northwest and the other northeast to link eventually with existing or projected pedestrian networks. By designing this complex, Sert once again seized the opportunity to transform a portion of the Harvard campus into his vision of what the modern city should be. Its inner network and the massing of its elements related to Harvard's circulation system and the scale and massing of buildings in the Yard. And by extension, the Science Center is an integral part of the city of Cambridge and its surrounding region.

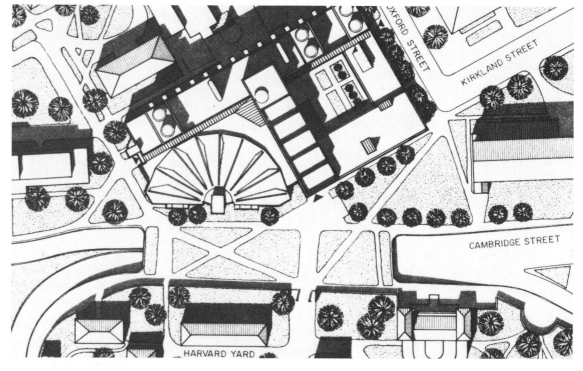

Jose Luis Sert has said of the urban campus, the RECORD noted, that it is "a cultural center within a city, and should set an example of good planning and design for the city. It is, in a way, a mini-city, and its urbanity is the expression of a better, more civilized way of life." And, as the RECORD observed, "this combined laboratory, library, classroom-administrative structure and power plant, in its density of use and complexity of function, is indeed a micro-city rather than a building. It completely fills a full city block to the north of Harvard Yard. This plot of land now holds 291,000 square feet of facilities for chemistry, biology and geology, physics, mathematics, statistics and astronomy, as well as four large lecture theaters, a cafe, three libraries and administrative offices. The chilled water plant which serves nearby and projected campus buildings occupies another 58,000 square feet. Prior to the construction of the Science Center, the Harvard University Planning Office had recommended that the University, in agreement with the City of Cambridge, turn a portion of Cambridge Street into a vehicular underpass with a park on top. Additional land for building was acquired by eliminating the intersection of Kirkland Street and Cambridge Street; but more important, by paying to sink the road, Harvard created a pedestrian connection linking the northern campus to Harvard Yard. This connection can be seen in the photo (top left), taken through one of the gates from the Yard. Since in Sert's hierarchy of architectural values circulation comes first, it should surprise no one that the Science Center is organized around a T-shaped pedes-

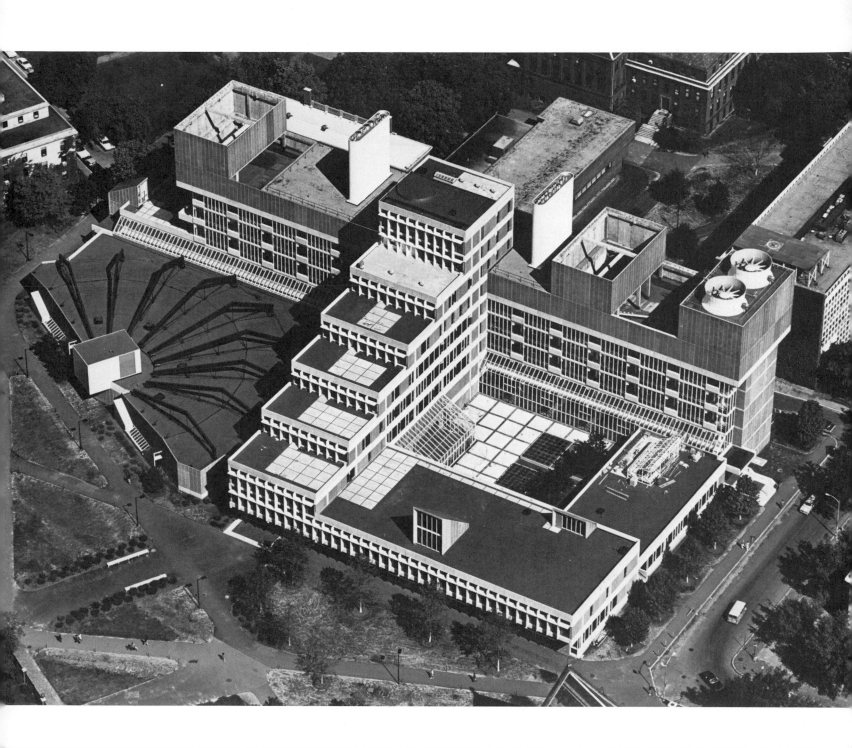

trian spine that reaches out to link with existing or projected pedestrian networks. Having created this spine, Sert and his team began to organize the elements called for by the program.

"For Sert, the most important problem was posed by the fact that, volumetrically, the building would be a monster. How could it be sized and massed so as not to overpower the buildings of the Yard, or the people who use them? The architects elected to keep the massing as low as possible on the side of the building which faces the Yard and the new lit-

tle park. The lecture hall element was designed as a pivot to turn the corner of the site as the orientation of the Cambridge Street geometry changes. To give it as little apparent bulk as possible, much of its volume is below ground and its roof is hung from an exposed space frame made of weathering steel and marine cables. The classroom wing for the mathematics department steps down to a series of terraces which end one story above the roof of the three-story library, an element scaled to harmonize with the Yard buildings directly across

the park. The laboratory wing with its penthouse cooling towers and exhaust ducts has the most combined height and is therefore set farthest back. Within the complex is a small courtyard, contained on one side by the low administrative wing. The lower elements of the Science Center give the little park a definite edge. In combination with the adjacent Harvard buildings, they transform the park into a new quadrangle rather than an amorphous open space."

A very large urban housing development designed to reinforce the potential of existing housing adapted planning concepts of the older buildings and invited public use of outdoor spaces

Lambert Houses
Bronx Park Urban Renewal Area
The Bronx, New York
Architects: Davis Brody and Associates

Low-rise buildings were designed to harmonize in scale with the neighborhood's existing six-story apartment structures, and to reinforce the whole neighborhood's value as a viable housing resource. The new buildings (center of photo above) occupied a five-block area and provided 731 apartments, many more than pre-viously on the site, but only 80 per cent of the maximum allowed by the zoning. Buildings were pulled back from the sidewalks to provide green spaces around the project perimeters. Semi-private residential courts were developed, but a pedestrian way invited public use. Angled projections of exterior walls were intended to provide vertical relief for long horizontal walls, varied and private views from within and such planning advantages as extra space for master bedrooms and dining areas.

"Urban renewal with a conscience," the RECORD called it. The owner was Lambert Houses Redevelopment Company, comprised of Phipps Houses (general partner), Bronx Park South Cooperative Development Committee (minority directors) and private limited partners. Phipps Houses became Lambert's sponsor in 1967 when a Bronx community group sought financial and management help. The group, headed by Barnett Lambert, had been successful in having the area designated for urban renewal by the city. The intent was to maintain the community's middle-class population, then housed mainly in the six-story apartment buildings (upper left in photo above) which had succeeded single-family dwellings of a still earlier era. But as in so many once-stable neighborhoods in cities around the country, an almost complete population change occurred within a very few years, with low-income ethnic minority families (in this case, black and Puerto Rican) replacing white middle-income families as the predominant residents. In the transition period, the area had become one of New York's worst by every social measure from felonies and gang warfare to infant mortality and poor school attendance. "The new Lambert Houses," the RECORD observed, "are strong physical evidence of a belief that the whole area can be a good place to live again, but the architects and the sponsor, Phipps Houses, emphasize that it will take more than new structures to make a viable community in which their project can function—and they are doing something about that. A neighborhood-wide Tremont Improve-

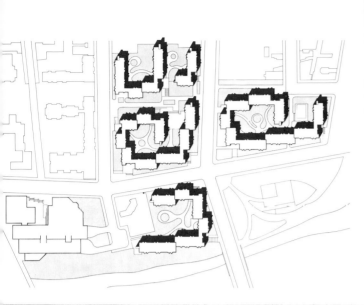

ment Association was formed by Phipps to initiate and carry on activities supporting community social needs. The staff consists of local residents, and the organization is privately financed through individuals and foundations. Within a year, crime and vandalism dropped markedly; continued funding is the problem.''

Describing the planning concepts, the RE-CORD said, ''Lambert Houses are generally arranged to enclose semi-private spaces used and visually supervised by the residents. But for the project to stimulate neighborhood feel-ing, the public could not feel excluded. So the currently popular notion of placing a hard line of buildings at the property line was not ob-served—although street containment is defined intermittently by buildings brought closer to the sidewalk. The closing of a public street provided the opportunity for a public pedestrian way through the larger block. Each new building is divided into segments (or 'houses') of approximately 45 apartments each. Some eight units share an elevator corridor on any given floor, and the result is the sort of living ambience found in the smaller old buildings nearby. The house concept has recently been recognized as a promising method of creating mutually interested groups as one deterrent to crime and vandalism. Apartments are duplexes except where apartments connect two houses and thus two exit enclosures. At a time when fire escapes had been disallowed by the city code as each apartment's required second exit, the architects saw duplexes as a solution, since access to different exit enclosures could then be achieved on two floors.''

"Lower Manhattan's new Police Headquarters, with its beguiling plaza, was commissioned more than a decade ago," the RECORD said. "Today, two mayors, six police commissioners and nine public works commissioners later, the building is complete and occupied. Through all these administrative changes, with their inevitable but vexing delays, architects Gruzen and Partners were the only continuing presence. Their patience and determination resulted in not only a splendid building but, perhaps even more important, a sound and coherent piece of civic planning in a portion of the city where this virtue has been absent too long. Chambers Street is a stop on Manhattan's West Side subway. Climbing to the street, up stairs softly frescoed in grime, the visitor finds himself near the intersection of Chambers and Centre streets under the broad vaulting of McKim Mead & White's colossal Municipal Building. This exuberant, faintly Italianate civic skyscraper, completed in 1914, houses a large chunk of the city's civil service. In a welcoming gesture, its colonnaded front opens, through an heroic central arch, to the southeast, and now reveals New York's recently completed Police Headquarters Building and Pedestrian Plaza. The 75-foot-wide pedestrian plaza, designed by Gruzen and Partners with M. Paul Friedberg Associates, is so carefully planted that the visitor scarcely realizes he is on a bridge with a busy traffic artery—Park Row—cutting underneath. Strongly axial, the plaza is lined with honey locust trees and fitted with benches, a large sculpture executed in weathering steel by Bernard Rosenthal and a

A Police Headquarters emerged as civic architecture after an 11-year struggle with the decision-making processes of a big city and its multiple bureaucracies

Police Headquarters, Pedestrian
Plaza and Parking Garage
New York, New York
Architects: Gruzen and Partners

The building was set squarely on its irregularly shaped site. The main entrance was put on axis with the Municipal Building and recessed under the cantilever of the tower. The lowest levels contain a large public parking garage, pistol range, detention cells and a large assembly hall. These spaces thrust outward in all directions, forming low projections over which the 10-story cube of office space rises. Tower and base are both clad in brick, but the separation between them is clearly articulated by massive concrete trusses that become walls inside, and that distribute the tower loads to heavy columns spaced on 30-foot centers. A deep band of brick forms the parapet on all sides and conceals the rooftop mechanical penthouse and helistop.

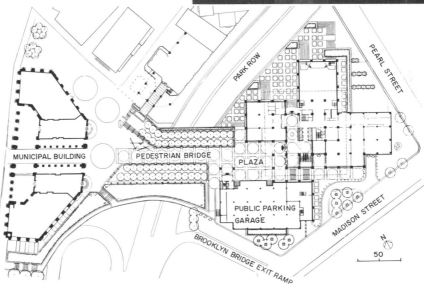

variety of small pedestrian amenities that encourage strollers to pause, lovers to dally, city brownbaggers to linger over sandwiches and apples. This grand space, with its seductive pedestrian ambience, seems so entirely appropriate that it is hard, in retrospect, to imagine that planners and police officials at first opposed its creation, favoring instead a narrow aerial tunnel reaching up over Park Row, and down again on the opposite side. The decision to depress Park Row and create the present plaza was agonizing. It required the shifting of

several approach ramps to the Brooklyn Bridge. That meant the cooperation of a spate of agencies and a helping hand from the Office of Lower Manhattan Development—as well as all the patience and persuasive powers the architects (and designer Peter Samton in particular) could muster. That the effort was worth it can no longer be doubted. Not only are the plaza spaces and subspaces handsome in themselves (though they show signs of hard use), but they bring to the edge of this civic district an amenity and a planning coherence that

it has long lacked. The Police Department is now physically and symbolically linked to the residential neighborhood to the south as well as to the courthouses along Centre Street, instead of being estranged from both in unapproachable, arterial limbo."

"Tufts-New England develops city site in Boston master plan," the RECORD reported. "Two new buildings have been completed in a long-range master plan for restructuring the Tufts-New England Medical Center in Boston. The architects have been closely involved in the growth of the center since 1965, when it was formed by the merger of three hospitals with the Tufts University School of Medicine and Dental Medicine. The objective is to upgrade and serve a densely urban community, Boston's South Cove section, and to continue matching long-range needs with urban renewal plans for the area. Accordingly, when the Boston Redevelopment Authority drew up its renewal plan for approval by Washington, it included assurances to local residents that the medical center would not expand unduly into residential areas. The plan involves reshaping some streets, closing others and replacing an old elevated railway with a new subway station directly under the center. The center will also provide various kinds of commercial and public spaces to serve both the staff and the neighborhood. The physical contours of the center are developing as continuous horizontal layers of health facilities above a ground floor commercial and traffic level. This is to preserve as much as possible a horizontal flow of medical traffic and to increase flexibility and efficiency. Informal contact among specialties is encouraged, and nursing floors can be linked vertically to treatment floors, while both can be expanded in increments of planned growth. The completed elements are a health services building and a dental sciences building, both

A medical center was designed as a piece of a city's master plan — health care facilities developed in layers above a commercial base

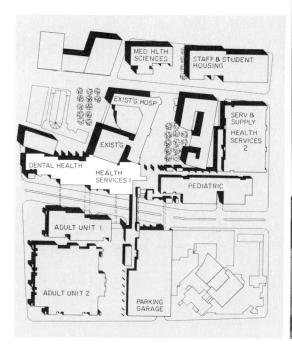

Tufts-New England Medical Center
Boston, Massachusetts
Architects: The Architects Collaborative

A health services building and a dental sciences building were the first new buildings completed in a long-range program for restructuring the medical center. The master plan of the ultimate development (right) shows placement of these buildings and the on-site replacement and/or linkage of existing and new buildings with the street system. Both to preserve as much as possible a horizontal flow of medical traffic and to increase flexibility and efficiency, the center was being developed as continuous horizontal layers of health facilities above ground-level commercial space and traffic.

served by a new parking garage for 925 cars that also contains restaurants and retail space. These first elements are closely interrelated and they anticipate the subsequent phases of growth that will bridge Washington Street and allow full realization of the horizontal megastructure concept. This integrated approach to the master plan requires great flexibility over time to respond to changing patterns of funding, evolving needs and space programs, changing economic patterns, developing structural systems and building technology, all still guided by the established framework and resulting in a unified building that functions well at any and all stages of growth. The Medical Center may take 20 years to complete, depending on availability of funds."

On expansive rural sites, topography and highways influenced architectural concepts as did connections among a variety of uses on dense urban sites

Thousand Oaks Civic Center
Thousand Oaks, California
Architect: Robert Mason Houvener

The architect of this building won a statewide design competition while serving as a "project engineer" in the Navy. His scheme, praised by the jury for "sticking to a very strong and simple idea," put a range of one-story buildings in a broad arc high on a hillside. From the freeway below, the complex is seen as a long white band curving across the land (photo above). Inside the building, individual offices tend to face the view, while larger interior spaces open onto landscaped courtyards, with stairways leading up to on-grade parking. On the uphill side of the building, the continuous sweep of the facade is broken into a series of small outdoor spaces by bridges that lead from the approach road to the rooftop parking.

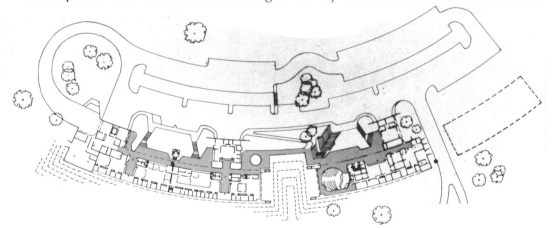

In the context of public environmental concerns in the 1970s, a natural landscape could offer an architectural challenge quite as complex as any dense urban site. Buildings shown on the last six pages of this chapter (122–127) reflect the sensitivity of both architects and clients to the need for designing buildings that were environmentally responsible as well as appropriate to their purposes. When the City of Thousand Oaks, California, announced a state-wide competition for the design of its new civic center, as the RECORD reported, architects were

invited to submit a master plan for the entire site, a conceptual design for the ultimate phase of the civic center, and detailed designs for the first two buildings—a city hall and facilities for a chamber of commerce. The site was a 30-acre parcel of land overlooking the town and adjacent to a major freeway. In spite of its fairly central location, it had an almost rural quality, and was made up of rolling hills dotted with oak trees. The challenge of the competition "was to make something on a difficult site (and within a fairly tight budget) that would be iden-

tifiable as a structure of civic importance and that would also be in concert with its environment—not just with the physical surroundings, but with the spirit of this growing southern California town." Entries came from 155 architects (representing some $1.5-million worth of work, according to one estimate). The jury included architects Charles Moore, then dean of architecture at Yale University, and Cesar Pelli, then a partner of Victor Gruen Associates (and later to become Yale's dean of architecture). "In their general comments," the RECORD said,

"the jury pointed out that while many of the entries were fine, many more were without concept, a lack that was 'camouflaged by highly complex and often, in detail, quite pleasant solutions.' They went on to conclude that such entries 'managed to miss the point of the simplicity and clarity that this building needed in order to work and in order to perform its symbolic function. That is what made the First Prize get the First Prize—sticking to a very simple and strong idea.' " In the RECORD's own view, "It is hard to imagine a more direct approach to the problem. The buildings make a clear image for themselves as they accommodate the required functions inside. They make it clear how you arrive and how you enter. They show that this is a public place, but one which nevertheless respects the natural site. They look as though they belong there. If preserving the strong concept has required longer than desirable walks from parking to building entrances, the architect has gone to considerable effort to soften the feeling of the uphill side of the building without actually changing his overall concept. On this side, the continuous facade is broken up into a series of small outdoor spaces by the bridges that lead from the approach road to the rooftop parking. These spaces are populated by stairs, ramps, small trees and plants that make this side of the building as inviting as the other side is imposing. The photograph (above) shows one of these spaces; it is the entrance to the Council Chamber which is also used for ceremonies."

A vertical solution for a small office building meant minimum intrusion on the site

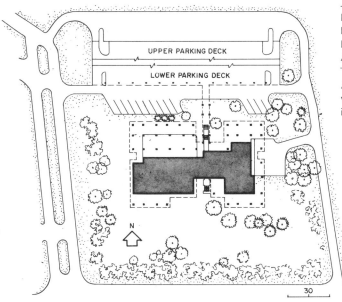

Headquarters Building for the
Progressive Farmer Company
Birmingham, Alabama
Architects: Jova/Daniels/Busby

A three-story office building was fitted into a wooded three-and-a-half-acre site without blemish to a tranquil rural landscape. Work spaces were put on the upper two levels to maximize views for employees. Editorial offices are on the top level, administrative and other shared functions on the second level. Service areas and cafeteria are on the lowest level. Employee parking and entrance were put at grade, with a visitor parking deck a level above. A bridge connects the parking deck with the entrance to the lobby.

If the bigger buildings in the bigger cities tend to get more attention in the general media, smaller buildings in smaller cities and along the nation's highways are far more numerous and, from an environmental point of view, equally important. As public consciousness of environmental quality spread beyond the urban centers where it had gotten its organizational start, so did client consciousness of environmental amenity as both an obligation of business citizenship and a significant component of public image. An approach to smaller-scale commercial architecture which a few years earlier would have required the proverbial "great client" was thus becoming a pragmatic commercial requirement. "Taking an approach to siting that is as public-benefit-minded as it is unusual," as the RECORD described it, "the architects have placed this building of 46,000 square feet far back from a parkway and have maintained much of the concealing natural growth. A vertical arrangement of office and parking areas was designed for minimum disturbance to the three-and-a-half-acre site. But the office building's three-story height was visually reduced on the entrance side by placing one story on the slope below the driveway level. Weathering steel sheathing and reflective glass blend into the natural surroundings. Editorial offices are on the top level. Administrative and other shared functions occupy the middle level, and service areas and cafeteria are at the bottom, where employees enter at grade. Visitors enter from the upper parking deck and cross the bridge to the lobby."

Stepping down a hillside both deferred to the scale of an older neighbor and created an impressive image from the highway

Heublein Corporate Headquarters
Farmington, Connecticut
Architect: Russell Gibson von Dohlen, Inc.

Stepping the building down the hillside was a topographical solution which also reduced the apparent bulk of the building in deference to the massive University Medical Center nearby. It produced an impressive view from the highway (above) and—from each rooftop garden—the ambience of a one-story building. Covered parking is reached by curving roads which follow the hillside contours. Mechanical equipment is contained in the angled roof spaces of each floor.

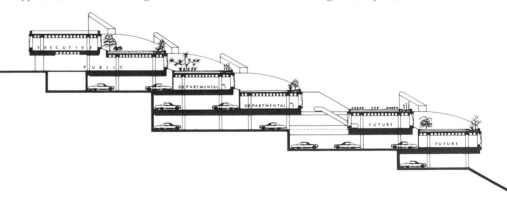

"The executive headquarters of an international food and beverage marketing corporation might be expected to reflect success by large size," the RECORD remarked, "but there are many more important credentials for a management staff of less than 100 persons; a high level of amenity speaks eloquently of substantial pursuits. The 75,000-square-foot building is located on 20 acres of wooded hillside, facing a major highway and distant views of Hartford, Connecticut. A stair-like building form was determined after three alternatives (including a thin tower) had been studied by the architect. It provides an agreeable image of respect for the terrain by conforming to the natural contours, while asserting its presence by a decisive form. It has a sensible lack of visual conflict with the massive University Medical Center nearby. From the interior, it also provides eye-level views of the surrounding trees, while the projecting roofs screen the highway below. The relationship of the floors in this configuration has a number of interesting functional consequences. The segmented structure allows for non-disruptive expansion that is planned to continue in repetitive increments down the hillside. Covered parking (110,000 square feet) is distributed so that many workers walk directly from car to desk. Vertical access is gained by a continuous line of escalators. Executive level is the highest floor, above the public entrance level that contains the cafeteria and Board of Directors' room, surrounded by audiovisual and entertainment facilities. Department levels are adjacent to parking areas."

"This regional headquarters houses the day-to-day operations of two recently consolidated health insurance corporations," the RECORD reported. "There are three phases planned, and this—the first—provides floor area of 225,000 square feet and accommodates 1000 employees on a 39-acre rural site near Durham. The headquarters has the internal functioning of a vertical building. Mechanical risers and elevators go straight up to the top, and the areas of the various floors remain constant. The clients required a large percentage of open-plan work area. There are few enclosed offices, and the potential problem of relating partitions to sloping glass junctures did not apply here. There was a preliminary worry that the shape of the building might concentrate wind forces on the ground floor, but wind tunnel tests proved the worry unfounded. In the steel structural system, groups of columns define mechanical risers, stairs and elevators, and are braced together to provide the building's lateral support. Distances between groups—62 feet—are spanned by deep beams. The cantilevered volumes of the building are supported by a series of triangular rigid frames, with a maximum projection of 50 feet, and with a height equal to the three stories. There are two types of frames, as the building ends required a special condition. The outer edges of each floor are supported by tensile or compressive members depending on the side of the building. Large floor areas are free of columns and accommodate the flexible planning."

A building appeared to float over a hilltop between two highways and became its own sign, reflecting the corporate seals from sculptured rods in the mirror glass sheathing of its facade

North Carolina Blue Cross and
Blue Shield Headquarters
Durham, North Carolina
Architects and engineers:
Odell Associates

Offices were "floated" above the crest of a highly visible hill in a three-dimensional rhomboid sheathed in mirror glass. Backup services, mechanical equipment and storage were accommodated below grade. With its long sides exposed to major highways on the north and south, the building became a literal sign, reflecting the corporate seals projected by the tops of rod sculptures. Slope of the exterior walls was calculated to be parallel with the sun's hottest rays so that, despite the greater area of exposure, direct energy gain was reduced by half compared with a glass-enclosed building of equal volume and vertical walls. Coupled with the reflective value of the chrome-plated glass, these conditions reduced the required air coolant compensation for solar heat gain by an estimated 90 per cent.

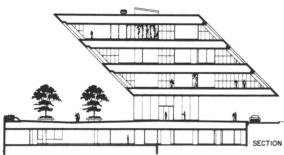

SECTION

New resources for community life were provided in a mix of new buildings and rehabilitated old buildings that were intended to provide local residents with a familiar context rather than a bold and impressive new architectural statement that might risk seeming forbidding. Pilot Center, Over-the-Rhine District, Cincinnati, Ohio: Woollen Associates, Architects.

1975

A combination of rehabilitation and "infill" retained sound old buildings and put new ones in between in a new kind of renewal effort .

Lenders were still shy, but "rehab" responded to public attitudes about renewal and preservation, and the public responded to "rehabbed" projects.

On a tight site along a downtown thoroughfare, the "interior plaza" appeared on the campus, and so did the requirement for providing links to connect new, existing and future buildings .

Correctional facilities designed for rehabilitation were built with public support as public concern about prison conditions caught up with correctional philosophy .

Townhouses that looked like home were appealing to more families in more places .

The house as architecture has both reflected and predicted design trends in all eras, like one large country house designed to seem smaller and evoking past and future with its combination of the familiar and the unexpected .

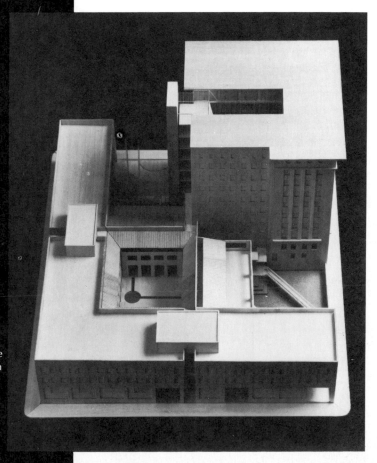

The winning design by Hastings & Chivetta in association with Mitchell/Giurgola Associates in a national architectural competition made Adler & Sullivan's historic Wainwright Building, dating from 1891, the dominant component of a new state office complex on a 19th-century urban block in St. Louis. The Wainwright is on one quadrant, with three new L-shaped units on the other three quadrants, emphasizing the block's parts and creating three courts. Walls of the new building were to be red sandstone like the Wainwright.

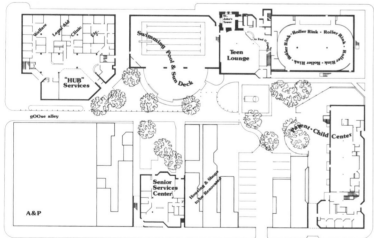

A combination of rehabilitation
and "infill" retained
sound old buildings and
put new ones in between

Pilot Center
Over-the-Rhine District
Cincinnati, Ohio
Architects: Woollen Associates

Four separate recreational and social service buildings were inserted among older
buildings in a two-block area which had
been selected as the "Target Area" for

launching a renewal effort for a much
larger decaying neighborhood. The new
buildings were woven into the existing
fabric so that they filled gaps at the street
line and created semi-enclosed public
spaces on the interior of the block. Old
buildings that were sound were retained,
and the area kept the image and character
familiar to residents.

"We have been able to add the things people
need in order to identify with a community,"
architect Evans Woollen told the RECORD. "And
we have been able to do it with a minimum of
disruption to the existing fabric." And, as the
RECORD described it, "The existing fabric is
Cincinnati's Over-the-Rhine district, a neighborhood that is 45 per cent black, 45 per cent
Appalachian white, and 10 per cent German
extraction. Over-the-Rhine has been suffering
from many of the familiar, self-compounding
ills of older urban neighborhoods—deteriora-

tion of housing, loss of population and low
average incomes. Thus what was once a well-
knit social (and architectural) fabric had
begun to unravel. But planners and residents
did not place their hopes on the once standard
panacea of wholesale urban renewal; they
opted for a more meticulous process of retaining whatever old buildings were sound, and fitting the new facilities in among them. Initially,
only one part of the district—dubbed the Target Area—was singled out for study by planners, and at its heart was the 1850 Findlay

Market, an open-air meat and produce market
diagonally across from the A&P store shown in
the photograph above. In the planners' view,
Findlay Market had an importance to the Target Area analogous to the importance of a
shopping center in a contemporary suburb.
Most of the key new buildings would be built
close by it. The Pilot Center is only one cog in
the Target Area wheel. It consists of four separate buildings that fill gaps between older buildings and enclose an interior green space. The
spire in the photograph at top right is the sur-

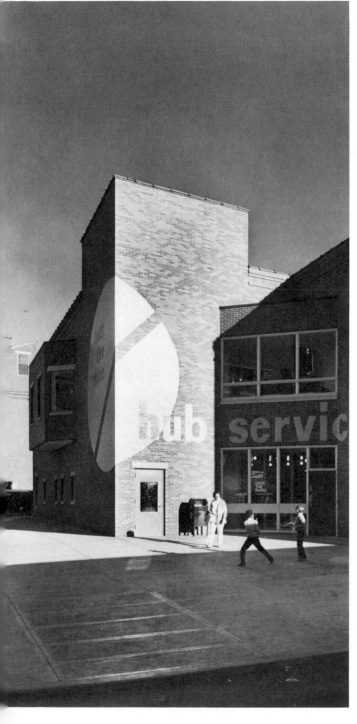

viving remnant of an 1840 Roman Catholic church, demolished to make way for a new gymnasium—a loss to the cause of adaptive reuse, and to the architect, who argued for its retention. In order to maximize contact with local residents, Woollen Associates planned the Pilot Center from a branch office in a store near the site. The largest of four buildings in the Center is the recreational building [seen in part in the photograph on page 128]. It contains a skating rink and a swimming pool. The pool is in a two-story space enclosed on one side with aluminum and glass doors that can be opened up on warm days to give some sense of connection between the pool and the outdoors. Two portholes give passersby the chance to look in at the pool and the swimmers. Across the pedestrian common from the recreation building is the Citizen Center; it provides low-cost meals, recreational and educational facilities for the elderly. Also across from the recreation building is a parent-child facility that houses a Montessori school and a day-care center; it contains a large community room for local meetings, parties, weddings and movies. In addition, the building provides employee training and placement services, a free store, a small health center and a post office. The architects hoped that this building, like the other ones in Pilot Center, would provide local residents with a familiar context, rather than a bold and impressive new architectural statement that would run the risk of being forbidding. Pilot Center was funded by the U.S. Department of Housing and Urban Development and the City of Cincinnati.''

Lenders were still shy, but "rehab" responded to public attitudes about renewal and preservation, and the public responded to projects like this one

Butler Square
Minneapolis, Minnesota
Owner: Development Associates
(Charles B. Coyer)
Architects: Miller Hanson Westerbeck Bell (in collaboration with Arvid Elness, project architect

A 70-year-old red brick warehouse on the edge of downtown Minneapolis had been unused for 10 years when it was recycled as a mixture of office, retail and public spaces arranged around a nine-story skylit atrium. The first two levels contained commercial and retail activities, with landscaped pedestrian walkways; the upper seven levels contained offices. The atrium was created by disassembling the original structural system toward the center of the building; material removed was then recycled to provide consistent details and finishes in occupied areas. The atrium served economic as well as esthetic purposes; if its volume had not been subtracted from the building's great volume, floor areas would have been larger than feasible for leasing.

"This massive encrustation of thick walls, deeply recessed windows, arched entrances, corbeled cornices and rampart-like towers is a lesson-laden example," the RECORD remarked, "of what that articulate Englishman, Alex Gordon, said should be the primary premises of design strategy in coming years—'long life, loose fit, low energy.' The Butler, idle for 10 years, is back in business as an eye-catching collage of commercial, retail and business activity that ranges up and around a skylit nine-story atrium. Here are office suites which look

out upon one of the most animated but articulate public spaces to be created anywhere in recent years. Lively shops, cosy corners to sip or sup in, landscaped promenades to stroll along, spots just to sit—it's all here, and as one secretary put it recently, 'I find that I'm in no particular hurry to leave at night.' A lot of people around town have been having a similar reaction to the explosion of life and light within the recently sandblasted austerity of the Butler's thick and slightly mysterious walls, which resemble some kind of Tuscan fortress. Inside,

these walls encase a not-slightly sensational experience, a bounteous and beautiful space bounded by the expressive edge of the building's fir-timber construction. This phase of the project, open about a year, takes up half the building's 500,000 square feet. Work is to begin shortly on the second half, which is being adapted as a 300-room hotel. [By 1979, work on the second half was still to begin, and it would involve not hotel but office space.] The original building, long known as the Butler Brothers Building, was designed by architect

Harry W. Jones and built by T.B. Walker, the founder of Minneapolis' prestigious Walker Art Center. The new work is being done by Miller Hanson Westerbeck Bell in collaboration with Arvid Elness, the project architect when he was with MHWB, who is serving as project manager on the second phase. The Butler's interior stems from a succinct structural system. The heavy fir timbers were put together on a module measuring about 16 feet by 14 feet. The columns, which receive the beams with cast iron brackets, gradually diminish in size from 22 inches square to a spindly eight inches near the top. The atrium was created by disassembling this timber system toward the center of the building, and the removed material was then recycled to provide consistent details and finishes in the occupied areas. No attempt was made to conceal elements of the existing structure. On the exterior, minimum change took place. The only visible alteration was the lowering of window spandrels to accommodate pedestrian access at grade level, and floor-to-ceiling glass in the office areas. The module of the building turned out to be marvelously flexible both horizontally and vertically; and every floor, reflecting a lively mix of tenants, has turned out differently. The space concept allowed for dividing floors into quadrants, with offices ranging from 114 to 400 square feet in each, and the possibility of shared reception, secretarial, storage and reference functions within each quadrant if more than one tenant were involved.''

On a tight site along a downtown thoroughfare, the "interior plaza" appeared on the campus, and so did the requirement for providing links to connect new, existing and future buildings

University Center, Cleveland State University. Cleveland, Ohio
Architects: Don M. Hisaka and Associates in joint venture with The Hoag-Wismer Partnership and Sasaki Associates

A multiuse building on a main thoroughfare in downtown Cleveland was designed to connect with campus buildings (two existing, one planned) on its other three sides, and to provide a communal space on a grand scale for the entire campus community. Self-contained working offices were put on the upper floors; the lower floors house a combination of small-scale public functions. The great space, six stories high, was framed in steel and, on two sides, glazed up to its full height. It became both the focal point and the visual reference for the whole campus.

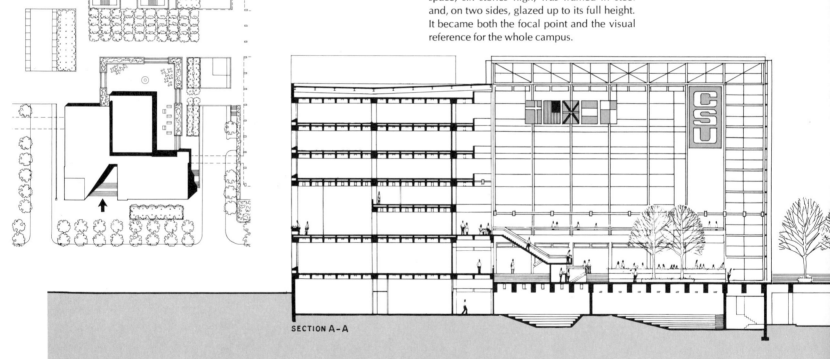

SECTION A-A

"For this University Center," the RECORD reported, "the architects worked with significant site restrictions. The building fronts on one of the city's main thoroughfares. It is bounded on the north by the existing campus library, on the east by an existing classroom building, on the west by the site of a future classroom building. In addition, all these buildings were to be linked by a network of all-weather corridors. Within these constraints, Hisaka's task was to develop a complex multi-use structure that would center on a student space of grand scale, a living room for the whole campus. The main entrance is set deep in the street facade. The approach is along an oblique wall turned to respond to the direction of pedestrian flow from the city center a few blocks away. The building section is particularly communicative. The upper three partial floors are self-contained working offices, the lower levels house a combination of small-scale public functions—any of which are readily accessible to students or members of the wider community. Relating to all—and reaching up the full six stories—is a monumental and exciting space, framed in steel and glazed up to its full height on two sides. The floor plane, printed with a shifting grid of shadows, is itself an extension of the outdoor plaza; and spaced out across its broad dimension are kiosks, a giant sculpture, a dining terrace and a planting bed for trees of substantial size. Each of these elements yields a little of its true scale to this heroic volume. From any vantage point, the space is active and alive, and its appeal to student users is obvious."

Correctional facilities designed for rehabilitation were built with public support
as public concern about prison conditions caught up with correctional philosophy

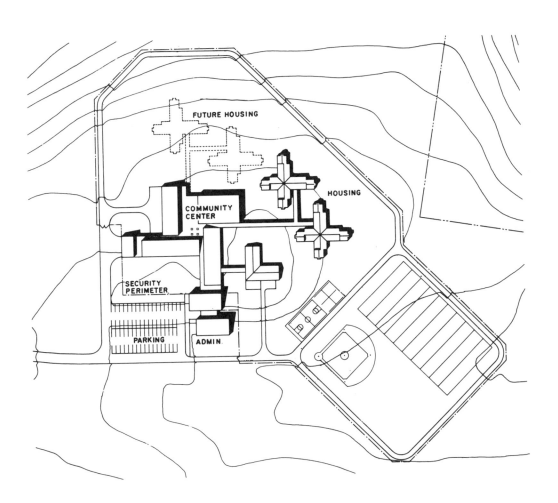

FUTURE HOUSING

HOUSING

COMMUNITY CENTER

SECURITY PERIMETER

PARKING   ADMIN.

South Central State
Correctional Institute
Eagle River, Alaska
Architects: Crittenden Cassetta
& Canhon/Hellmuth Obata
Kassabaum

A state correctional facility with a campus atmosphere reflected in its design the new approach to prison programs. Buildings were residential in scale and character and composed of non-institutional materials and forms—wood and plywood siding, pitched and shed roofs and large windows (of security glass). Except for split-level housing units, all buildings were one-story. The architectural concept of the housing units was of prime importance in the rehabilitation program, giving inmate and counsellor maximum exposure to each other. Each housing unit had rooms for 40 men and the staff responsible for the custody, counselling, education, work and recreation of the unit's residents. All sleeping rooms were single, organized in 10-room groups. Each group shared a living room and a "quiet room" with adjacent counsellor's office; dining room with small tables was provided for meals, which staff and inmates eat together.

"In its radically different architectural concept," the RECORD observed, "the South Central Correctional Institute at Eagle River, Alaska, represents the new approach not only to prison design but to prison programs. The living environment that it provides is as nearly normal as possible, permitting small freedoms within the larger, necessary restrictions of the institution as a whole, but providing, along with the counselling system, strong incentives to development by the offender of individual responsibility. The site, virgin land with mus-

keg ground cover and many small-diameter trees, is 13 miles north of Anchorage. Many of the trees remain, even within the perimeter fence, and the overall effect is of a small private school or college campus. Covered walks connect the housing units and the administration building. Inside, color is used to enhance the open, light character of the rooms, and good-looking modern furnishings are used throughout."

At the Federal level, the first of several regional youth correctional institutions reflecting

"the reforms in prison programs" was built at Pleasanton, California (pages 138–139), the RECORD reported. "It is a minimum/medium security institution for first offenders 18 to 25, controlled not by guard towers but by perimeter fencing and an electronic detecting system, with television monitors inside. The environment which results from the rehabilitation program and its implications permits more normal living conditions than older prisons. Here, a 'village,' planned around a manmade lake on an almost featureless 87-acre site 30 miles

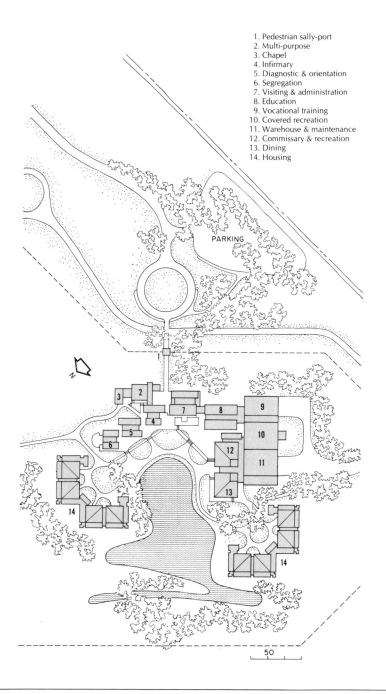

1. Pedestrian sally-port
2. Multi-purpose
3. Chapel
4. Infirmary
5. Diagnostic & orientation
6. Segregation
7. Visiting & administration
8. Education
9. Vocational training
10. Covered recreation
11. Warehouse & maintenance
12. Commissary & recreation
13. Dining
14. Housing

Federal Youth Center
Pleasanton, California
Architects: Frank L. Hope and
Associates

A non-institutional look was required by the Federal Bureau of Prisons to support its program emphasis on community reintegration. Each feature of the complex was designed to be part of the institution's program and to contribute either openly or more subtly to the individual inmate's rehabilitation. The architectural concept grouped buildings around a manmade lake created specifically to heighten the humanizing experience of the place. All the views, whether near or distant, were planned to be worth looking at — the focus always outward, not inward.

from San Francisco, consists of two 120-person housing units and the necessary core facilities: admission and administration, education and training, dining and recreation. The heart of the village and of the program is the 30-person housing sub-unit, where direct contact between counsellor and inmate takes place on a continuing basis, with the counsellor and the program the main deterrents to security problems. Vandalism to date has been minimal, inmates showing an exceptional regard for the buildings and grounds. The materials used are

atypical for prisons: wood frame with redwood plywood, built-up roofing and asphalt shingles, reinforced concrete block and precast concrete floor and roof decks. Laminated security glass is used throughout, affording vistas to courtyards, lakes and distant foothills."

It seems unlikely that any building type ever lagged longer behind professional thinking in the field it served than the "prison" or "jail" in the mid-20th century. By the early 1950s, an influential minority of the penological community was convinced that "correction" or

"rehabilitation" should supersede punishment as the primary goal of incarceration; and that prisons, jails and related places of detention should be thought of as "correctional" facilities. In these circles, it was recognized that existing penal institutions — most dating back to pre-Depression days and many to the turn of the century — were designed not for correction (or rehabilitation) but for punitive incarceration, and were completely unsuitable for rehabilitation programs. And there began to be efforts — at the Federal level, under an enlight-

ened and courageous director of the Federal Bureau of Prisons, the late James V. Bennett, in a few states, notably Louisiana and California, and in Canada—to rethink the architecture of prisons, to conceive them as correctional facilities designed to rehabilitate offenders and equip them to return to their own communities and lead constructive lives. But the leaders of the reform movement faced two key obstacles. First, legislators at local, state and Federal levels, who had always dragged their feet on funding for prisons and jails as the least "justifi-

able" (to taxpayers) expenditure of tax dollars, were even more reluctant to authorize funding for any projects taxpayers might consider were "country clubs" designed to "coddle criminals." Second, the overwhelming preponderance of staff at penal institutions with their historic and continuing focus on punitive incarceration was non-professional—"guards" whose chief duty was to keep "inmates" in line. While there were notable exceptions, legislative reluctance combined with opposition from old guard staff to delay widespread im-

plementation of the new correctional philosophy until the prison riots of the 1960s led to public demand that human rights be recognized inside as well as outside of prisons. Thus public concern, belatedly catching up with professional concern, made it possible to design and build institutions like these.

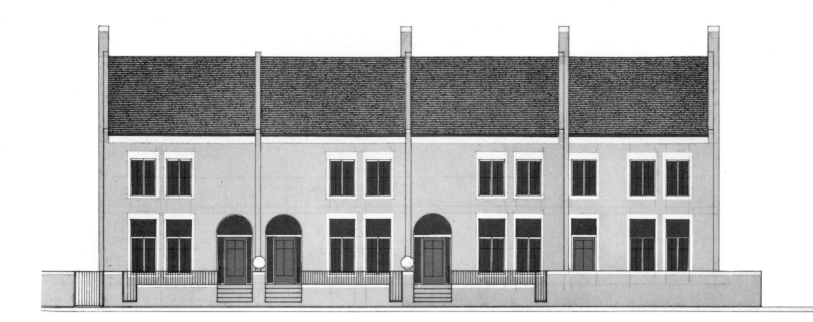

Townhouses that looked like home were appealing to more families in more places

Whitman Village
Huntington, New York
Architects: MLTW/Moore-Turnbull

This townhouse development was shaped around two characteristics of its site. One was that in the middle the site was open and grasssy with large, handsome old trees. The other was that on one side it was bounded by a busy four-lane road separating it from the local train station parking lot. Accordingly, on this side, the housing units turn their back on the street and on their parking in order to face the interior greensward. On the other side of the site, freestanding fourplexes make a much softer boundary.

The townhouse became a familiar building type to a new generation of homeowners in the 1970s. The high cost of land, whether in city or suburb, had much to do with it. So did the apparently increasing inclination of young homebuyers to opt for the cities instead of the suburbs, hoping that they did not have to give up all the advantages along with the disadvantages of suburban living. Developers found it more and more difficult to assemble sites for apartment developments in the face of public resistance to out-of-scale or out-of-character intrusions in any neighborhood. And the market potential for townhouses was suggested by the popularity of the pioneering modern townhouse developments of the fifties and sixties — Southwest Washington; Reston, Virginia; and Society Hill in Philadelphia, among others — as well as the evident interest of young homebuyers in rehabilitating old row houses in cities from New York and Baltimore to San Francisco. The need to be acceptable in a neighborhood of single-family houses and the need to appeal to people accustomed to living in houses both tended to encourage an architectural character that expressed the idea of "house" rather than the idea of "apartment" (or anything too "different"). The result, as in this group of townhouse developments, was often a look that some might have called "traditional." But by 1975, modern architecture was not bound by looks, though that may not have seemed so obvious at the time.

"All of these designs," the RECORD reported, "make efforts in many directions at once to form residential environments not so much

Eastover Gates
Charlotte, North Carolina
Architects: Wolf Associates

Unlike many new developments in existing neighborhoods, this small townhouse development (left) was organized along curving tree-lined streets like the older single-family houses around it. The architects' first concern was to create a place that could be comfortably inhabited by people and cars, whether stationary or in motion. But they were also careful to make the soft delineations—for instance, between street and sidewalk, or sidewalk and front steps and gardens of the houses—that tell what belongs to whom.

Kingsmill R-3 Housing Development Kingsmill-on-the-James, Williamsburg, Virginia. Architects: Charles W. Moore Associates

In this townhouse development, density was about eight units to the acre. Most of the parking was provided on the street in small parking areas behind one of the two basic types of unit clusters. The building, which might recall an old-fashioned garage or stable, acts as a gateway between the street and the parking area, and is, in the process, two houses. Each unit sits on its own plot of land, designed to be sold outright rather than as condominiums.

around a diagrammatic conceptual consistency as around the consistent sensibilities of the inhabitants. They are housing designs which organize themselves around community spaces (almost all of them streets) in an active attempt to enliven those spaces while at the same time making private places to live adjacent to them. Finally, readers will notice that the designs on these pages look startlingly, or perhaps discouragingly, traditional—a fact which is not easy to explain. One explanation was offered by Marley Carroll, head of the de-sign team for Eastover Gates (top left). 'We didn't start out to design traditional houses,' Carroll says. 'We just wanted to be sensible about the function and the imagery of each of the parts. So we used chimneys because fireplaces are nice, and chimneys visible on the outside seem to say "house." Pitched roofs let the rain drain off easily, and they have a nice profile; and large arched front doors tell you clearly where the entrance is. We were surprised when the design turned out to look traditional.' "

The house as architecture has both reflected
and predicted design trends in all eras,
like this large country house designed to seem
smaller and evoking past and future with its
combination of the familiar and the unexpected

Private residence
Philadelphia, Pennsylvania
Architect: Hugh Newell Jacobsen

This house was designed in response to the
clients' wish for a house that looked like a "country house," a big house that didn't look big, with
plenty of space for all the activities of a sizable
family. The various functional areas of the house
were organized as elements of the plan and staggered, row-house fashion, to reduce the size visually and to camouflage the overall length. The
sense of scale is even further manipulated by defining the elements with pitched roofs and with
fenestration — ranging from narrow vertical slits to
wide sliding glass doors — that does not have the
usual proportional relationship to the house.

A house by a serious architect for a sensitive
client — affluent or not — may summarize tendencies in architecture at any given time, or
even foretell them, more eloquently than the
biggest building. Perhaps it is because the
communication between architect and client,
always the heart of the architectural process, is
never more direct and personal. Perhaps it is
because the client and the client's family are
also the users; and the architect can see them,
talk to them, know them all, at least a little, not
through a veil of statistics or as represented by

committee, but as human beings. A house calls
forth the most specific architectural interpretation of life — as it is lived by a particular family
in a particular place in a particular time — and
the most intimate architectural expression of
human aspirations. This great house spoke
eloquently of trends in modern architecture in
the mid-1970s while it evoked both past and
future. It looked almost (not quite) as though it
had always been there. It was very large, because its multiple functions required it to be,
but it was presented as a group of small-scale

elements. It combined the familiar with the
unexpected so that they seemed to belong to
each other. It deserved but did not seek attention.

"The restrained elegance that has become a
hallmark of the work of Hugh Newell Jacobsen," the RECORD observed, "has been honed
to an even keener level of detailing in this big,
beautiful house. The owners had a rural, rolling site in suburban Philadelphia, land that
overlooked a small, distant pond and that
seemed to call for a 'country house.' In com-

missioning Jacobsen, the owners stressed the desire for this 'country' quality, and for 'a large house that didn't look large,' to accommodate a sizable family. Jacobsen deftly solved the problem by deliberately breaking up the massing of the house to reduce the size visually and to screen the overall length. The various units of the house are contained between the white-stuccoed concrete block walls — in a staggered, row-house fashion — and are given even further definition and form by using 'traditional' pitched slate roofs. The overall sense of scale

in the house is further baffled by the fenestration: narrow vertical slits and wide, sliding glass walls that don't have the usual size relationship to the house. The end effect is that of a country place, of somewhat indeterminate size, that has occasionally had a room added here and there. Inside, however, the real spaciousness is emphasized. The rooms are big, with high ceilings following the tall, steep-pitched roofs. And they are made to appear even bigger by a series of devices: all-white walls and ceilings; continuous black slate

floors and terraces; a calculatedly underfurnished look; a monochromatic color scheme, only occasionally brightened by paintings, plants, and rugs; a succession of planned vistas, many of them unexpected, through glazed transoms, slits and skylights; and extremely well-planned and dramatic lighting. Jacobsen has grouped all major family and service spaces in the center of the house, so they can be used separately or all together for big gatherings. These rooms are flanked by the two bedroom wings.

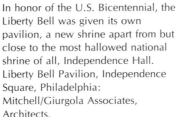

In honor of the U.S. Bicentennial, the Liberty Bell was given its own pavilion, a new shrine apart from but close to the most hallowed national shrine of all, Independence Hall. Liberty Bell Pavilion, Independence Square, Philadelphia: Mitchell/Giurgola Associates, Architects.

1976

A new library under Harvard Yard linked three existing libraries of which it was an extension and emerged above ground as a grass-covered embankment, the planting and pathways of its roof reinforcing the existing circulation network.

Buildings with very different programs in very different settings responded to functional requirements, made complexity comprehensible, and expressed the essence of their social and cultural context.

A 10-foot-wide slit of space separated twin towers that connected at ground level in an interior plaza, and had links at concourse level to nine other downtown blocks.

A tower that was both hotel and office building had commercial space at ground level, and a canopy that serves to shelter passersby and users alike.

Even shopping centers which were hugely successful as horizontal malls began to expand vertically as the cost of land mounted, and multi-level parking garages replaced expanses of parking.

Subsidized housing and private housing were no longer so easy to tell apart, with more amenities designed into both.

A very large house was made to seem unpretentious and much in the spirit of the local vernacular by the disposition of functions in four separate units with no connecting roofs, their only link a wooden deck.

Clients were asking for references to the past in otherwise modern houses, and hand-craftsmanship was increasingly prized.

A house might recall indigenous structures of centuries ago, or be a minimal structure within which occupants could arrange space for their own special and changing needs.

The real impact on design of solar possibilities or even of energy scarcity was yet to come, but all over the country, even in less than ideal climates, experiments were under way.

A mixed-income housing development became community architecture, with four acres of plazas and a river-edge promenade open to the public, and a pedestrian bridge making access easy.

On a sprawling urban renewal site, Venturi put a building that wanted to belong where it was and that had aspects both ordinary and extraordinary . . . on a new university campus, a building that evoked Aalto both in spirit and vocabulary and was intended to invite the users "to make the building their own."

A new library under Harvard Yard linked three
existing libraries of which it was an extension
and emerged above ground as a grass-covered
embankment, the planting and pathways of its roof
reinforcing the existing circulation network

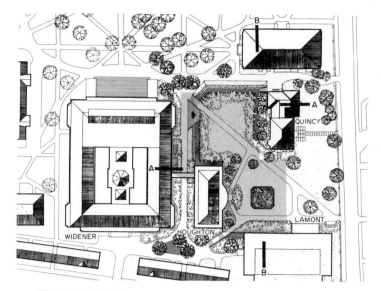

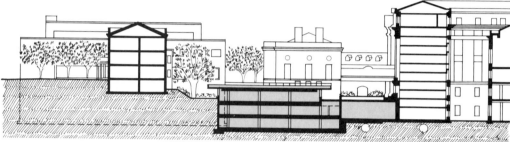

Nathan Marsh Pusey Library
Harvard Yard, Cambridge, Massachusetts
Architects: Hugh Stubbins and Associates

On a site too constricted for a building above
ground, this three-level library was put for the
most part below grade; but windows concealed
by sloping berms along two sides of the exterior,
and a central court, introduced natural lighting to
staff and reader areas. The new library was designed to be an interconnecting link between
three existing libraries (Widener, Houghton and
Lamont) and an extension of each. The landscaped roof (seen at right from the front of Widener) became a link as well. The steps lead to the
principal diagonal path, which connects with the
circulation system of the Yard. The main entrance
to Pusey Library is below grade at the foot of a
staircase to the right of the stairs visible in the
photo. The entrance staircase, between Houghton and Lamont, also leads to the landscaped roof
of Pusey.

"In deference to its environment," the RECORD
wrote, "Pusey Library was built beneath Harvard Yard. By partially burying this three-level
library, and covering its roof with grass, planting and paths which reinforce the existing circulation patterns of Harvard Yard, the architects have added an essential structure while
preserving open space. Glass windows, concealed by sloping berms along two sides of the
exterior, and a central light court, introduce
natural lighting to staff and reader areas. Harvard Yard is, of course, a place of great historic
interest, a museum of native American architecture of every period and an environment
revered by generations of Harvard students,
Cambridge citizens and lovers of campus architecture. Originally, it had been thought that
the proposed libary should be completely subterranean, but new concepts of landscaping
led to the idea that the building could emerge
at least slightly above ground. The architects
foresaw an opportunity they have since effectively capitalized upon—that of designing the
library in a way that would open up new vistas
within the Yard as seen from the inside of the
new structure, or from its landscaped roof. Just
as importantly, allowing the building to surface
brings daylight into the interiors. From the beginning, the Pusey Library was seen as an interconnecting link among three existing libraries—Widener, Houghton and Lamont, and
an extension of each. Its roof has become a link
as well, its paths and landscaping reinforcing
the existing circulation network in the Yard. Inside the library, the principal circulation corridor is directly beneath the main diagonal

path on the roof. The three major entrances are at important campus nodes. The principal entrance is directly to the east of the grand staircase of the Widener Library; the second is at the corner formed by Houghton and Lamont; the third is adjacent to 17 Quincy, the former official residence of the president of the university, now used for miscellaneous functions. The new structure adds 87,000 square feet to the buildings that comprise the Harvard College Library, which is a subdivision of the Harvard University Library, the largest university library in the world. The new library accommodates the expanding general collections of Widener Library and the manuscript collections of Houghton. In visible exterior form, the Pusey Library is a slanting grass-covered embankment. Its roof is a stone-rimmed platform of earth containing a lawn, trees and shrubs, diagonally bisected by paths and stairs. On axis with the neo-Georgian bow-front of Houghton is a square sunken courtyard which admits light to major interior spaces. The portion of the building that appears above the surface is surrounded by a broad band of brick paving which forms a wall between the berm and the window wall. At the top of the berm is a deep concrete trough planted with shrubs and vines. The courtyard is two levels deep. It is faced with panels of shipsaw granite alternating with bands of glass. The court is a small garden with a brick surround.''

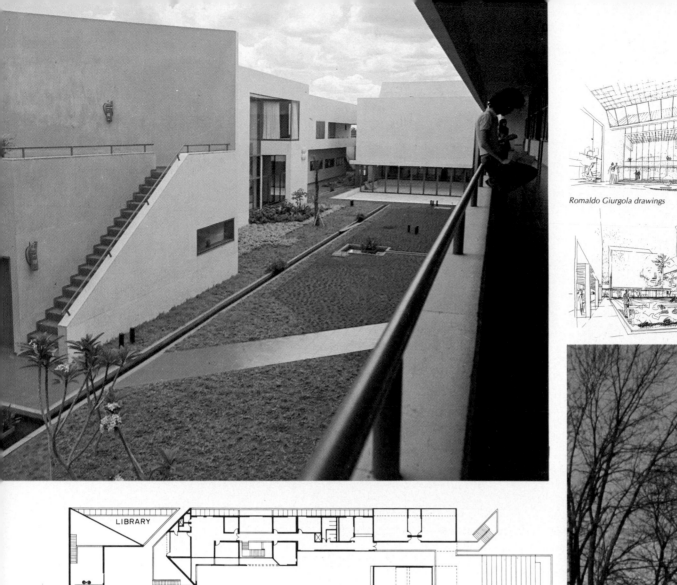

Romaldo Giurgola drawings

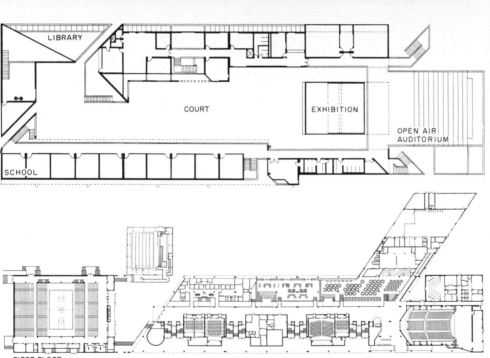

LIBRARY

COURT   EXHIBITION

OPEN AIR
AUDITORIUM

SCHOOL

FIRST FLOOR

"In contrast to the pylon-studded polemic of much of Brasilia's architecture," William Marlin wrote in the RECORD, "the Casa is a nice neat hit for humanism, with some of the spontaneity of a *favella* in Rio. A functional mix is contained within several two-level structures that are smartly scrunched together. Like iron filings, these fragments gravitate around a landscaped interior courtyard, a deliberately magnetic, unifying field of space with colorful flowers, exotic trees and cooling pools of water. At several points, the courtyard seeps out to the surrounding streets in the form of shoulder-squeezing slit-like walks which, cut between the fragments at the far corners of the overall composition, offer intriguing glimpses inside. Wider entranceways are positioned in the middle, but on either side of the courtyard, second-level overhangs give a sense of intimacy as one comes upon the inner space, supplying a clear clue to the complex, yet cohesive nature of the architecture that edges it. The functional fragments include 20 classrooms and two language labs; offices for the school faculty, the USIA and the Fullbright program; a 25,000-volume library; and a two-story skylit exhibition hall. Seen through the skylight, the rooftop tiers of the amphitheater edge upward, and beneath it is a 250-seat multi-use auditorium. Interpenetrating lines of sight pull the interior spaces, done in white, bright plaster, into a spritely continuum. The reddish-pink stucco of the exterior, the hue of local clay, closes around this variegation—both a countenance of and a check upon the traits of complexity."

Buildings with very different programs in very different settings
responded to functional requirements, made complexity comprehensible
and expressed the essence of their social and cultural context

Casa Thomas Jefferson
Brasilia, Brazil
Architect: Mitchell/Giurgola Associates

A bi-national cultural center built by the U.S. Information Agency (USIA) in collaboration with a local group, the Thomas Jefferson Cultural Council, had unpretentious stucco walls which related it comfortably to its surroundings. Entrances, alternately wide and low and high and narrow, opened into a lively landscaped courtyard that disclosed the functional fragments of the whole composition—library, exhibition hall, classroom and office wings and amphitheater.

Columbus East High School
Columbus, Indiana
Architects: Mitchell/Giurgola Associates

Spaces for flexible uses were put on the upper two floors, spaces for more specific uses on the lower two floors, a difference clearly expressed on the exterior. External surfaces of the upper floors, laid over a steel-frame module 44 by 32 feet, were composed of glossy white aluminum sandwich panels with integrally gasketed windows set flush with the external planes of the wall. Recessed lower floors were clad in clay tile.

This was a building designed to reflect the overlapping rural and industrial moods of a town famous for its evolving collection of fine contemporary architecture. Designed for a student capacity of 2100, and providing more than 363,000 square feet of floor area, the school was planned with a time module in mind—a 15-minute module. "In addition to specific subjects of study," the RECORD reported, "the architects had to consider various speeds and styles of study, ranging from the needs of the individual, to the level of the seminar, to the more familiar classroom format, and on up the hierarchy to general lectures. Studying the frequency and density of flow as students or faculty move from one activity to another, the architects made the principle of circulation the premise of design. Vertical circulation is punctuated by the skylights above the stairwells which, reading on the exterior, denote the linkage of levels. Columbus East is a reconciliation of disparate elements, both of its functional program and of its community context. Its taut character reminds us that for all the talk about 'complexity and contradiction,' there can be a still higher relationship, 'complexity and complementarity.'"

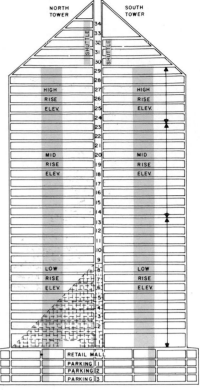

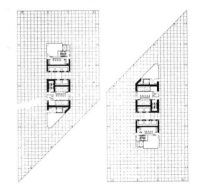

A 10-foot-wide slit of space separated twin towers that connected at ground level in an interior plaza, and had links at concourse level to nine other downtown blocks

"In plan, section and elevation," as the RECORD described it, "Pennzoil rises 36 stories (495 feet) from its block-square downtown site, 250 feet to a side, with a flourish of 45-degree angles in a geometric exercise worthy of Euclid. Its 1.4 million feet of leasable space are a sizable increment of the whopping 36 million square feet of commercial space booming Houston has added in 16 years to its 1960 stock of nine million square feet. The two identical shapes, flipflopped to be mirror images of each other, are separated by a sky-scraping slit of space, ten feet wide, and, down at groundside, by a landscaped air-conditioned plaza that takes up 27 per cent of the 62,500-square-foot site in the form of two right-angled triangular areas—this space being what is left over after the two trapezoidal-plan towers. The plaza, or two plazas to be more precise, contains 36,000 square feet of commercial space, including that of the concourse level below, which interconnects with a pedestrian tunnel system that threads below the streets. The plazas are enclosed by truss-sup-ported slopes of glass which slant skyward at 45 degrees to the eighth floor. Here the slopes join, the ten-foot slit starts, and the towers are seen to thrust vertically through the white-painted filigree of steel trusswork—straight up to the 29th floor. At this level, the wall becomes a 'roof,' as the skin of the towers, composed of bronze-tinted glass and anodized aluminum, breaks from the vertical at yet another 45-degree angle rising to the apogee of each shape. These topside slopes enclose executive offices and suites—six of them in the

Pennzoil Place
Houston, Texas
Owner: Gerald D. Hines Interests
Architects: Johnson/Burgee
Associate architects: S. I. Morris
Associates

Pennzoil Place consists of twin 36-story towers, trapezoidal in plan, that are mirror images of each other. At ground level, they define connected triangular plazas that are enclosed by 45-degree slopes of glass, supported by a white-painted trusswork of steel. Towers thrust vertically through the plaza spaces to the 29th floor, where the 45-degree-angle slopes repeat.

north tower, four in the south. Reached by shuttle elevators, these tiered spaces, with stepped-up mezzanine levels, represent a fundamentally new slant on the old story about starving in a garret. The concrete sheer-wall core of each welded-steel-frame tower contains utilities and the banks of elevators, but, more to the point of rentability, permits minimal columns and beams and maximum leasable open space of 20,500 square feet per floor. Of the three banks of elevators serving each tower, six move between 2nd and 13th floors,

five between the 14th and 23rd floors, five between the 24th and 36th floors, plus those special shuttles 'up in the garret.' Thus the configuration of Pennzoil, its towers and enclosed plazas nudging right out to the sidewalk, makes intensive use of its site: 550 parking spaces are taken care of on three subsurface levels. The plaza provides temperature-controlled year-round comfort in Houston's hot humid climate, creating a kind of 'city room' in which a mix of people and purposes can rub elbows. Convenient linkage with any of nine

downtown blocks (and 14 buildings) by way of the two concourse-level tunnels, 12 feet wide and 8 feet high, will make Pennzoil a primary ventricle in the city's circulation system. Although cost of the tunnels is around $4000 a foot, the one leading to the Houston Club Building is already open, the one to the south is awaiting future development of that block—heightened accessibility is thought to be justification enough for the added cost. And in the case of the eastern link half of its cost has been picked up by the Texas Commerce Bank.''

A tower that was both hotel and office building had commercial space at ground level, and a canopy that serves to shelter passersby and users alike

One United Nations Plaza
New York, New York
Owner: United Nations
Development Corporation
Architects: Kevin Roche John
Dinkeloo and Associates

The first building in New York to mix office and hotel functions had a skin of blue-green reflective glass and aluminum. The curtain wall was engineered for energy savings, with walls of office floors (1-26) composed of four bands of glass per floor, two clear and two insulated; and walls on hotel floors (28-38) of three bands of glass per floor, one clear, two insulated. Setbacks are 45-degree "slant-backs," which on the north facade occur twice, angling up from the 12th and the 28th floors; on the southeast corner, a "slant-out" angles up to the 12th floor.

"A friendly neighborhood skyscraper," the headline on the RECORD's article read. "During what is being called the 'post-modernist' phase of 20th-century architecture," William Marlin wrote, "it may strike some as unseemly to extol another tall building. Yet if the Skyscraper Age is over, and one suspects that those who say so for philosophical rather than economic reasons are being precipitate, there are some lyrical, resonant swan songs being composed. One such is One United Nations Plaza. While it may well be that the profession has moved beyond its fascination with solitary, stunning shapes that are all wrapped up in themselves but little else, One United Nations Plaza, being wrapped up in a lot else, is a needed reminder that tall buildings, designed to come down off it and take cues from their environment, can still help architecture to turn its corners nicely—and will probably be doing so long after post-mortems on the 'post-modernist' phase are complete. Svelte of build and spiffily draped in a toga of blue-green glass, the 39-story One United Nations Plaza, located across from the Secretariat and General Assembly and next door to the U.S. Mission, is a friendly neighborhood skyscraper which, leaving a lot to the imagination, has a lot going on inside its 586,000-square-foot bulk. At 505 feet in height, the building is three feet shorter than the Secretariat, in line with zoning restrictions for the district, and is the first in New York to combine office and hotel functions. Just in from the two sidewalks that bound it is a lobby. The one off First Avenue (center photo) leads to elevators for the office floors, 360,000 square

feet on the first 26 floors of the building. The one off 44th street, around the corner (photo at right above), leads to the reception desk and elevators for the United Nations Plaza Hotel, run by Hyatt International, which contains 288 rooms and suites, occupying floors 28 through 38. The Turtle Bay Tennis and Swim Club, named for the old surrounding neighborhood, is on 27; and 39 provides 24-hour tennis facilities. A branch of Chemical Bank and Bernie's International News Corporation occupy retail space at ground level. The rest of the ground floor is given over to the hotel-managed Ambassador Grill and Lounge, accessible through both lobbies; and on the second floor there are a European-style eating spot called the Coffee Mill and three divisible meeting rooms. Outside, the building's material mass meets the street in a pleasant way, hovering over passers-by with a wrap-around shed-style canopy of glass that slants out as a continuation of the curtain wall above. It is a building with a certain quizzical quality about its sheer surfaces, implying the animation and mix of activity inside, but leaving open the question of its exact nature. In a genre where the 'form follows function' thesis was most cogently pioneered, this skyscraper negotiates a new variation of *detente* between the two. It reads 'true,' all right, but because its formal character was as consciously conceived to evoke, or to point up, the many dimensions of its external environment as it was to house an amalgam of internal needs. It is an especial obligation of the tall building to take such pluralistic, contextual factors into account, and this one does.''

A vast expansion of this highly successful regional shopping center in a Dallas suburb reflected the changes that had come to shopping center design in the ten years since it was first built. When the RECORD first published it (April 1966), it was cited as "a culmination of the horizontal concept of varied but visually unified retail stores in a single building." In the same article, the RECORD predicted that "the next phase of evolution after Northpark will almost surely be the vertical shopping center because of the high cost of land." In 1976, the

RECORD reported, "That evolution has come about, at Northpark itself. And the new multi-layered parking structures have wed the existing structures to the neighborhood that surrounds it by creating physical presences that both 'define' the surrounding public streets and visually break the former expanse of flat parking areas. Each parking structure takes advantage of changes in grade levels by offering direct access to upper and lower decks without ramps. The decks are precast concrete plank on poured-in-place columns and were

erected very quickly (one of them in six weeks) to avoid interference with shopping at a peak season. They are faced in white brick. The basic problem of multi-level shopping malls is creating equal exposure for all of the stores. To encourage pedestrian traffic on both levels at Northpark, the levels were set half a story above grade and half a story below, and the entrance arrangement of a central escalator up and side stairs down encourages shoppers to go up to the 'problem second level'—as does the direct bridge entrance from the second lev-

Even shopping centers which were
hugely successful as horizontal
malls began to expand vertically
as the cost of land mounted,
and multi-level parking garages
replaced expanses of parking

Northpark
Dallas, Texas
Architects: Omniplan

Expansion of Northpark continued the successful original for-
mula of placing the department
stores in prominent positions at
the corners of the overall massing. The new Lord & Taylor
store boldly solves the visual
problems of windowless structures by appearing to be a gigantic sculpture of folded
planes at a comfortable scale
for the large site. It is entered
from a new parking structure
by a bridge—and from the
ground—by doors within the
angled recesses. Northpark's
extension exhibits an even
greater manipulation of bold
forms and planes than the original, but is unified with the 10-
year-old section by a single
material both outside and in.
While the architects had hoped
for development of fountains
at the Lord & Taylor entrance,
the present simplicity is almost monumental, and certainly pleasing.

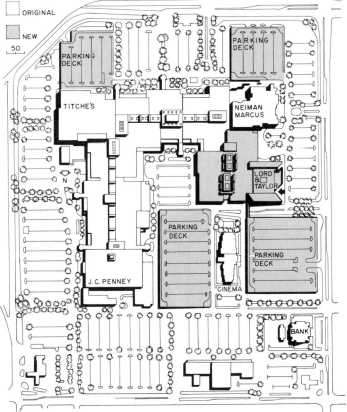

el of the adjacent parking structure. Visual
contact between levels is encouraged by the
double-height mall and glass railings on the
upper story's access galleries and bridges. In a
section of the country noted for personal independence, Northpark was one of the first major
shopping centers to demand control over
stores' graphics (by a review board of repre-
sentatives of both the developer and the architects). While the concept was difficult to en-
force in the beginning, the popularity of the
center has largely erased resistance. In the
malls, the diverse storefronts are further unified
by a strong visual framework of sandblasted
white brick, which has been carried over from
the center's exterior cladding. Natural light is
provided by translucent skylights put above
deep beams to reduce glare. These supply
most of the mall illumination required during
the day, though this natural light is supple-
mented by photo-cell-controlled artificial
lighting. The concept was an energy-conserving 'first' with the original building. Stairs and
escalators have been deliberately kept out of
the center of the mall to eliminate what the
architects call a busy space full of 'things.'
While the building was made of concrete, the
new extension, for construction speed, has
been built of steel with precast concrete decks.
Here, ground floor tenants were able to start
finish-work while second-level construction
was being completed.''

"A prime site in Marin County north of San Francisco—with spectacular views to San Francisco and man-made lagoons—is the location of Hilarita apartments, a Section 236 Federally assisted housing project," the RECORD wrote. "While only 102 units occupy the 12.8-acre site, there was a limited area on which to build, because of a commitment of 4.5 acres as open space (as part of Tiburon's trail and park system) and poor soil conditions. The instability of alluvial clay soil throughout, and the necessity to meet building codes for earthquake resistance, meant extensive soil preparation before construction (including earth fill, installation of drains, benching and earth buttressing to contain fill). Foundations consist of drilled concrete pier footings and poured-in-place concrete grade beams. The buildings' low profile on the hill was a solution to the twin objectives of preserving views for neighbors and keeping construction costs as low as possible. The project was nonetheless designed to give every apartment unit a view. Other amenities include a private entrance to every apartment; parking near, though separated from, each unit; and, for noise control, little abutment of the units. Community spaces are grouped near the entrance, with a playground adjoining an all-purpose center which contains the manager's office, maintenance offices, laundry facilities, a meeting room and space that can be converted to a day-care center. Exteriors are rough-sawn redwood plywood."

Subsidized housing and private housing
were no longer so easy to tell apart,
with more amenities designed into both

Hilarita Apartments
Tiburon, California
Owner: Tiburon Ecumenical
Association
Architect: Kaplan/McLaughlin

The low profile of the project is enhanced by the clear, sharp line of roofs.
Most units have fenced-in private terraces; each six units share a common
open area. Interior spaces responded
to needs defined by tenants in meetings with the architect during the planning process. The steep slope of the
site permits multi-level apartments and
diversity in ceiling heights.

The Islands
Foster City, California
Architects: Fisher-Friedman
Associates

On one third of the units, glass enclosures—often used as greenhouses—
add another dimension of light to the
space, and also enhance visual interest
along the street. All balcony railings
were constructed of tempered glass
panels, providing shelter from strong
winds without obstructing views to
either water or street.

"Located on two large islands in a large man-
made lagoon near the southern tip of San Francisco Bay," as the RECORD described it, "this
condominium development provides a fascinating geometrical configuration in which all
apartments have a view to the water. Excellent
site planning and design amenities in individual units create one of the most pleasant new
housing developments in the area. Of the three
phases of construction, only the third phase—
half the island—is incomplete; completion is
expected by the end of 1976. All condominiums are organized into six-unit rectangular
buildings, each with four flats and two townhouses. Ground level consists of two flats facing the water and either an eight- or twelve-car
garage facing the street. The upper level consists of two two-story townhouses flanked by
two one-story flats. On the smaller of the two
islands, buildings are positioned around the
perimeter, with a circulation spine in the center to serve both pedestrian and automobile
traffic. To obtain views to the water for each
apartment and provide visual interest from
across the lagoon, the buildings were staggered. The clubhouse—as focal point of the
development—is located in the middle of the
island near the entrance. As an intentional
contrast to other housing in the area, the project was painted white, and accented with yellow awnings, cedar wood details and blue ce-
ramic tile on roofs and as trim on windows
and stair rails. Extensive landscaping, especially along streets, includes trees between garage
doors." Townscape, not "development," was
the ambience of projects like these.

A very large house was made to seem unpretentious and much in the spirit of the local vernacular by the disposition of functions in four separate units with no connecting roofs, their only link a wooden deck

Vacation house in Maine
Mt. Desert Island, Maine
Architect: Edward Larrabee Barnes

A vacation house in a spruce grove on the coast of Maine responded to a program that suggested flexibility and a site that suggested modesty. It was composed of four separate structures: a studio tower with laundry below; a one-bedroom house with living room, dining room and kitchen; a two-story guest house; and a high-ceilinged library-study. No roofs connected the four units. Each of the structures was shaped in simple vernacular forms finished in wood shingle, each artfully placed in relation to the others, and all spun together by a rambling wood deck that opens at intervals to arresting coastal views. The whole composition kept a respectful distance from the shoreline. The access road stops 200 feet short of the house.

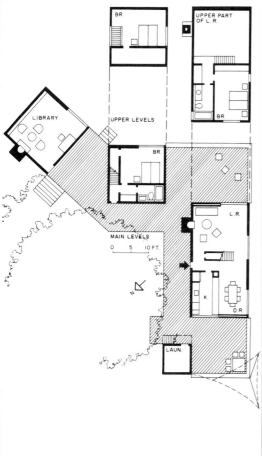

David Franzen © ESTO, (Photos opposite)

In the second generation of modern architects, the work of Edward Larrabee Barnes was notable from the beginning for its sense of place, its sophisticated restraint, and its fine detailing. While Barnes has long been involved with very large-scale urbanistic projects, from campus planning (for example, see page 63) to downtown development (pages 94–95), he has continued his interest in the house as architecture, as this house indicates.

"Though elegant in its details," as the RE-CORD observed, "the house has some of the same hardy character and stern New England virtues that we associate with the Maine fishing villages its massing seems to reflect. This beautifully restrained vacation house was built for a man who is an author/scholar with an interest in public service. Among his wife's varied interests are calligraphy and cooking. Their children are grown and living away but often visit, bringing family or friends when they do. The detailing throughout the house is spare, and elegant in its simplicity. The roof planes turn down into wall planes, for instance, without the interruption of large board or fascia. Trim around openings is so reticent it all but disappears. At one corner of the deck, however, just off the kitchen, the need for a shaded outdoor living area produced a pleasantly flamboyant series of details. The architect set a spinnaker on booms—a sail that can be adjusted to a range of sun angles by hand-operated winches mounted on the deck."

Clients were asking for references to the past in otherwise modern houses, and hand-craftsmanship was increasingly prized

House for Mr. and Mrs. John Wierdsma
Nantucket, Massachusetts
Architect: Louis Mackall

Given the client's request for heavy timber framing, the architect suggested this "architectural anachronism" be placed in quotes, so to speak. Prominently exhibited, the oak 10 x 10s actually support the second floor, but the exterior walls of the house are conventional framing, with the rafters—sawn from 3×12s—two feet on center, tied in pairs by tension rods. The house is shingled in white cedar, and interior flooring is tongue-and-groove fir.

This hand-hewn house crosses the upland at the head of a long marsh stretching out of Pulpis Bay across from the town of Nantucket. "With its silvery bowed roof," the RECORD remarked, "it resembles a weather log, ax-cut once in the center for a tall interior porch, and notched toward the ends for skylights. Beneath the master bedroom (right above), a low ceiling slides over the giant beams, making a more intimate family space. Whaling artifacts hang on the fir columns and beams. In front of the tall fireplace, the children can hash out a game of Monopoly.

" 'We can extrude almost anything now,' says architect Louis Mackall. 'People are surrounded by objects which are there only because people can afford them. But eventually they realize that their whole environment is foreign to them, that they have no personal attachment to anything in it. That's why so many people are turning to handcraft . . . making things for themselves, or having things made for them.' Mackall built many of the parts of the Wierdsma house himself in his Connecticut shop—the skylights, cabinets, doors and screen doors, the stairs—everything that could be conveniently carried in a moving van. 'I could go on forever making stuff for this house,' he says as he eases out one or two of the drawers in the kitchen. Feeling a slight hesitation in the glide, he goes out to find his plane. 'I hope all this wood, this handcraft, will be an important part of these kids' childhood and recollections,' Mackall says. 'I hope it makes a difference.' "

"In addition to being a graceful and interesting solution for this exposed but isolated hilltop site," the RECORD observed, "the parti is reminiscent of earth mound buildings developed centuries ago by the various Indian tribes that inhabited central Florida before its present settlement. Reinterpreted here, the earthform idea seems just as compelling today. The house is built into the crest of a hill that overlooks citrus groves on the valley floor 230 feet below. From its uppermost level, tucked under a hipped roof, the owner can look out in every direction across enormous expanses of view that reach into five surrounding counties. The architect reports that on one occasion from this vantage he was able to count seven separate thunderstorms in progress simultaneously. In sharp contrast, views from the lower levels are confined and intimate. The ends of the cruciform plan open through glass doors to small partially-enclosed courts which, by their different orientation, architectural treatment and planning, provide a variety of sensory experiences. The structure is reinforced concrete block with tie beams, pilasters and a concrete slab poured in place. All exterior walls are earth-insulated except where glazing occurs. Partitions are plaster board on wood stud, glass is solar gray tinted and the roof is finished in clay tile. The original elevation of the hilltop was just about the level of the first floor slab. The pyramidal flanks of the building, therefore, represent an extension of the hill inclined upward at about 18 degrees."

A house might recall indigenous structures of centuries ago,
or be a minimal structure within which occupants
could arrange space for their own special and changing needs

UNDERFLOOR ACCESS SPACE

Private residence
Central Florida
Architect: William Morgan

A house built into the crest of a hill was bermed on its other three sides to create an "underground house" above ground. The house had sweeping views from its top level, more confined and intimate views from its lower level. The ends of a cruciform plan opened through glass doors to small partially enclosed courts. Structure is reinforced concrete block with tie beams, pilasters and a concrete slab poured in place. The original elevation of the hilltop was just about first-floor level. Pyramidal flanks of the building extend the hill.

Ron Davis Residence/Studio
Malibu, California
Architects: Frank O. Gehry Jr. and Associates

A trapezoidal form was developed from a close collaboration between architect and artist, and relates to Davis' paintings, mostly abstracts based on strong use of perspective. From a 30-foot-high corner, the roof slants steeply to a 10-foot height at the opposite corner. Windows—in varying sizes and shapes, with reflective glass on the south wall—and a large 20- by 20-foot centered skylight allow more than adequate natural light for the artist's work. These unconventional shapes add a new dimension and different perspective to each side of the house.

"An unusual concept for a residence is this design for an artist, Ron Davis," the RECORD wrote. "A temporary combination of residence and studio (a separate studio is planned for later), is located on a three-and-one-half-acre site in Malibu with views of mountains to the north and east and views of ocean to the south and west. The objective of the architect was to create a minimal structure in which Davis could arrange space for his own special and changing needs. The use of corrugated galvanized metal on the exterior—which kept costs down—permitted an enlargement of the house size to 5000 square feet within the owner's budget. The angular and high ceiling allows a flexibility in the use of the space, including loft space, which could be expanded to a complete second floor within the structure, thus doubling the floor area. Openness for work area and display of art was achieved through the use of only three center columns and few partitions. To increase the flexibility for the artist, Gehry originally proposed that everything, including wall partitions, be on wheels, allowing spaces to be changed according to need and function. This was not done; but there are very few permanent partitions; none full ceiling height. A partial second level was built to allow an unusual place to sit, talk, sketch or view art work. One of Gehry's aims is to create spatial illusions. In designing for these, he uses unusual shapes—and the design of this house avoids the obvious and the predictable."

The real impact on design of solar possibilities or even of energy scarcity was yet to come, but all over the country, even in less than ideal climates, experiments were under way

House in New Castle, New York
Architects: Raymond, Rado, Caddy & Bonington

A conventional developer plan was remassed to adapt it for solar heating by stacking elements to gain a more compact volume. Heavy insulation coupled with a modest use of glass kept heat loss to a minimum; but except for the heating systems, construction and finishes were conventional. A standby oil-fired heater was provided as backup to the solar heating system during protracted periods of overcast or rainy weather. Domestic hot water is also supplied by a solar system backed up by an electric heater. One duct system distributes both solar and conventionally generated heat.

Kelbaugh House
Princeton, New Jersey
Architect: Douglas Kelbaugh

A massive concrete wall, set back six inches from a south-facing glass curtain wall, was the key to the solar capabilities of this experimental house designed by an architect for his own family. The 600-square-foot concrete surface absorbs and stores heat from the sun and radiates it continually into living spaces that are nearly uninterrupted spatially upstairs and down. Backup space heating was provided by a gas-fired hot air system independent of the solar system but with ductwork cast into the concrete wall. The house was sited to avoid shadows cast by its neighbors.

A house in New Castle, New York, was designed to meet at least half its heating demand with flat plate collectors, an indication, said the RECORD, of how a conventional developer's plan could be remassed and adapted for solar heating. "The decision to use solar collectors, together with the sloping site, suggested to the architects a compact volume and a stacking of elements. Six inches of glass fiber insulation fill the wall cavities, and 12 inches are applied at the ceiling of the second floor and at the first floor under the deck. This heavy insulation, coupled with a modest use of glass, keeps heat loss to about 100,000 Btus per hour—this in a region with an average winter temperature of 42° F and approximately 4900 degree days. The deeply sloping roof faces just west of due south and is inclined at 50 degrees—an angle assumed to be optimum for solar collection at this latitude. This roof is fitted with a system of flat plate aluminum collectors with a surface area equal to nearly one half the square footage of space to be heated. The liquid medium (water treated with an antifreeze solution) is picked up in manifold pipes between collectors, then conveyed to a heat exchanger in the basement. Here the heat is transferred to a conventional forced-air distribution system before being recirculated to the collector system on the roof. In case of a protracted period of overcast or rainy weather, a standby oil-fired heater trips on automatically when the water temperature in the storage tank drops below a certain level."

This 2100-square-foot house designed by an architect for his own family is frankly experimental.

Princeton is a community with a 40-degree-north latitude and a climate that typically includes 5100 heating degree days and a 50-55 per cent sunshine factor in the winter. "By obtaining a variance," the RECORD reported, "the Kelbaughs were able to push the house to the northern side of their 60- by 100-foot lot, thus clearing the pattern of shadows cast by neighboring houses and, at the same

time, giving the lot an ample outdoor space instead of a mishmash of shallow yards. Insulation, of course, is critical. Kelbaugh provided an average 4-inch wall insulation of cellulosic fiber (recycled newspaper) and a 9½-inch roof insulation that achieved an R-factor of 40. In addition, he used a one-inch thickness of polystyrene on the perimeter foundation wall to a depth of two feet. The resultant heat loss, by conventional analysis, is about 75,000 Btu per hour—32,000 of which is lost to the small greenhouse on the south face of the building.

After double glazing this greenhouse, and fitting it with rolling shades, the heat loss should be considerably less next winter. Other adjustments and fine tuning will be necessary to balance temperature differentials between upstairs and down. Kelbaugh says that if he were beginning again, he would enlarge eave vents and/or install operable windows in the south wall to increase cross ventilation. During its first winter, a mild one with about 4500 degree days, the system worked well, with savings estimated at 75 per cent."

" 'Waterside' is a misnomer," the RECORD noted, "because the project's 1440 housing units, 50,000 square feet of commercial space and 900-car garage are actually built *over* the water—on 2200 specially designed piles. The suspended six-acre site is the first step in a master plan prepared by the architects in the late 1960s to reclaim a 13-block-long area for an existing community and a new one along New York's East River. The new area would occupy a recess in the shoreline now defined by the major highway that still isolates all but the most intrepid from most of the water's edge. Similar groups of buildings at both ends of a future park would provide not only badly needed housing but 24-hour activity. As it now exists, Waterside provides four acres of plazas and a river-edge promenade, all linked to the older community by an elevated pedestrian bridge. The main public plaza is surrounded by a higher level of plazas reserved for strictly resident use. The river-edge promenade is intended to be continuous with planned future development to the south, and is reached from the public plaza by broad steps. Boats can dock at the promenade, and among amenities planned is a restaurant with spectacular views up and down the river. Semi-private outdoor resident areas connect the four towers and ring the public plaza, which has shops open to the public as well as residents. Townhouses above shops have private yards a half level above general resident spaces. Despite the public presence, controlled access offers security through easy surveillance, and heightens a sense of community."

A mixed-income housing development became community architecture, with four acres of plazas and a river-edge promenade open to the public, and a pedestrian bridge making access easy

Waterside
New York, New York
Architects: Davis, Brody and Associates

A spectacular site on the East River in midtown Manhattan was "found" for this mixed-income housing development, which incorporated four acres of public plazas and a river-edge promenade, also open to the public. The six acre site was suspended over the water on piles and was part of a master plan to reclaim a 13-block area to occupy a recess in the shoreline defined by the East Side Highway. A pedestrian bridge links the Waterside site with the older neighborhood west of the highway. Four towers were less economical than fewer, more massive buildings, but developer Richard Ravitch agreed with the architects they were needed to preserve maximum views of the river.

167

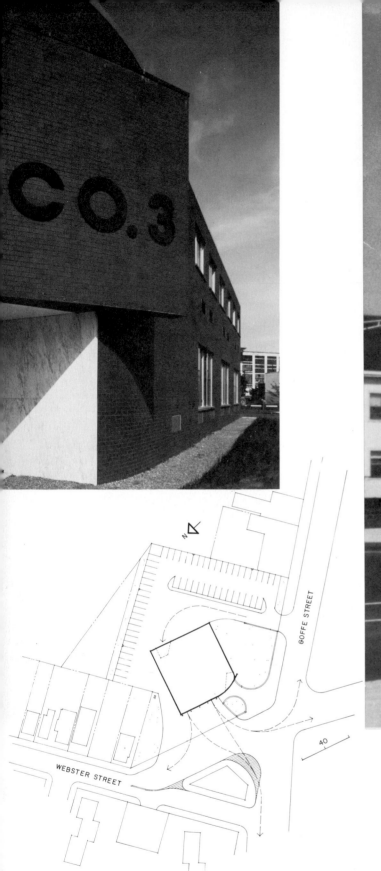

On a sprawling urban renewal site, Venturi put a building that wanted to belong where it was and that had aspects both ordinary and extraordinary

These two buildings (pages 168–171) began to suggest what the architecture of Robert Venturi might become. Robert Venturi the critic — the author of *Learning from Las Vegas* and *Complexity and Contradiction in Architecture* —and Robert Venturi the brilliant polemical designer had long tended to obscure the architect; but with these buildings, Venturi the architect at last seemed to transcend the rhetoric. The Dixwell Fire Station was published in 1976, the Humanities Building at Purchase in 1974. In the only departure from the book's organization by publication years, these buildings are shown together in the 1976 chapter for their very revealing view of the architecture of Robert Venturi as it had emerged by the early 1970s. (Dixwell Fire Station dates are given in Academy Editions Architectural Monograph #1 as 1970–1973; Humanities/Purchase dates as 1968–1973).

"It is not the purpose of this, or any other Venturi and Rauch building, to look *precisely* ordinary," Robert L. Miller observed in his RECORD article, "to imitate, in this case, one of the nearby auto body shops, as if on a movie set. What the firehouse tried to do instead, with considerable success, is to be a special, even monumental public building, *and at the same time* to be part of the factory town of New Haven, as the garages of automobile row so clearly are. To the extent to which it succeeds in doing this, Venturi and Rauch's small building, symbolically located on the border between Yale's turf and the black Dixwell neighborhood (and very near the proposed site of the dividing ring road), rejoins the halves of the

Dixwell Fire Station
New Haven, Connecticut
Architects: Venturi & Rauch

A building to house three formerly separate fire companies and a rescue unit was placed on its site so it accommodated the turning circle of the fire engines. The scheme is essentially a box within a box—the two-story apparatus room and the almost-square building that encloses it and everything else. The big doors open not on either of the two intersecting streets, but on an angled lane that connects them, and a wide apron provides maximum maneuverability for the trucks.

On the Goffe Street corner, the building is truncated to provide a pedestrian entrance. Upper-level brickwork is cantilevered out like a billboard, with lettering that spells out a long list of engine company names and asserts the civic character of the place, as does a marbel wall at the entrance and a flagpole out front.

city's dual identity, grandiose fantasy and grubby reality. It is very nearly the first Modern building of any architectural ambition to deal in the vocabulary of the 'real' New Haven. The Dixwell Fire Station is a celebration of the traditional dullness of municipal architecture, which by being celebrated, is somehow no longer dull in any pejorative sense. It is the overall image of the building, however, in relation to its time and place, that seems particularly well-chosen. The earlier Venturi and Rauch firehouse in Columbus, Indiana, reflects in its form a different program, but also represents the desire for a strongly graphic, Pop image. The Dixwell Fire Station—although it uses a kind of brick billboard as its main 'architectural feature'—rejects specifically Pop devices because of the nature of New Haven. That is, there is a perception that in a place where every architect has an angle, the most impact is made by playing it straight. The impact of straight but intense and highly selective *reportage,* seen in the work of the photorealist painters and the photographers who employ similar methods, represents a natural outgrowth of Pop to which this building clearly owes a great deal. This is, then, a photorealist building, very much of its time, and thus not entirely escaping New Haven's insistence on fashion. It is, also, however, a real building, a super-real building, among the first architect-designed buildings in New Haven that can make that claim."

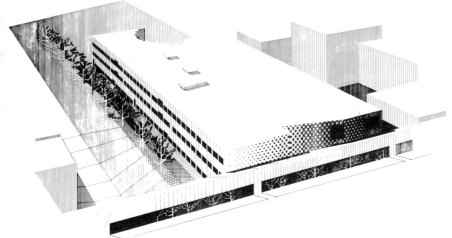

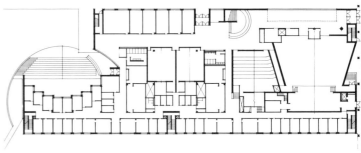

"In the Humanities Building," the RECORD reported, "the architects tried to incorporate ideas they had arrived at as faculty members and students themselves. These ideas focused more, for instance, on the design of the circulation space than on the design of the rooms themselves. And so the 'Street' came to be thought of as a place where waiting would be pleasant and informal, where discussions started after lectures and could continue over a cup of coffee, where notice boards and telephones were easily accessible. Along the length of the street, the architects designed a series of sitting places which were not explicitly benches but which could be sat on in various implicit but not altogether clear ways."

In notes on a post-construction evaluation (by Denise Scott Brown, Elisabeth Izenour and Steven Izenour of Venturi & Rauch), the architects describe reactions of users they interviewed on three occasions during the first school year when they visited the building to observe it in use. The first complaint of most people, they reported, was that windows can't be opened. "No one seemed aware that a sealed building was part of the program of the university and was in answer to the noise problem of an adjacent airport. When we told them, some still questioned the importance of airplane noise compared to personal control of fresh air. As a result, future buildings on the campus will have windows that can be opened, especially in offices. People seemed to like the 'street,' and students mentioned the 'airiness' of the building at the entrance and the width of the 'street.' And we found

On a new university campus,
Venturi's building evoked Aalto
both in spirit and vocabulary
and was intended to invite users
"to make the building their own"
by altering and adding to it

Humanities Building
State University of New York
Purchase, New York
Architects: Venturi & Rauch

A building located within the master
plan for Purchase designed by Edward
Larrabee Barnes, it was required to be
within a 130-foot zone extending out
from a covered pedestrian mall and to
use the brick, the anodized aluminum
window sections and the coping details prescribed for the whole campus.
The building is organized with two
scales of circulation—a broad and
busy "street" between classrooms and
lecture rooms and a narrow quiet hall
along the other side of the building for
the offices. Outside the large lecture
hall there is a high narrow gallery
which is—as the architects put it—the
only "rhetorical" space in the building.

people sitting on non-benches as we'd hoped
they would." But "while we had hoped that
the people who used it would make the building their own by altering it and adding to it, this
happened only rarely. It seemed to us that
many users felt themselves at the mercy of an
'institution,' and that this had generated an
inertia. They complained but did not act."

1977

Louis I. Kahn's last constructed building was completed the year after his death, and it revealed a return to the Miesian volumetric envelope from which he had departed 20 years before, and to the use of glass "at its maximum capacity," as Vincent Scully put it, "for visual magic in translucency and in reflection".

A museum designed to display Indian artifacts took its primary form from one of them, and site plan and landscaping were a metaphor of the kind of village from which the artifacts came.

Rational and disciplined architecture evoked the Mediterranean vernacular and the Catalan grand tradition of the octagon without being nostalgic.

A street-like gallery 1400 feet long made a one-building college of 13 loft-like structures.

Architecture becomes a performing art in a building for dance instruction that used sky-lights to manipulate spaces as well as light and to define the building profile.

Architecture as serene and poetic as Camelot derived from solving a complex problem in a creatively rational way.

A reflective glass tower in Boston's historic Copley Square suggested the possibilities of the glass tower designed as a "background" building to celebrate its environs with reflections of them.

On a garden site in the center of Tokyo, high and low buildings were positioned to enclose a tranquil garden court.

A curtain wall of glass blocks enclosed spaces arranged in tiers around a light well six stories high, covered not by a roof but by a steel "hat" hovering above roof level and tied down by diagonal and horizontal members.

A new government center spanned a major street with a pedestrian plaza.

A building in the desert enhanced its landscape by the way it was placed on the site, and mirrored the changing light from a wide open desert sky in glass and aluminum walls.

One house suggested a humble rural farm building of no particular time or place, the other was modeled on a great antebellum mansion, both were by the same architect, both were intensely particular as response to client needs.

A new building was designed to relate to an old building not because it was THERE, but because it was BROUGHT there from its own site to help create a character for a new development that would be compatible with the architecture of a community.

A cascading garden, a Grand Atrium and a shiny glass elevator made an irresistible target of a seven-level shopping center beginning two floors above ground level in a commercial tower.

The principle of "valid continuity" was triumphantly exemplified in the restoration of a historic marketplace.

Louis I. Kahn's last constructed building was completed the year after his death, and it revealed a return to the Miesian volumetric envelope from which he had departed 20 years before, and to the use of glass "at its maximum capacity," as Vincent Scully put it, "for visual magic in translucency and in reflection"

Yale Center for British Art
New Haven, Connecticut
Architect: Louis I. Kahn—
Completed after his death by
Pellecchia and Meyers, Architects

Kahn used exposed reinforced concrete for the structure of the building and, to define the non-structural parts of the wall, he used glass and pewter-finish stainless steel. The main part of the building is 200 feet by 120 feet and it rises four stories above the street level. Kahn continued the visual line of the street by placing the building right up against the sidewalk and by relating its height to that of the buildings across the street. The rhythmic unit at street level is 40 feet—double the 20-foot spacing of the columns on the three floors above. Photo at right shows the three-story interior court.

Louis I. Kahn was a great teacher as well as a great architect, and his conviction that "order" was an essential ingredient of architecture influenced generations of students at Yale, where he taught from 1948 to 1959. His search for order in his own work was eloquently summarized in the RECORD when this building was completed, two years after his death at 73. Vincent Scully, Jr., professor of art history at Yale and former colleague and biographer of Kahn, wrote: "Louis I. Kahn's Yale Center for British Art was an unexpected culmination of

his career. Two decades earlier, Kahn had set out to free himself from the volumetric envelope of Mies van der Rohe's design. He had also done his best from that date onward to eliminate glass, or its visual expression, from his work. But in the British Art Center, effectively his last constructed building, he not only went straight back to the volume and the bay system of Mies but also brought glass forward to operate at its maximum capacity for visual magic in translucency and reflection. The British Center's special site and function surely

had something to do with these surprising developments. Directly across the street from it stands the earliest of Kahn's mature buildings: the first in his great sequence of inventive designs. It is Yale's Art Gallery of 1953. There Kahn had employed the Miesian envelope and had also fought it, as something inherited and unwanted, with every resource at his command. Kahn had then gone on, like Wright before him, to break out of the classicizing box and the ubiquitous classic bay. He had thus done much, by the time of the Richards Labo-

ratories of 1960, to bring the last phase of the International Style to a close by connecting architecture once again with its more material 19th-century traditions and by breaking an agonized path toward new, apparently more varied, certainly physically more convincing, forms. But now, in his last urbanistic dialogue, he went back to Mies. He produced a perfect box, its long side pressed flat to the street and stretched along it. The bay system, very moderately scaled, reappeared and was released to act as the major visual determinant of all the facades. The box was thus made pure, like one of Mies' at IIT redone in concrete . . .

"Avoiding the signs, symbols and above all the gestures of his [Mies'] greatest successors, ignoring the 'linguistic' virtuosity of so much recent architecture and criticism, which may well have challenged, even annoyed him somewhat, Kahn *builds*. Long before, in the 1940s, he had prowled between the drafting tables in Weir Hall and, having as yet built almost nothing himself, talked passionately about what he called 'order.' In the British Art Center, he finally arrived at a kind of building order which was not far from the old classicizing mode. Avoiding speech, it is the wordless image of Kahn's deep constructor's soul, his incomparable memorial.''

A museum designed to display Indian artifacts took its primary form from one of them, and site plan and landscaping were a metaphor of the kind of village from which artifacts came

Museum of Anthropology
University of British Columbia
Vancouver, British Columbia
Architects: Arthur Erickson Architects

The museum has been shaped primarily as a container for the massive totems and longhouse frames brought in from remote Northwest Coast villages. Most of these had to be enclosed in a controlled atmosphere in order to preserve them. As the last poles to be found in the region, they are extremely valuable. A man-made lake will fill in the now-bare foreground in photo at right. Section shows (1) entry; (2) lobby; (3) ramped gallery; (4) great hall. Photos below and right show interior and exterior of the great hall.

"The museum was designed to effectively display such splendid Northwest Coast Indian artifacts as the Kwakiutl longhouse frame shown (above right)," the RECORD reported. "The precast posts and precast, post-tensioned beams of the museum, inspired by the primitive house frame, were tied together by invisible bolts. Erickson has revealed that his decision to recall the primitive structure for the primary form of his building was not a conscious one. He became aware of what he had done only after the building began to assume its final shape on the drawing board. In designing the museum, his conscious concerns were the basic ones common to all his work — considerations of site, light, cadence and space. The placement of the building on the site and the overall landscape design were conceived as a metaphor of a Northwest Coast Indian village. The museum has large areas of glass wall and skylights to open it up toward the pale, evanescent, mist-filled light of the region. And the cadence and dimensions of its spaces were designed to contain powerful art which, in a less carefully differentiated and scaled grouping, might have been too overbearing to be endured.

"The museum is built upon a cliff edge within the campus of the University of British Columbia, and overlooks the Straits of Georgia and the North Shore Mountains. An artificial lake will be built between the edge of the building and the cliff edge in such a way that, as seen from within the exhibition space, it will simulate an inlet of the sea as it appears to merge with the waters of the strait below. Thus,

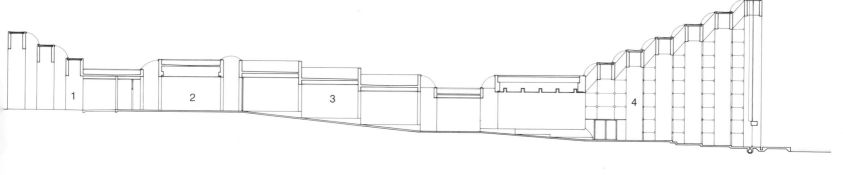

when the lake is finished, a setting will be created metaphorically similar to the sites of the Old Northwest Coast Indian villages, which were all located on the beaches between the two main sources of food—the sea in front and the forest behind. In the old villages, the totem poles stood close to the forests behind the village longhouses and the beach. Those poles and village longhouses in the museum's collection that are in good enough condition to remain outdoors will be arranged in a manner approximating the traditional setting of house and pole—at the line of conjunction between forest and sea. Showing the typical village this way and surrounding it with ethnobotanically significant flora will be an important anthropological statement of the museum.

"The new museum is as transparent as structure and function allow it to be. Bands of double-glazed, barrel-vaulted skylights bring daylight to the displays, and the great hall has a suspended glass wall 45 feet high. The artificial lighting system blends unobtrusively with the structure and the exhibits. The enclosure of the great hall followed the preliminary layout of the carvings. The hall itself is the climax of a spatial sequence which proceeds along an asymmetrical path beginning at the main entrance. Spatially, the hall expands outward and upward to the view of the sea and the distant mountains by means of concrete frames with spans of 40 to 100 feet."

Rational and disciplined architecture evoked the Mediterranean vernacular and the Catalan grand tradition of the octagon without being nostalgic

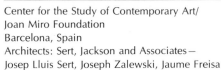

Center for the Study of Contemporary Art/
Joan Miro Foundation
Barcelona, Spain
Architects: Sert, Jackson and Associates—
Josep Lluis Sert, Joseph Zalewski, Jaume Freisa

Use of the outdoor areas and roof terrace for exhibitions more than doubles the available exhibition area. There are four courtyards: (a) central courtyard; (b) court with Miro sculpture (left) serving as a balcony to the city below and the mountains beyond; (c) the old walled garden with cypress trees and cypress hedges; (d) the multi-use court space for happenings. The first-floor plan includes (1) entrance; (2) exhibit rooms; (3) room for temporary exhibits; (4) bookstore; (5) auditorium; (6) service.

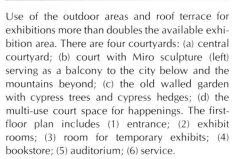

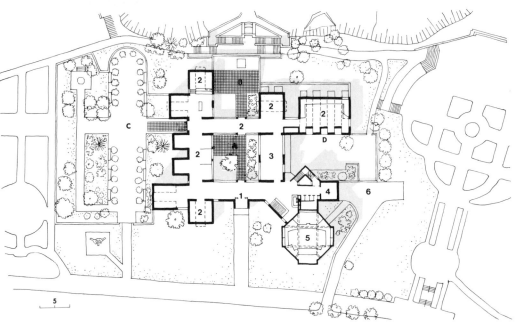

"Because Sert's eminently rational, conscious architecture is in powerful juxtaposition to the joyfully irrational effusions of his friend Miro, the building and its contents are excitingly dissonant," Mildred F. Schmertz observed in the RECORD. "Sert has dramatized this fundamental esthetic polarization, and the effect is wonderful.

"The Foundation Maeght in St. Paul de Vence, designed by Sert and built in 1974, served as a pattern for the programming of the new museum, which was to house a large collection of Miro's paintings, sculpture, ceramics, prints and books donated by the 84-year-old artist to his native city of Barcelona. Friends of the artist raised half the funds to build the museum, and Sert [also a native of Barcelona] donated his architectural services. Sert credits Andre Maeght with having taught him much about the programmatic, display and storage needs of museums for contemporary art. Sert points out that, like the Foundation Maeght, this new building is composed of carefully proportioned spaces that have a va-

riety of shapes, ceiling heights, sources of light and degrees of openness. The work and research spaces have been differentiated from the gallery space by inclusion in a three-story octagon. This shape strongly articulates the active as opposed to the contemplative side of the building. The octagon as a shape is very much part of the architectural tradition of Catalonia—appearing often in the monasteries, churches and fortresses of the Romanesque and Gothic periods and in the various Islamic monuments left by the Moors. While Sert's use

of the octagon partakes directly of this grand tradition, the building also draws from the Mediterranean vernacular. It is white, vaulted, lit by clerestories and oriented toward tiled patios and gardens. For all its subtle eclecticism, however, the building is not nostalgic. It is as intellectual and disciplined as Miro's work deliberately is not. The painter wisely chose as architect a fellow Catalan become cosmopolitan, whose work by contrast enhances his own and whose knowledge of the culture of their birthplace is shared. Sert sees the building as a series of varied volumes linked by a continuous, well-defined circulation pattern. The way people move through these spaces is the key factor governing the plan. Circulation is strongly oriented in one direction so that people need not go twice through the same spaces unless they want to. The courtyards, gardens and roof terraces are part of this circulation pattern and are used for the display of sculpture, ceramics and mosaics and for gatherings of people on special occasions. In everyday use, they are quiet spaces with benches permitting restful enjoyment of the gardens and the art. The plan has been devised so that some of the rooms are to be used principally for display of the Miro collections. These displays will be changing continuously because much of the work donated by the artist will be kept in storage or in traveling exhibitions.''

Stockton State College
Pomona, New Jersey
Architect: Geddes Brecher Qualls
Cunningham

Stockton State College is the expression of procession, which is, for GBQC, a fundamental and
longstanding principle. At Stockton, the primary
organizational element is the street-like gallery,
two levels high, which threads through the long
linear plan. The principle of circulation was the
premise of the overall design. The structure that
enfolds it, a composite of off-the-shelf systems,
reads clearly and consistently throughout, set off
by colorful graphics, woodland views to the outside and an all-hours, all-seasons mix of people.

A street-like gallery 1400 feet long made a one-building college of 13 loft structures

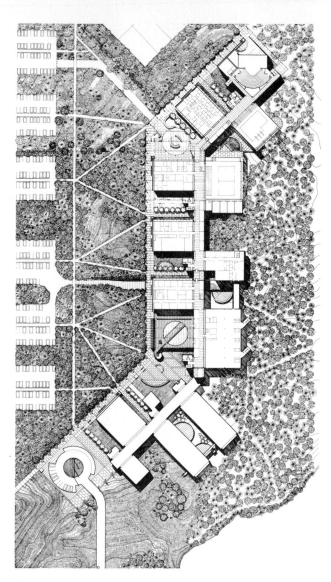

"Stockton State College is the expression of
procession, which is, for GBQC, a fundamental and long-standing principle," the RECORD
observed. "The campus site of almost 1,600
acres is in New Jersey's famous Pine Barrens, a
deep-pile carpet of dense dark green and
brown over an underweave of soft sandy gold.
This texture edges right up to and in some cases into the low-lying latticework of the college
buildings. Stockton is organized on a five-foot-
square module. A long, linear, street-like gallery, two levels high and 30 feet wide, links

everything up. The second level, overlooking
the first in many places, varies in width from
10 feet to the full 30. One can walk Stockton,
end to end, in ten minutes. Thirteen major
loft-like structures are alternately arrayed, off
to either side of this street, which becomes, in
use, an ebullient, banner-hung harmonizing of
bull sessions, hand-holding steadies, and
strolling or hurrying pedestrians. These loft
buildings, mostly given over to classroom,
seminar and office facilities, are meant to encourage meshing of programs and discourage

superdepartmentalization. Other loft structures
house library/learning resources, the multi-
science laboratory and the main lecture room,
elements which are more 'fixed' in design. And
at the far western end of the complex, there is a
trilogy of more finite buildings — 'fixed' in function, but still very flexible: gymnasium, swimming pool and lecture hall/theater. Stockton
emphasizes lifetime sports and physical culture no less and no more than *culture* culture."

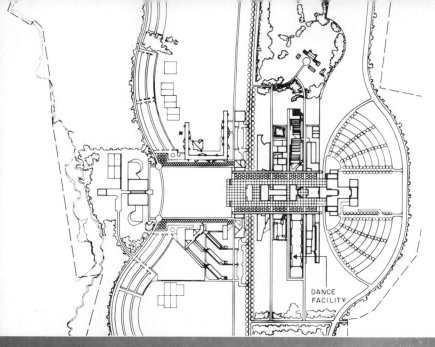

Architecture became a performing art in a building for dance instruction that used skylights to manipulate spaces as well as light and to define the building profile

Dance Instructional Facility
State University of New York
Purchase, New York
Architects: Gunnar Birkerts and Associates

The master plan for the Purchase campus (by Edward Larrabee Barnes) is essentially axial and symmetrical, and requires that the buildings on the edge of the mall be contained in rectangles. The entrance facade of Birkerts' building is set back from the mall arcade, a setback which brings light into the entrance halls and first-floor administration space. The section/perspective is a composite which on its left side shows the typical skylight as it illuminates first the office, then the corridor and its tilted reflective plane.

"The Dance Instructional Facility for the State University of New York at Purchase cannot be seen nor assessed as an isolated building. It was designed by Birkerts within a strongly controlling master plan by Edward Larrabee Barnes. It is one of a row of four buildings like parallel fingers at 90-degree angles to an arcade. Each building occupies a plot 130 feet wide and can extend to an ultimate length of approximately 650 feet. Across a mall 300 feet wide by 900 feet long, an identical arcade connects four identical finger sites. Of the eight buildings (in addition to Birkerts' building), two are by Venturi and Rauch, facing each other on opposite sides of the mall (one shown on pages 170-171); one is by Philip Johnson, one by TAC, one by Paul Rudolph, and two by Barnes. Each of the six architectural firms had different ideas as to the degree to which their buildings were to be 'background' to the mall, its parallel arcades and its dominant focal buildings (all of the latter also by Barnes). Venturi attached each of his buildings to the arcade bluntly and directly, thus subordinating them to the ensemble. So did Barnes. The TAC and Johnson buildings are more connected than disconnected, more supporting players than stars. Only Rudolph and Birkerts have given their buildings a distinct presence by pulling them back almost completely from the arcade and away from the mall, thus giving them fronts.

"The dance facility, part of a School of the Arts that also includes facilities for music, theater, film and painting, is a two-story structure as wide as its site (again, 130 feet) and approxi-

mately 475 feet long. The building is symmetrical on either side of its major axis. On the top floor, offices line the long exterior walls and these are paralleled by long skylit corridors which give access to the dance studios. The walls of the dance studios are not a continuous plane but alternately project and recede, adding to the spatial complexity and interest of the corridors, and making them appear less long. The section/perspective is a composite which shows the typical skylight as it illuminates first the office, then the corridor and its tilted reflective plane. This tilted plane throws daylight through the parallel glass planes of the dance studios, lending them a beautiful diffused light which aids the dancers' concentration. The right side of the section shows the skylit lounge, one of the two located at each of the opposite points where the major transverse corridor interconnects with the corridors on the long axis. Here Birkerts juts the skylight forward in a V-shape, forcing the interior space beyond the rectilinear constraints of the master plan and creating an unusually happy and spir- ited space for the students to relax in. Birkerts has also created smaller lounges at the intersections of the narrower transverse corridors and the main corridors. These have the same V-shaped skylight projection but are only two modules wide.''

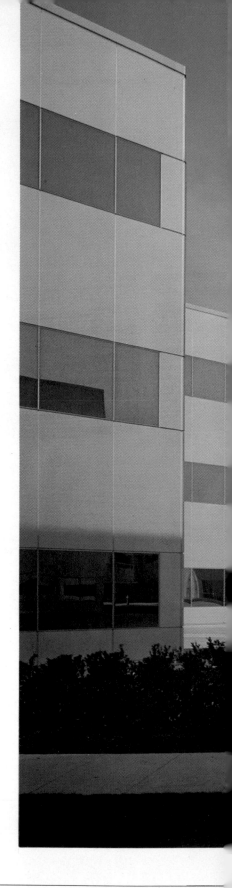

Architecture as serene and poetic as Camelot derived from solving a complex problem in a creatively rational way

IBM Santa Teresa Laboratory
San Jose, California
Architects: McCue Boone Tomsick
and Associates (now MBT Associates)

Eight four-story office buildings surrounding a second-level plaza were designed to share ground-floor service facilities, including the visitors' lobby, the library and the computer center. All the buildings are linked at ground level, and most are also linked by bridges at upper levels. The concept made it possible to respond to the client request for a maximum number of private offices, as many as possible oriented to outside views, for nearly 2,000 computer programmers, without making a building either enormously long or enormously high. Ground level linkages offered some single-building advantages while the multi-level office blocks responded to user needs at a scale appropriate both to function and to site.

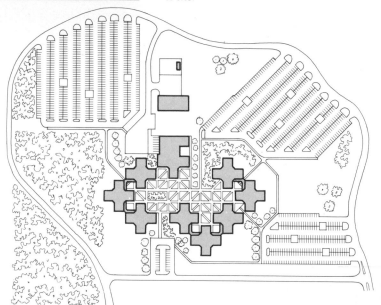

"This big, handsome complex for the General Products Division of IBM was designed for use by 2,000 persons, mostly computer programmers, and it solves a long list of seemingly incompatible problems," the RECORD reported. "These include providing for (and doing the most for) a beautiful, but earthquake-prone, natural setting; a large group of technical people needing both extreme efficiency and compensating human comforts and pleasures; and the highly special and demanding requirements of computers. A campus-like set of eight cruciform buildings surrounding a plaza responded to these requirements and—in particular—to the client's request for private offices for the programmers, with as many as possible oriented to the outside views. All buildings are linked beneath a second-level plaza and most of the buildings are also linked by bridges at the upper floor levels. The core of each building is surrounded by the primary circulation corridor and contains stairwell, elevator (in five of the buildings), restrooms and 'administrative support centers.' Radiating from the corridor are identical arms of private offices, a large conference and common computer terminal room, all serviced by a secondary U-shaped corridor. Therefore all corridors are short, no longer than 50 feet, with no office more than 15 feet from a window. The clustering pattern of three buildings offset from the other five marks the entrance from the visitors' parking area and reduces the scale of the complex from the roadway. It also creates a variety of spaces on the plaza, including six courtyards between the buildings, and directs views

from the plaza outward to the hills on the north and to the valley on the south. The site plan also opens up 'vista corridors' diagonally and at right angles throughout, and views are architecturally emphasized by grass-lined or paved walkways on the plaza level. Each building is color-coded for identification, in brilliant hues of magenta, red, red-orange, orange, yellow, green, teal and blue. Coding is complete from office tackboards to stairwells, carried to the exterior only where the wings of two adjacent buildings form a courtyard, so there are two

colors in each courtyard, predetermined as complementary pairs.

"The complex was designed to withstand expected earthquake forces. A moment-resisting steel-frame structure, it is dynamic, capable of moving relatively freely in an earthquake. The skin of the building, therefore, needed to be lightweight, and aluminum was chosen for that quality and for its high reflectivity. Solar reflective glass, set flush with the aluminum curtain wall panels, completes a totally reflective facade and contributes to an

energy-efficient design.

"Harmony with the site is achieved through scale and proportions. 'The building was meant to flirt with the landscape,' says McCue. 'It does not try to change it. The building ought to become an interesting contrast. It is the juxtaposition of manmade forms and colors to nature's forms and colors that heightens the intrinsic values of both.' "

A reflective glass tower in Boston's historic Copley Square suggested the possibilities of the glass tower designed as a "background" building to celebrate its environs with reflections of them

John Hancock Tower
Boston, Massachusetts
Architect: I. M. Pei and Partners

The narrow north facade of the 60-story tower edges Copley Square on the southeast, where the site is filled out with a seven-story base which is the same height as the venerable Copley Plaza Hotel. The diagonal face of the eastern facade creates an angular plaza that brings the Clarendon Street side of Trinity Church into full view—just as H. H. Richardson, who first conceived and drew it from this direction, always hoped. Composition of the glass and metal curtain wall was carefully studied to minimize the tower's apparent bulk, and there are 10,344 glass panes in all, each measuring 4½ feet by 11½ feet.

This building more than any other may have suggested to architects the civic possibilities of the glass tower as a "background" building that celebrates its environs by its presence. When the preliminary design was first published in 1968, many critics and some architects saw it as a "monumental" intrusion in a historic setting. Until it was built, the new architectural vision was not fully communicated; and the design concept tended to be interpreted in terms of familiar shibboleths.

"The building has turned out," William Marlin wrote, "to be a strong, energetic, civil presence—giving the Square, if anything, more closure, definition, and even delight. Looking from the west, along Boylston Street (opposite), existing edges and elements have been enlivened, not enervated, by the 60-story building's rhomboidal shape. From the eastern plaza entrance (top right), beyond Copley Square on Clarendon Street, H. H. Richardson's Trinity Church is seen for the first time in the round."

Those sheer monochromatic walls made kinetic with changing reflections of the historic architecture which surrounds them were not easily achieved. But the highly publicized problems of glass breakage have not deterred architects from continuing to apply contemporary technology—as Pei had done in this building—to design a generation of glass towers which sometimes evoke, often surpass, the dreams of modern visionaries.

On a garden site in the center of Tokyo, high and low buildings were positioned to enclose a tranquil garden court

United States Embassy Office Building
Tokyo, Japan
Architects and Engineers: Gruen Partners/
Cesar Pelli, partner in charge of design

Another of those elegant sheer curtain walls that architects were wrapping around buildings in the second half of the 1970s enclosed the long sides of the Tokyo embassy; on the ends, the concrete structure was revealed. Anodized aluminum and reflective glass made curtain walls that are thin, light, flat and shiny, a meticulously crafted mirror for their environs. The site was like a garden in the middle of the city, and this character was preserved when the old embassy was demolished and the new one built.

The new embassy was built on the site of the old, which had been demolished. A garden-like site in the middle of densely-built-up Tokyo, "it would be a good site anywhere," Pelli said, "but in Tokyo it is extraordinary." As the RECORD described it, "the building is set at an angle to the main axis of approach in order to seem somewhat informally composed, and it seems as well to grow out of the hillside behind—a finely honed, eminently manmade object set in a natural context. The sides are the thinnest of curtain walls, made of anodized aluminum and mirror glass; and on the ends the concrete structure is revealed, like so much building cut from the stock of an elegant supplier.

"The State Department provided the architects with a very specific program which set strict limits on the amount of glass that could be used and which seemed to require a series of standard office spaces along double-loaded corridors. The building that resulted is in two parts, one high and one low, that together enclose the courtyard (above). Major spaces, when they occur, are multiples of the standard building bay. 'Two systems play against each other,' Pelli says, 'enveloping skin and expressive structure.' One admirable result of all this is a building that is at once commonsensical and elegant. 'The design is straightforward,' says Pelli. 'We strived for the simplest, most direct answer to each problem. This also resulted in an economical building.' Pelli's whole approach to design, indeed, actively involves simplicity, directness and (above all) do-ability. It is not just that do-ability is impor-

tant if a building is to get built, according to Pelli, but that the questions of what can be done (and what really needs doing) are critical esthetic chasteners—reducing the realms in which the imagination takes fire, but allowing it to do so with more point."

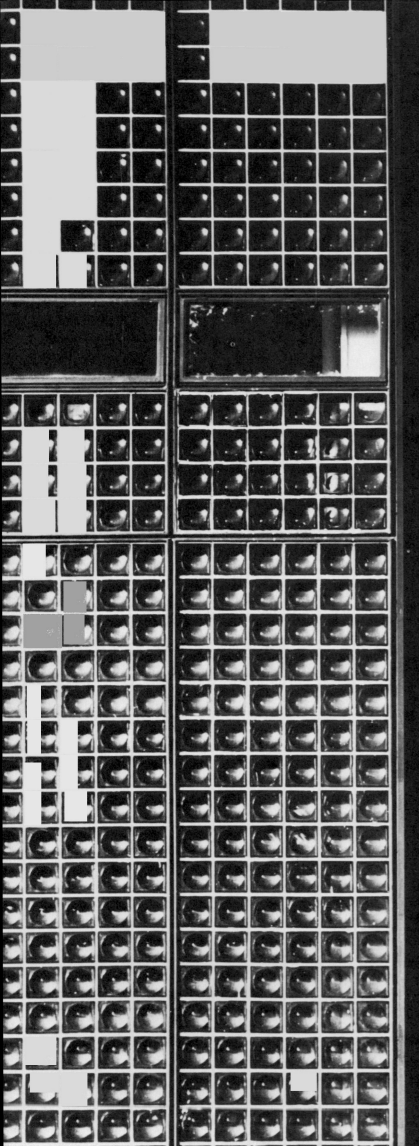

A curtain wall of glass blocks
enclosed spaces arranged in tiers
around a light well six stories
high covered not by a roof but
by a steel "hat" hovering above
roof level and tied down by
diagonal and horizontal members

Central Building for
the School of Art
and Physical Education
Tsukuba University
Ibaragi Prefecture, Japan
Architects: Fumihiko Maki
and Associates

This gateway to Tsukuba University, a research and academic center
60 miles north of Tokyo, was designed to anchor the overall university plan, straddling the main
route between north and south sections of the campus. A curtain wall

of eight-inch-square amber-colored
translucent glass blocks enclosed
some 216,000 square feet of space
arranged in tiers around a six-story
well of light. The central well is
actually "outdoors," but protected
from the elements by a big steel hat
hovering just above roof level and
tied down by diagonal and horizontal members. The curtain wall
was created from fully prefabricated 4.1- by 12.4-foot panels, each
consisting of glass blocks set in
steel frames and a transparent operable window.

"This is a very humble building," the RECORD
observed, "and instead of throwing a high-tech
tantrum in the manner of the now calcified
Metabolists, this curtain wall creates a subtlety
of light and texture that owes more to the tradition of *shoji* screens than to the bionic assert-
iveness of structural, mechanical, plumbing
and electrical systems. Maki has become long
since involved in a more lasting movement—
the flow of people and activities and feelings.
In this building, Maki has related technology
and philosophy, fact and feeling, form and
idea."

A new government center
spanned a major street
with a pedestrian plaza

Hennepin County Government
Center
Minneapolis, Minnesota
Architects: John Carl
Warnecke and Associates

Twin towers with a 350-foot-high atrium between them were set on an elevated pedestrian platform that spanned a major street. County administration offices were put in one tower, district and municipal courts in the other. The building was sited to align the atrium with the towers of the old Municipal Building (Long and Kees, 1906). Facilities most often used by the public were concentrated on a "public service level" one level up by moving stairs from the plaza level. Seven elevated walkways, spaced every third floor above the public service level, connect the two towers. The structural system devised by engineers Ketchum Konkel Barrett Nickel and Austin positioned and exposed diagonal wind-bracing on the interior walls facing the atrium. The total space frame acts like a cage, stiffening the building's frame, minimizing building drift and allowing 85 per cent usable floor space in the towers. It accepts lateral loads transmitted from the composite floors through diaphragm action, and distributes the stresses throughout the 180-foot building length. The cage is supported below the public service level by 30-inch-thick shear walls, constructed on bedrock.

"Completion of the Hennepin County Government Center," the RECORD noted, "marks the beginning of a new civic center that will encompass an 18-block area when completed. The civic center's master plan (also the work of the Warnecke firm) was premised on the design of this building as the focal point of the area. The plan establishes guidelines for future public and private development within the parameters including the location, height and bulk of buildings, and the position of open spaces, all interconnected by elevated pedestrian walkways. The Center's design concept was based on an exemplary planning process by both the architects and a facilities analysis and design firm, SUA, Inc. SUA began an extensive, detailed space utilization study in 1965; its recommendations subsequently stimulated passage of 23 bills by the state legislature that reorganized the county government. One major recommendation which affected the design was separation of county administration offices from district and municipal courts. The oustanding feature of the building, however, is the atrium. It is a great indoor space enjoyed by both public and employees, fully appreciated as a controlled year-round environment not affected by the changeability and severity of Minneapolis weather. A large skylight and glass end walls flood the atrium with light. At the roofline, enormous exposed steel tetrahedrons frame this skylight and the corridors of the top floor."

A building in the desert enhanced its landscape by the way it was placed on the site, and mirrored the changing light from a wide open desert sky in glass and aluminum walls

Johns-Manville World Headquarters
Jefferson County, Colorado
Architects: The Architects Collaborative

A competition-winning building was sheathed in an aluminum and glass skin of spectacular beauty that changes continually with the changing light from a wide open desert sky. The wonderful smoothness and flatness of the wall was made possible by a system developed by TAC and the fabricator's engineers. The panel skin is not welded to the stiffeners; instead it is essentially "hung" on the stiffeners and allowed to "ride free" or "float." The stiffeners are anchored to the building and provide the necessary bracing to meet performance specifications. As temperatures change, the panel skin changes dimension but, as it is not confined by welds, it does not distort. A brilliantly innovative structural solution by engineer William LeMessurier exploited the plasticity of steel and the composite action of steel and concrete to achieve an economical design which provided the required long spans as well as the required earthquake resistance.

"TAC won the competition," the RECORD reported, "for the masterful way Joseph D. Hoskins [then a TAC principal] and his team placed the building on its site [see photo in photographic essay inside front cover], using the foothills as a backdrop and building up against them; for the bold manner in which the architects took advantage of the vista toward Denver across an undefiled valley; for their elegant and minimal design of the roadway approach with its dramatic arrival under the building; and for their unobtrusive insertion of parking space on the roof and in tiers carved into the natural bowls at the rear of the building. TAC's design was commended by the jury for combining all the elements—parking terraces, helix ramps, reflecting pools, greenhouse (unfortunately not built) and open ground—into a sculptural composition of great interest and variety which had the potential of forming a very distinctive image from the air. The program established a poorly conceived ratio between linear feet of building perimeter and net square foot floor area. Unlike their eight competitors, TAC boldly deviated from the program because it could not have been solved as written except by a high-rise building, which was not considered a suitable option by any of the competitors, including TAC. What TAC did was to work with the established floor areas, reducing the linear feet of perimeter wall. The result was a simpler building which took brilliant advantage of the opportunities offered by the site."

One house suggested a humble rural farm building of no particular time or place, the other was modeled on a great antebellum mansion, both were by the same architect, both were intensely particular as response to client needs

A small house by Charles W. Moore
Long Island, New York
Architects: Charles Moore and Associates
(now Moore Grover Harper)

This little house owed something to a 1683 settler's house in Topsfield, Massachusetts, the Capen house, one of those relevant memories Charles Moore can pull out of a head where he sometimes seems to carry the history of architecture whole. Rooms are arranged around a central chimney for warmth in winter; one circulates through the house from room to room in the absence of a hall; the "kitchen" is also for dining and living.

A large house by Charles W. Moore
Architects: Charles W. Moore with
Richard B. Oliver

The model and metaphor for this house was Stratford Hall (Westmoreland County, Virginia), with its great square room centered between two pavilions. In this house, two conservatories known as the Orangerie and the Jungle form the main foyer and hall. Although asymmetrical, Moore's derivation is similar to the 18th-century space in that it is the basis for arranging everything else, yet it is so complex and deflected that it emerges as idea rather than discrete form.

"Charles Moore carries the whole culture of architecture in his head," Mildred F. Schmertz observed in an article on these two houses. "His art lies in his power over the art of the past, his ability to bring forth out of memory timeless forms to convey unchanging human feelings.

"The little Swan house suggests a humble rural farm building of no particular time or place, while the model for the larger house was an antebellum mansion. Designed in collaboration with Mark Simon, the Swan house

was the first small house Moore had designed for several years. It was done for no ordinary client. Simone Swan is an artist, and a friend and patron of artists, who is the mother of two grown children. Charles Moore became her architect after the death of her first choice, Louis Kahn, who had not yet begun to design her house when he died. Before his death, he had encouraged her in her wish to buy and tear down an old farm building to obtain a stockpile of hand-hewn joists, flooring and beams; and these, as arranged by Moore, are Kahn's

legacy to the house. When she met Charles Moore at a dinner party, Simone Swan didn't know that he was a 'Post-Modernist Movement Radical Eclectic,' but she intuitively felt that he was the right architect for her. He began, like a psychoanalyst, to help her discover and express her own inner fantasies and dreams as well as her everyday needs. She had sought a subtle variety of experiences in her house-to-be. In her words, she wanted 'bathing while looking at the trees, sitting in the winter sun protected from the winds, a secret tower

terrace . . . .'" After an earlier design which met all these specifications, but seemed "too cosy, rather worldly, a bit 'suburban classy,'" the design for this house evolved.

The large house designed for a family of four on a beautiful rural site has very special requirements. The husband, who is blind, wished the new house to speak to his remaining senses, especially those of smell and touch, not only to give him pleasure but to orient him within the spaces of the house. "So the house has many textures, smells and breezes that tell him where he is. The air moving through the house is a signal to him—he knows from which direction it is coming by the scents it carries, whether from the lawn or a particular grove of trees, from the garden or one or the other of the two indoor conservatories which form the main foyer and the hall. The hall is paved tile which by its resonance tells the client he is not in the living room or in the dining room, which have their rugs centered on hardwood floors. The sound of trickling water in a fountain located in the Jungle garden is another orienting element, as is the texture of the stone walls, which are the boundaries of living room, dining room and study. Snaking through this main hall, becoming a banister at the stair and ending in the second floor hall is a beautiful wooden guide rail. More subtly, the client can tell where he is by means of what he calls ambient sound, which communicates to him the size and dimensions of the room he is in. For this reason among others, he wished the rooms of his house to be discrete and contained rather than flowing into one another."

"What one sees, sauntering along the streets that bound it, or on the bordering C&O Canal," as the RECORD described it, "is an architectural event, or, better, a well-coordinated set of events, that thoroughly embrace the location. Indeed the Canal setting itself was approached as an integral element of the design. A park-lane ambience edges the opposite side, while 1055 edges its side of the Canal with a generous landscaped esplanade. Entrances to both The Foundry and The Foundry Mall are off the esplanade. The Foundry

Mall is a shop-lined two-level internalized 'street' that threads through the new building at an angle, actually an enticing shortcut between the canal side and the Thomas Jefferson Street side. Its culmination is a two-level 'piazza,' and in its center there is a reflective pool with a generous stair poised above it. The Mall provides a lively indoor space for the public — that 'street' and 'piazza' — and, because of its siting and massing, the new building, as a whole, defines a lively outdoor space for the public. The Mall is a room with a roof. The

Canal and park create a room without a roof. Both must be counted as architecture — architecture as the courting of a public constituency and as the countenance of human encounter. The restored Foundry and the new building are carefully placed with respect to each other. The old element, in effect, anchors the new amidst the old. The lobby level nudges against it, its walls parallel to the Canal but set back a distance to create part of that outdoor room. The second floor, where office spaces begin, is angled back from the roof of the lobby level,

A new building was designed to relate to an old building not because it was THERE, but because it had been BROUGHT there to help create a character for a new development compatible with the architecture of a community

1055 Thomas Jefferson Street
Georgetown, Washington, D.C.
Architects: The ELS Design
Group and Arthur Cotton
Moore Associates

A 19th-century foundry building was moved from its own site so it could be incorporated in this retail and office complex developed by Inland Steel Development Corporation on a site along the Chesapeake and Ohio Canal in historic Georgetown. A new building was designed to relate to an old neighbor not because it was *there* but because it was *wanted* as an element of the architectural complex, to help create a character for a new development that would make it compatible with the architectural character of the community around it. The foundry was recycled as a restaurant and as exhibition space for the C&O Museum. The new building, with its two levels of shops and five office floors above, and its old neighbor were sited to create a wide esplanade on the Canal for public use.

which thus gives a terrace. The second floor, in turn, gives a small terrace to the third floor. The third floor juts out toward the upper roof peak of The Foundry, and this jut gives yet another terrace up on the *fifth* floor. The intervening fourth floor and the top (sixth) floor (both without terraces) give clear definition to the overall mass."

A cascading garden, a Grand Atrium and a shiny glass elevator
made an irresistible target of a seven-level shopping center
beginning two floors above ground level in a commercial tower

The Malls at
Water Tower Place
Chicago, Illinois
Consulting Architects:
Warren Platner Associates
Associated Architects: Loebl,
Schlossman, Bennett & Dart
and C. F. Murphy Associates

A cascading garden that begins at street level and goes up with the escalators to the main floor of the "Grand Atrium," where seven levels of shops begin, was designed (with Dan Kiley and Partners) to lead people to The Malls. A shiny glass elevator shaft was made the central focus of the Atrium, which acts as anchor for an otherwise random plan.

"Seven floors of small- and medium-size shops, beginning two floors above the ground, are buried within the building," as the RECORD put it. "Was there any way to bring in the business? Was there any way to make people, once they were there, feel like they were in a real place? The first step was to create the 'cascading' garden. Once inside the Grand Atrium, the shopper's attention is grabbed by the shiny glass elevator shaft that slickly rises the full height of the interior court. Balconies on the middle floors are set back to give the space a central bulge, and all around it the individual shops are located. The precise placement of these atrium stores, as well as the exact amount of space allotted to them on each floor, is determined by the amount of space left over after the two 'magnet' stores of Water Tower Place—Lord & Taylor and Marshall Field—have been accounted for. Since these two stores wind irregularly through and around the building, the arrangement of the atrium stores is similarly irregular. One of the only constants is the presence of the central court, made more memorable by the strong presence of the glass elevators, and acting as an anchor for the otherwise random plan. Another constant is the fact that the long corridors that radiate away from it are not allowed simply to end in a blank wall, but are instead (for the eye, at least) open through small wells to a similar corridor either above or below."

The principle of "valid continuity" was triumphantly examplified
in the restoration of a historic marketplace

Faneuil Hall Marketplace
Boston, Massachusetts
Architects: Benjamin Thompson
and Associates

The restoration and transformation
of Boston's historic Faneuil Hall
Marketplace by architect Benjamin
Thompson and developer James
Rouse turned it into a triumphantly
successful downtown center. Quincy Market (opposite) opened in
1976, South Market in 1977. Two
streets closed to traffic have become great public plazas, paved
with brick, cobblestone and
granite and newly planted with
trees. Outside Quincy Market,
glass canopies extend the retail
space into the plazas. The drawing
shows how the Marketplace looks
now that the North Market is finished. Faneuil Hall is in the foreground and directly behind it is
Quincy Market, with its great dome
and Classic Revival porches. The
three rows of buildings were designed as an ensemble by Alexan-
der Parris and built between 1824
and 1826 on landfill facing the
harbor.

The approach to preservation, rehabilitation
and new use which made Faneuil Hall Marketplace what it is has been summarized by Benjamin and Jane Thompson: "Two rules of
restoration seem well accepted now after some
recent years of confusion: First, do not improve
on history; do not 'restore back' to a fixed cut-
off date; history is richer in time than any one
period or style. Second, when repair or replacement of building elements is required,
new material should be subtly distinguished
from the original. If such distinctions are not

made, the genuineness of the original is confused, and the viewers' perception of time is
confused. A third precept is longer in coming,
but achieves more acceptance daily. This is the
principle of *valid continuity*—the joining of
successive styles in elegant and compatible
ways. If the joining of what is old and what is
contemporary (in whatever year) is clearly differentiated, the genuineness of each can be
established and enhanced. Throughout Europe
and America, buildings of successive periods
have used differing materials, proportions and

details. Cumulatively, these changes express
the depth of a time line in the life of a building
which is one of architecture's most important
perspectives on history. Buildings, like people,
must be allowed to age, develop and change—
and the changes must show. We should not
attempt to freeze history but rather attempt to
enhance its flow. The Market should be neither
'historic' nor 'modern' but simply the genuine
continuation of a special place in city life
growing out of genuine urban commerce and
answering human needs."

1978

"Post-Modern," critics said of a building that derived from Raymond Hood and wore a "recognition cap" on top; but its architect said he was still a "functional modernist" and that his new buildings reflect the "new" pluralism of American life and the new freedom architects gain from new attitudes of consumers.

The first mixed-use building in the Federal City was designed three years before 1976 Federal legislation authorized mixed use in Federal buildings, and it required special Congressional sanction.

A milestone in Federal architectural policy was reached with the decision by the U. S. General Services Administration to use the design competition method in selecting architects for the most important Federal buildings, and rehabilitation of the Old Post Office in Washington, D.C. was the first test. The Post Office and Custom House in Sᴛ. Louis was the second; and that never-completed Neo-Classical mish-mash, the Federal Triangle, was the third, with the competition winner expected to do a master plan for the whole Triangle, Old Post Office included.

A building that enriched city life like none since Rockefeller Center was completed in New York City, the first to realize the true civic potential of the urban design tools New York had been developing since the late 1960s.

While critics wrote obituaries, modern architecture continued to develop, and an addition to the National Gallery of Art in Washington revealed how urbane and dynamic it could be while still deferring to its setting.

A new building embraced an old library relocated on its site to create a cultural center that gave civic presence to the area around city hall and that looked (almost) as though it had always been there.

"Interpretive restoration" re-established the formal themes of a great Beaux Arts Building.

Text and captions for pages 206–227 were written by Mildred F. Schmertz, Executive Editor of ARCHITECTURAL RECORD. —J.M.D.

As RECORD writer Barclay F. Gordon points out: "Gold Medalist Philip Johnson is one of a small handful of architects who can make the profession flinch—or at least reverberate with a tremor of incomprehension—by simply holding up a sketch." Johnson's own views, extracted from a talk with the RECORD's editors, are provocative and challenge some of the Modern Movement's most sustaining and consoling myths. Using this controversial new skyscraper as a context, the great architect describes his intentions, his outlook and his

hopes for architecture's future. Says Johnson: "I don't believe in revolution, I'm not post anything, and I'm still a functionalist modernist." Rather, he argues that his new buildings including this one reflect the new pluralism that has entered American life and thought. "Who thinks of the melting pot any more as a solution for America? We now think of ourselves as a pluralist society. Look at *Roots*. What's best for one isn't necessarily best for all. . . . It's the attitude of the consumer that's changed, and what this change has done for the architect is

to give him a most significant sense of freedom." Another point that Johnson makes is that we are tired of two particular attitudes of the Modern Movement, first: "the-architect-will-tell-you-what-you-should-like"; and second: "we'll-conquer-the-problems-of-the-world-with-architecture." Instead Johnson proposes that architects rejoin the esthetic mainstream. "The painters showed us the way and we can rejoice once more in the mainstream of taste and public sensibility." Like the painters we are paying more attention to the

"Post-Modern," critics said of a building that derived from Raymond Hood and wore a "recognition cap" on top; but its architect said he was still a "functional modernist"

Headquarters for American Telephone & Telegraph
New York, New York
Architects: Johnson/Burgee

This 660-foot-high stone and glass tower is rising on Madison Avenue in midtown Manhattan. It will have a largely open plaza at street level that ties to a mid-block pedestrian arcade to the west. The main building volume begins above the 60-foot-high plaza space shown in these model photos. The office floors with central cores have been conventionally designed, but will have greatly reduced window areas — approximately 30 per cent glazing. The stone veneer will be of pinkish granite. The controversial top will house mechanical equipment.

symbolic content of form. We are also, according to Johnson, paying more attention to regional vernaculars. "This delight in inexpensive buildings, unpretentious buildings, has eroded the base of the International Style." As a by-product of our growing interest in both preservation and symbol, argues Johnson, we can look back today and reevaluate and reappreciate much of what was discarded earlier. This new spirit finds expression in Johnson/Burgee's design for AT&T. "The shaft of the building," says Johnson, "is symmetricized

Raymond Hood: the gathering of columns, the play of shadows, the recessed windows. The bay spacing is on a Renaissance model: 50 feet to 20 feet to 17 feet. At street level, 60 per cent of the space is open — and leaving it open is wonderful. The top of AT&T? Oh, that's just a recognition cap. People say it looks like a Chippendale something-or-other, but that never occurred to us when we were designing it. To us it is reminiscent only of Hellenistic or Roman design features . . ." Johnson's central point, however, is that nothing about his new work is

truly revolutionary: "It's a perfectly normal development," he says. "The river of architecture has split apart into a number of streams and architects are free to follow any stream they wish. I think we should just enjoy the freedom and variety we now have. One great change is the fact that architects can be playful again — that they can laugh. That's why I'm not at all bothered by the Chippendale jibes. If you can't do something just because you want to do it, then we have all been hemmed in too much."

The first mixed-use building in the Federal City was designed three years before
1976 Federal legislation authorized mixed use in Federal buildings,
and it required special Congressional sanction

The criteria this building meets was established in 1975 by a National Endowment Task Force which in its report suggested that "Federal buildings used by the public should provide the widest possible range of uses along with public use—including commercial, educational, civic, cultural and recreation uses"—in short, mixed use. This goal was written into public law in October 1976 as part of the Public Building Cooperative Use Act. Several buildings incorporating mixed use were in construction or being fitted for reuse in 1978—

but the first building to demonstrate that government can in fact "live over the store" is this one, designed by Max O. Urbahn Associates. Indeed the mixed-use concept of this building was born long before such uses became policy—and was suggested by Max Urbahn as part of his presentation to the GSA/FHLBB selection committee, which chose his firm for the work back in 1973. The plot plan at right shows the quality of the scheme: the L-shaped, six-story office building (and the older Winder Building on the same block) wrap around and shelter a

handsome and inviting plaza, with broad pedestrian walks, a waterfall, a reflecting pool around which people sit in the summer (which becomes a skating rink in the winter); large shade trees and a glass-roofed galleria (which becomes an outdoor restaurant in the summer)—all well lighted at night. Surrounding the plaza are a series of ground floor shops and another restaurant. The darker shading on the site plan indicates the small amount of ground floor space devoted to bank use. The new building is six stories—with 250,000 net

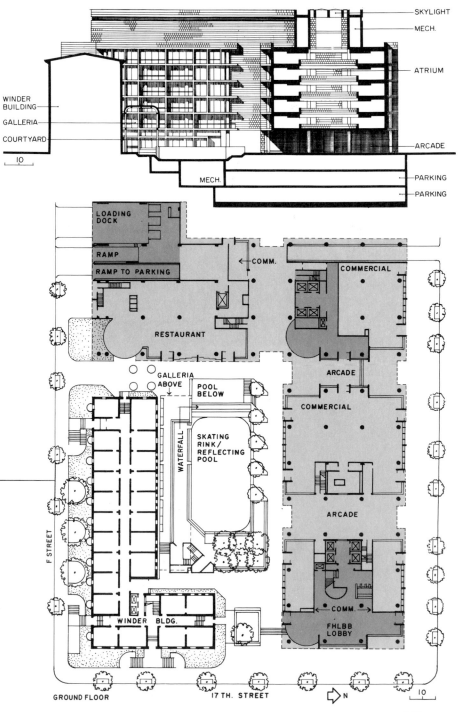

Federal Home Loan Bank Board Building
Washington, D.C.
Architects: Max O. Urbahn Associates

A high degree of interagency cooperation was required throughout the design and construction process. For one thing, while the General Services Administration served as the construction agency, the building was financed by the FHLBB and its district banks. For another: to create the plaza and galleria, land that was part of the Winder Building (see plot plan) which is owned by the GSA, had to be incorporated with the FHLBB land. The National Capital Planning Commission was involved in approval of every phase of the design. NCPC enthusiastically endorsed the mixed-use plaza plan, and was deeply involved in some of the design decisions—specifically widening both of the major entrances to the court and keeping it open without gates or fences.

square feet of commercial space. The cornice line of the older building was maintained in the new, and a maximum of space is built below grade to minimize the building's mass. This handsome building has become an excellent prototype for the kind of building the Federal government hopes to continue to build.

A milestone in Federal architectural policy was reached with
the decision by the U.S. General Services Administration
to use the design competition method in selecting architects
for the most important Federal buildings, and rehabilitation
of the Old Post Office in Washington, D.C. was the first test ...

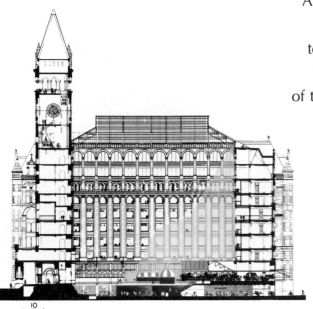

The Benjamin Franklin Post Office
Washington, D.C.
Architects: Arthur Cotton Moore &
Associates; Stewart, Daniel, Hoban and
Associates; McGaughey, Marshall &
McMillan; and Associated Space Design

Moore has left the metal frame of the lightwell
skylight intact, a metaphor for the filigree of
commercial, cultural, and Federal office space
that will interlace the building. Solar collectors
(not shown) were eliminated to accommodate
real available dollars.

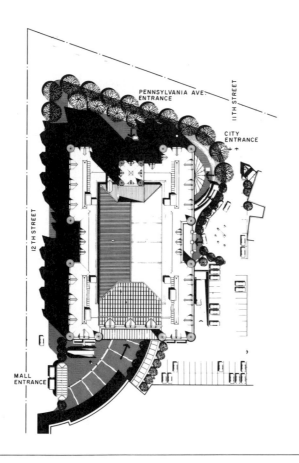

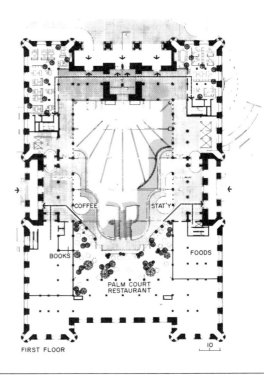

Lois Craig, author of *The Federal Presence: Architecture, Politics, and Symbols in United States Government Building,* has described the GSA's Level 3 competitions for the RECORD. In her words: "The new breed of competitions is called Level 3 simply because the first step in architect selection, the review of credentials and experience, has been, in GSA parlance, Level 1; and interviews of the short list of architects selected by regional GSA advisory boards has been Level 2. For a growing number of buildings, 'consideration of alternative design solutions'—in short a design competition among the short-listed firms—has become Level 3. . . . The Old Post Office and Clock Tower in Washington, D.C. was the subject of a Level 3 design competition to study proposals for the mixed reuse of this sturdy turn-of-the-century building. Each team which participated in the design competition was paid a stipend of $46,000. The program incorporated both the adaptive-use and mixed-use provisions of the Public Buildings Cooperative Use Act. (The latter, passed by Congress in re-

sponse to recommendations of a task force on Federal architecture appointed by the National Endowment for the Arts, opened Federal buildings to commercial and cultural uses to combat the deadening effect of large office buildings in urban areas.) The act also encouraged acquiring and reusing historic and architecturally interesting buildings for public use). The winning proposal for the adaptive reuse of the Old Post Office (known officially as the Benjamin Franklin Post Office) was done by Arthur Cotton Moore & Associates, teamed with Stew-

art, Daniel, Hoban and Associates, McGaughey, Marshall & McMillan, and Associated Space Design, Inc. This is the project, now in construction, that got the whole Level 3 process perking, and the result, in turn, generated interest in using the process for the entire Federal Triangle. The Neo-Romanesque building was completed in 1899 to the design of W. J. Edbrooke, the U.S. Supervising Architect of the period. From the time it was completed it was scorned, even by the likes of Cass Gilbert, who disliked it not for

its style but for its 'undue height and excessive prominence' relative to the lower scale of Washington. One senator criticized it as a cross between a cathedral and a cotton mill. In the 1930s, its presence of Pennsylvania Avenue impeded completion of Secretary of the Treasury Andrew Mellon's Beaux Arts extravaganza, the Federal Triangle. Well, the 1970s changed all that, and the Moore scheme dramatizes that what is thought of as frightening in one century can turn out to be fashionable, certainly fun, in the next. The

most struggle, the most adverse criticism, the most laudatory celebration surrounded this first Level 3 competition. And the winning entry did in fact so far exceed the stipulated budget limit that complaints about unfairness were justifiable. Architects, of course, have always risked breaking competition rules to capture the imagination of a jury, and juries have risked ignoring their own restraints to get the design or designer they want. The question endures of how much is too much—until a real building redirects critical attention.''

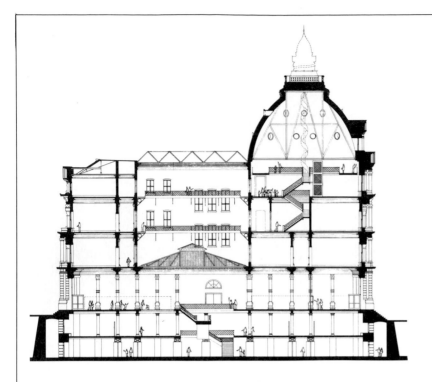

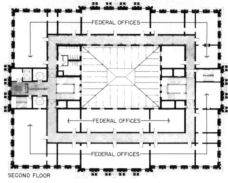

SECOND FLOOR

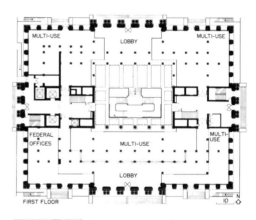

MULTI-USE LOBBY MULTI-USE

FEDERAL OFFICES MULTI-USE MULTI-USE

MULTI-USE

LOBBY

FIRST FLOOR

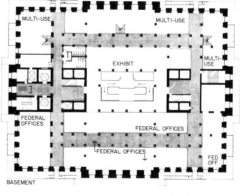

MULTI-USE MULTI-USE

EXHIBIT MULTI-USE

FEDERAL OFFICES FEDERAL OFFICES

FEDERAL OFFICES FED OFF

BASEMENT

... the Post Office and
Custom House in St. Louis
was the second, focus again
on adaptive reuse, and ...

Post Office and Custom House
St. Louis, Missouri
Architects: Patty Berkebile
Nelson Associates/Harry
Weese & Associates

This wonderful late-19th-century building is in the style known as Second Empire in honor of Napoleon III. It was completed in 1884 by a little-known American architect, Alfred B. Mullet, who worked for the Federal government with the title of U.S. Supervising Architect. The building is greatly loved by the architecture buffs of St. Louis, who informally let it be known to the competition jury that they would not tolerate any radical change to the structure.

Lois Craig, writing for the RECORD, described the winning proposal for adapting this grand structure as follows: ''The architects' basic approach involves removing all additions since 1884 that do not directly bear upon the esthetic integrity and functional efficiency of the building; restoring missing or mutilated elements that were basic to the artistry and ingenuity of the original designer, U.S. Supervising Architect Alfred B. Mullet; and inserting new elements only to meet contemporary functional standards, doing so in such a way to minimize physical and visual disruption of the original. Out of a projected 200,000 square feet, about 25,000 is given over to commercial or cultural space. The existing skylight, hovering in the big light well, is to be restored. Up over the light well, a new insulated reflective and clear glass skylight is to be constructed. Thus the light pouring in will once again be introduced to the deeper lower levels where, by way of this adaptation, balcony-like esplanades and staircases will heighten appeal. For this competition the GSA took a tighter look at budgets than in previous Level 3 programs. Reportedly, it also tightened deliberation procedures. Local interest in St. Louis ran high and some objections were made to suggestions in the press that the community would not tolerate an intrusive transformation of the historic building. The most radical solution did in fact lose—for whatever reason. But public sessions can make the jury more responsible and, as one losing competitor suggested, subjecting a jury to local lobbying is a reasonable side effect of a public process in a democracy.''

... that never-completed neo-classical mish-mach, the Federal Triangle, was the third, with the competition winner expected to do a master plan for the whole Triangle, Old Post Office included

A Redesign for the Federal Triangle
Washington, D.C.
Architects and planners: Harry Weese and Associates with Zion & Breen

The area covered by this competition by no means includes the entire Federal Triangle—only the most difficult intersection between the once-scorned

Another Level 3 design competition called for initial re-design schemes for the Federal Triangle in Washington, D.C. Begun in 1928 and brought to its present incomplete state in 1938, it is a great Neo-Classic pile with a particularly fine curving facade designed by Delano & Aldrich. The prod to GSA in getting a Federal Triangle competition under way was the earlier one held for the Old Post Office building and Clock Tower on Pennsylvania Avenue (pages 210-211), the results of which reminded everyone that some connection had to be

made with its Neo-Classic neighbor. Harry Weese and Associates in association with Zion & Breen won the competition over two other submissions—one from Sert, Jackson/Jerome Lindsay in joint venture with the SWA Group and Monacelli Associates, and the other from Sasaki Associates in joint venture with Shepley Bulfinch Richardson & Abbott and Gindele & Johnson. The selection by the GSA ended a year-long search for a way to bring the two styles together. The Weese firm's design extends the horizontal plane of the great semi-

circular plaza to intersect the rectangle of the Old Post Office. The plaza, now almost a circle, becomes a pedestrian precinct closed to cars. The Weese design was selected because the jury believed it would succeed in forming a strong connection between Washington's commercial district to the north and the Mall and museum area to the south. The proposal would also establish a lively pedestrian environment with shops and arcades. Moreover, Weese's proposal incorporates existing and new art works into the plan and responds to

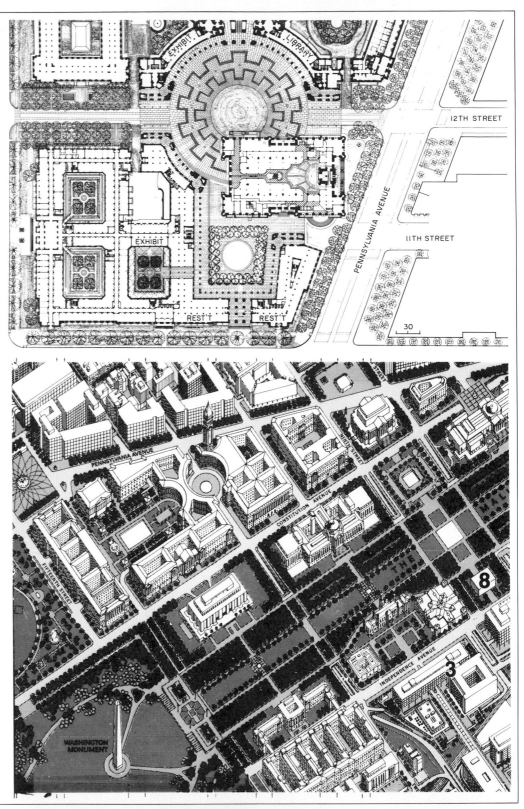

Old Post Office and Delano & Aldrich's curving facade. Now a landmark, the Old Post Office and its Clock Tower will live on in spite of the pronouncement by the late President Kennedy's Council on Pennsylvania Avenue which declared that to retain the old Post Office as a whole would be "chaotic beyond relief."

the government's call for such social benefits as access for the physically handicapped. Original plans for the Triangle called for the demolishment of the Old Post Office and Clock Tower. A decade ago, as in the isometric above, the preservation of the Clock Tower became the goal. Today, it seems correct that the Neo-Romanesque building, tower and all, be preserved as an acceptable interruption of a fine Beaux Arts complex.

A building that enriched city life like none since Rockefeller Center was completed in New York City, the first to realize the true civic potential of the urban design tools New York had been developing since the late 1960s

Citicorp Center
New York, New York
Architects: Hugh Stubbins
and Associates
Associated architects:
Emery Roth and Sons

Architects working on the next generation of New York City skyscrapers should be paying attention to Citicorp, but not merely for its dramatic silhouette or glistening skin. They should be studying its public space. The church, plaza and galleria at the ground level of Citicorp actually *invite* ordinary people to use them, offering such small pleasures as comfortable places to meet, sit and eat. Think of the plazas of the skyscrapers of the past decade, each empty except for its single correct, nonobjective and nonobjectionable sculpture of brightly colored bent steel— sensitively placed, of course. Think of the grudging, gloomy public space in other recent New York buildings like the Galleria and Olympic Towers; public space put there by the owners in exchange for the profits to be made from higher floor area ratios granted by the City Planning Commission's incentive zoning program. Few citizens know that these empty concourses are supposed to be amenities, hard won by the Mayor's urban planners, for public enjoyment, but people know, because the architecture is inviting, that Citicorp is for them.

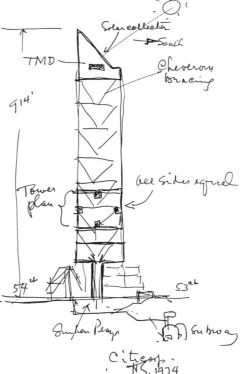

"To make Citicorp Center stand out against its neighbors," the RECORD wrote, "and become a recognizable and memorable corporate symbol, architect Hugh Stubbins decided to give it a light, bright, easily cleaned curtain wall with natural aluminum spandrels. And he wanted to do something interesting with the roof. Early in the design process he began to study the possibilities of a diagonally sliced pinnacle as a powerful mark against the sky. Stubbins at one stage proposed that the slanting surface become a solar collector, but this proved not yet

practicable. He believes that eventually, as solar energy develops, it will be. The street environment of Citicorp Center is a triumph of urban design—the first project influenced and helped to fruition by the New York City Mayor's Office of Midtown Planning that demonstrates convincingly what the Planning Commission's Urban Design Group has been trying to accomplish since 1967. The top management of Citicorp, fortunately, were determined to meet their obligation to give the city fair return of handsome usable public space for the right to build at a floor area ratio of 18. The two most important public spaces are the skylit galleria with its restaurants and shops and the church. It is not necessary to have money to spend to enjoy the public spaces of Citicorp; and depending on the time of day you see a sprinkling of older people relaxing at tables in the treefilled, skylit atrium. And the church is there for quiet meditation. The lantern of the church is at the upper plaza level. The sanctuary floor, however, is one story down at the level of the lower plaza. The sanctuary is a magnificent surprise. Passers-by look down and into it from a large window on the sidewalk. No one expects to suddenly come upon a church interior without actually entering a church—and many stop, look and find their way in."

The structural system of the Citicorp tower is also of interest. As the RECORD noted, "the tower is very economical in its use of structural steel. The 915-foot-high wind-resistant columns are placed at mid-point under each face. By lifting the tower in this daring and imagina-

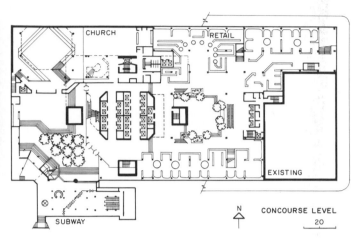

The skylit galleria or atrium is open to the public, who may bring their own food to the tables shown, or patronize the food shops adjacent to the court. There are several good restaurants and shops within the galleria. Office landscaping (below) is used on typical tower floors.

CONCOURSE LEVEL

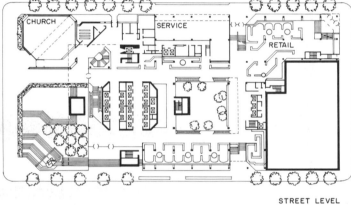

STREET LEVEL

tive way, Stubbins and structural engineer William Le Messurier created the space in which Saint Peter's church exists as a separate entity with its own sky overhead. They also opened up the space at the ground. Since the tower touches ground at only four points, and since the columns are only 24 feet square, the design permitted the construction of a 9,000-square-foot sunken plaza located twelve feet below the street level and interconnected with a new subway station. Most of the building's load—half the gravity and all the wind load—is

brought down the trussed frame on the outside of the tower. The remaining gravity load is carried by the core. The tower is divided into eight-story tiers (see diagram on the preceding page) defined by the steel chevrons that feed the loads into a mast column at the center of each face connecting to one of the four visible supports. The latter, according to Le Messurier, could have been designed to appear much thinner. They were made wider and deeper to enclose space for ductwork and stairs, and as the plans indicate, there is room to spare in-

side them." The wide spandrel at the top of the columns is not "structurally honest"— since it appears to be a beam transforming the tower loads to the columns. RECORD editor Mildred F. Schmertz noted, however, that "the giant piers and the wide spandrel are esthetic, not functional, choices to make the building look and feel right. Giant buildings need to appear to be heftily supported—and huge pilotis must at least appear to carry big beams. Good architects put art before the expression of structure, and Stubbins is no exception."

While critics wrote obituaries, modern architecture continued to develop,
and an addition to the National Gallery of Art in Washington revealed
how urbane and dynamic it could be while still deferring to its setting

The East Building of the
National Gallery of Art
Washington, D.C.
Architects: I.M. Pei & Partners

The photo at left shows how the
new building relates to the diagonals of L'Enfant's 18th-cen-
tury plan for Washington, John
Russell Pope's great Neo-Classic gallery and the U.S. Capitol.
Shown below at left is the
ground level plan which includes Pope's building, the interconnecting plaza and Pei's
new East Wing. The main gallery plan and the mezzanine
level are shown at the bottom
of the opposite page. The
sketch is an early one by Pei,
which studies the scale relationship between the Capitol to
the left, his building in the middle and Pope's gallery to the
right. The principal entrance
plaza (right) is graced by tetra-
hedronal skylights which illuminate an underground concourse which connects Pope's
building with Pei's. The interior
court and more exteriors are
shown on the next pages.

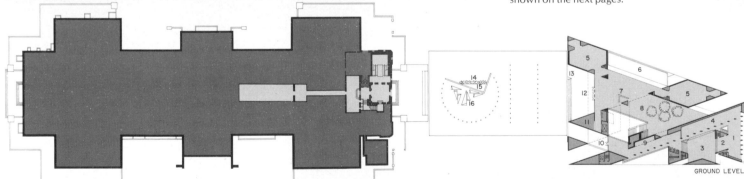

GROUND LEVEL I

Impressed by what he considers a masterpiece, William Marlin wrote for the RECORD: "In many respects this building is for all seasons and architects. It is also a calm commentary about the commotion, inquiry and cant that have lately been heard about the supposedly limited language of modern architecture. It could not be less modern, actually, or more modern. It could not be less post-modern, or more." The East Building of the National Gallery of Art reflects the geometry of its trapezoidal site, adjusting itself to the scale of Pennsyl-

vania Avenue and the Mall. This geometry is articulated by the interlocking and interplay of two basic triangles—an isoceles section containing the exhibition areas and a right triangle containing the Center for Advanced Study in the Visual Arts. The isoceles section is entered from Fourth Street, passing a burnished bronze by Henry Moore, symmetrically aligned across a new plaza from the original Gallery building. Also in from Fourth is the entrance to the Center, through a deep indentation which not only introduces the section composed of the right

triangle but is also a subtle but definite shift to asymmetry in the direction of the Mall. Entering the exhibition area either from the plaza on Fourth Street or by a low tunnel leading to it from the cafeteria below the plaza, the upper galleries are enfolded within three "houses" or "pods," one rising up from each of the three corners of the isoceles triangle encasing this section. Each "house" is a parallelogram, with elevators or spinal stairs set into the corners. The room-like scale of the galleries is thus arranged with great flexibility of expression and

Ezra Stoller © ESTO

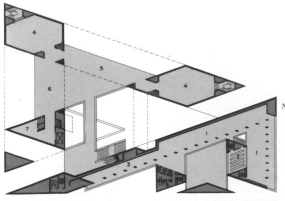

MEZZANINE LEVEL 2
1. Library offices
2. Stacks
3. NGA Press
4. Gallery
5. Sculpture
6. Sales Desk
7. Office
8. Toilets

LEVEL 2   MEZZANINE

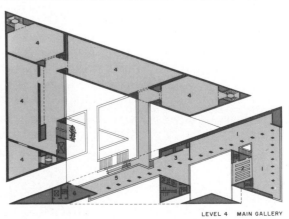

MAIN GALLERY LEVEL 4
1. Offices
2. Stacks
3. Lounge
4. Gallery
5. Terrace cafe
6. Kitchen

LEVEL 4   MAIN GALLERY

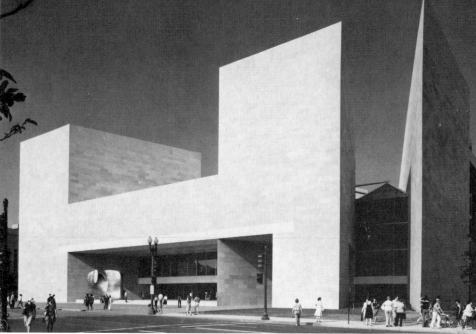

installation, within basic hexagonal hollows within these ''houses.'' Walls can be newly built to suit the scale and spirit of the art being shown. The uppermost ceilings in each ''house'' can be adjusted up or down, assuring the correct vertical scale. The courtyard (next page) rises 80 feet above the concourse-level entrance to the exhibition areas. This concourse speaks of space, light and movement. The building is of some structural interest, particularly its 500-ton welded-steel space frame skylight above the courtyard. The double pane glass of the 25 tetrahedrons composing the skylight includes a safety laminate and filters ultra-violet rays. Each tetrahedron is 30 by 45 feet, its chords held by cast steel nodes of two to six tons. The main air supply is through marble air scoops beneath the skylight; main air return is beneath the stairs. The building is clad with Tennessee marble which has been detailed, even at the most acute exterior corners, to maintain a quality of solidness. The individual pieces of stone, each 2 by 5 feet, are individually attached to precast blocks in the backing wall. Steel plates support the bottom corners, anchors restrain the tops and neoprene lining accepts expansion. The building, however, is much more than a technical marvel. As Marlin concludes: ''Culture may sometimes appear to be, as Buckminster Fuller has said, the flotsam and the jetsam saying to each other that there should be a law against having any waves. The East Building of the National Gallery of Art is a wave that architecture, and its relationship to the values of culture generally, has very much needed.''

Some critics have dubbed the new Biloxi Library and Cultural Center "Faculty Club South," a reference to the well-known faculty club building which William Turnbull and his partner Charles Moore designed for the University of California in the 1960s. The collection of shapes and the look of the materials in the newer building help recall the older one, and here as well an irregularly composed plan is covered over with a relatively simple set of roofs which drape like a giant tent over the complexities which lie beneath. Layers of part-

ly pierced walls, both inside and out, also help complete the stylistic recall. But the overall effect is somehow sharper and clearer: largely because the building comprises a relatively simple program organized in an extremely straightforward way. Near the center of the building is a two-story circular space. The library is to one side, stretching itself around the courtyard outdoors. On the other side are administrative, service and display areas. Two traffic systems reach into the center, and one of them does triple duty of serving the public

rooms on the second floor doubling as exhibition space and, most importantly, by simply being a memorable space in its own right. Missing, however, are what Gerald Allen, writing in the RECORD, calls the "jarring and shocking cacophonies of the faculty club," to be replaced by something calmer as indeed befits a library. "Fans of the earlier building will no doubt detect a loss," Allen points out, "but others will detect something quite else—an altogether different kind of building." Turnbull's building sprouts a pair of wings which

A new building embraced
an old library relocated
on its site to create a
cultural center that gave
civic presence to the area
around city hall and that
looked (almost) as though
it has always been there

Biloxi Library and Cultural Center
Biloxi, Mississippi
Architects: MLTW/Turnbull Associates

The new building performs three important urban design functions in downtown Biloxi. It extends its arms in a friendly gesture and enfolds the town's original library, relocated on the site. It also defines a space shared by the city hall to the east and establishes a strong architectural presence to the west by means of a major entrance gate to be seen in the isometric below.

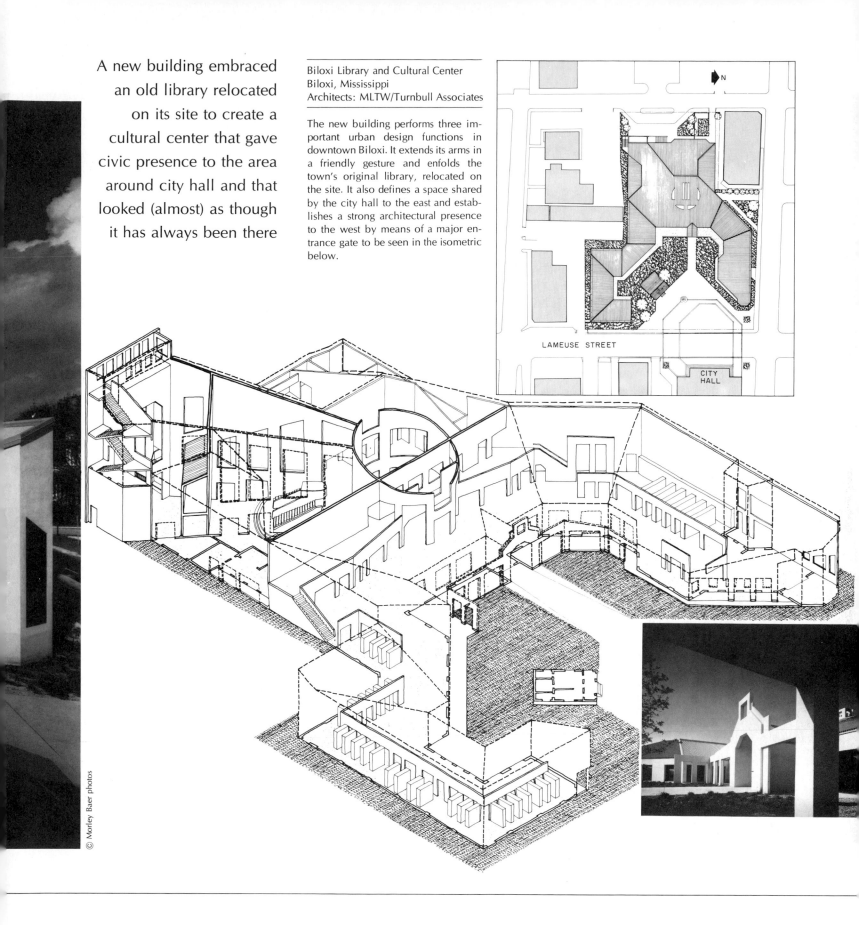

LAMEUSE STREET

CITY HALL

© Morley Baer photos

embrace a newly created courtyard—originally conceived as Biloxi's bicentennial gesture—where the town's original wood frame library has been spruced up and relocated (as can be seen to the left of the photo above). The courtyard—which Turnbull calls a walled garden—also forms a foreground for Biloxi's city hall across the street (shown in the plot plan above right). In the courtyard is one of the building's two main entrances, leading straight into the library. The other entrance, to the west, serves the second traffic system described above.

As the photos and drawings indicate, the entrance from the courtyard is a very welcoming door. Architect Turnbull clearly knows his gates, doors and porches down through the history of styles and it is refreshing to see a door with the quality of "doorness" appear once more in architecture. It is not easy to design such a door. Borrowed forms do not necessarily combine in a way which has resonance for today, but Turnbull has done it successfully here.

MLTW/Turnbull of San Francisco got the

job, by the way, through an interesting teaching assignment. In May 1975, the RECORD reported that teams of students from six southern architectural schools, led by six nationally known architects, had camped out for a week in Biloxi, Mississippi, to develop a series of alternative designs for the new library and cultural center which the town was then proposing. Turnbull was one of the team leaders and subsequently received the commission for the building.

"Interpretive restoration" reestablished the formal themes of a great Beaux Arts building

The St. Louis Art Museum
Restoration
St. Louis, Missouri
Architects: Hardy Holzman Pfeiffer
Associates

Down through the years the architectural significance of this noble Beaux Arts building was little understood. Cass Gilbert's formal axes make a lattice of movement which surrounds and contains the exhibition spaces. Museum curators who should have known better cluttered these passages, blocked them off, sealed their windows and created fake period environments for their genuine art. In order to reestablish the lattice the architects had to cut new openings in certain walls and restore existing doorways and frames.

Cass Gilbert was the original architect of the Museum. As RECORD editor Mildred Schmertz pointed out: "Like other American Beaux Arts architects he looked to ancient Rome in his search for the timeless architectural values he hoped to bring to his work." He fashioned the combined concourse and sculpture hall of the museum after the tepidarium of the Thermae of Caracalla. (A few years later McKim, Mead and White were to turn to the same source for Pennsylvania Station). As in the Roman bath, the hall has three great bays with arched recesses at opposite ends of each bay. The whole is roofed by a barrel vault interrupted by lunettes. At each end of the main axis are three arched doorways spanned by a balcony and crowned by a lunette. All of these elements, thanks to the perceptions and craft of architects Hugh Hardy, Malcolm Holzman and Norman Pfeiffer, have become readable once more and a magnificent room has emerged. The architects, who call what they do "interpretive restoration," have also rediscovered and successfully restated the formal dynamics of other spaces within the museum. They clearly love the building. In Hugh Hardy's words: "This major work by a once-forgotten architect gives delight in its audacity and solidity, its remembrance of the past and its commitment to the future." Through the 74-year life of the museum, Cass Gilbert's design was little understood, and many depredations were made upon it (above right). The Hardy Holzman Pfeiffer firm began by removing these piecemeal accretions, thus restating Gilbert's axial and spatial themes. The main axis and the

minor axis were clarified and enhanced. The museum insisted that the fountain at the crossing of the two axes remain and the architects agreed. Though not part of Cass Gilbert's original design, it helps turn the concourse from a channel to a room. According to the RECORD: "By making the most of the fountain the architects had all of architectural and town planning wisdom behind them, for every intersection of paths of movement is transformed by a monument or fountain into a place to stop and be."

Further, the architects wished to celebrate Gilbert's arches and vaults. They made exhaustive lighting studies with the firm of Jules Fisher & Paul Marantz, Inc. The architects also investigated Gilbert's ornament and color palettes in buildings in which they were better preserved than in the art museum (the St. Louis Public Library, for example). They found that he loved bright colors and rich decorative devices. Despite what they learned, Hardy Holzman Pfeiffer elected to use color and ornament sparingly in the belief that color and decoration of extreme subtlety were better suited to today's esthetic standards. Cass Gilbert's skylights were reconstructed, reglazed and augmented by incandescent light. The quantity of daylight was greatly reduced and the combined light better directed. The architects did everything possible to conceal the sophisticated new climate control and security systems required to meet the standards of environmental quality for today's museums. All such equipment has been located within the original walls and fan rooms and in a new, partially buried concrete structure.

1979

This final chapter is the only one in the book for which the material has been selected from current work in architects' offices rather than from the pages of ARCHITECTURAL RECORD. By representing 1979 largely with work in progress rather than completed buildings, it was intended to reflect the thrust of architecture as it entered the 1980s. That thrust is urbanistic, humanistic, perhaps even approaching the "organic" of Frank Lloyd Wright's philosophy of modern architecture. Nothing here is a departure from what has gone before, everything is an evolution of architectural convictions, efforts and tendencies that had been expressing themselves increasingly throughout the 1970s, and that had their roots in the architectural experience of the 1960s and the 1950s.

The big change in the 1970s was the context in which architecture is done. Once the public had asserted its right to a voice in any decision with an impact on the built environment; once processes had begun to be invented and institutionalized to ensure that the public voice *could* be heard; once clients, public and private, had come to understand that these circumstances were the inescapable conditions for building: then vast new possibilities as well as new constraints had been established for the doing of architecture. The architectural results are visible in every chapter of this book.

Content of this chapter has been selected to suggest the increasing assurance with which architects were responding in varied ways to varied problems in the new circumstances.

Rejuvenation by design of a major street in a major city (pages 230–231) was recognized (12 years into the process) by a special AIA chapter award.

Design of a government center for a smaller city (pages 232–233) preserved the front half of an old city hall, while rebuilding (but not "restoring") the interiors; created a network of courtyards that linked the buildings within the center and connected the complex with the city's pedestrian circulation system; and, with a fenestration concept that maximized views for occupants while minimizing glass areas, made facades for new buildings that related in scale and spirit to facades of older buildings.

A downtown development project that mixed uses and created connections between its activities and those of the city around it (pages 234–235) was one exemplar of what Edmund N. Bacon calls "the city as an act of will," which can become reality when architect, developer and community work together in the most intimate conceptual collaboration.

A new generation of skyscrapers was evolving (pages 236–251). They are designed to engage both earth (or street) and sky; to involve, celebrate and sometimes transcend their surroundings. In contrast to towers of a decade or so earlier (pages 2–5), which sought to humanize tall buildings by manipulating their facades to enrich them, and in contrast to more recent towers which relied on decoration (pages 206–207) or reflections (pages 186–187) for enrichment, these towers are most often enriched by manipulation of their volumes, while facades are kept quiet, as close to monochromatic as possible. The manipulation of volumes derives from concern with scale and massing of buildings conceived as elements of the cityscape.

Towers shown in this chapter include both institutional and commercial projects, and you can't tell them apart by the quality of their architecture. That is a fact of substantial significance to architects and architecture. In the speculative office building booms of the 1950s and the 1960s, developers did not worry about prestige architecture. Now, it seems, you can't compete in a world of apparently perpetual rental escalation without offering the kind of "something extra" that only creative architecture can provide.

Architects working on spacious sites far from congested urban centers are often faced with the need to assert a presence, to *create* a "place," which can be done (pages 252–255) with every respect for environmental context. Neither "infill" nor "background" buildings are any more universally appropriate than monuments are, even for building types designed to serve everyday needs.

Conversations with all of the architects whose work is shown in this chapter (except one who was too busy) discovered none who considered that the end of modern architecture is at hand, or even in prospect. To quote Hugh Newell Jacobsen, an architect whose work is represented elsewhere in this book but not in this chapter, "There are no revolutions in architecture . . . It just *continues*."

Text and captions for pages 230–255 have been written by the editor of ARCHITECTURAL RECORD, Walter F. Wagner, Jr. —*J.M.D.*

A building in the heart of New York's Harlem was infill on the street side, made a little oasis of almost sylvan tranquility on the other, and, within, created a world apart for learning and doing. Harlem School of the Arts: Ulrich Franzen and Associates, Architects.

The rehabilitation of San Francisco's Market Street is an example of the urban-scale work architects find themselves involved in: here much more than a "fix-up" of a major street but rather a bold commitment to reshape the core of a city

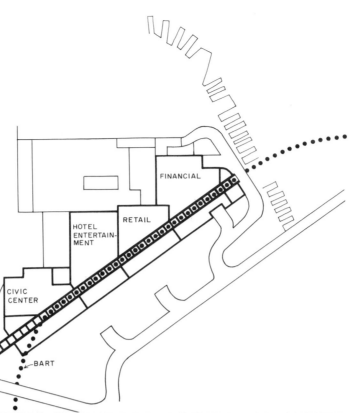

The great majority of the pages in this final chapter on the final year of the 1970s are given over to the design of urban spaces and the design of buildings for those urban spaces — yes, including a lot of those controversial new skyscrapers. The reason is a fundamental one: the biggest problems of architecture (and the biggest changes in architecture) related to design in and for the cities — and we enter the 1980s with a conviction that things are going to stay that way.

This is not to minimize the importance of architecture everywhere — the creation of beautiful houses on exurban sites; design of all manner of residential, institutional and commercial buildings in our small towns and smaller cities (which are, by the way, and for the first time in a long time, growing faster than our major cities). But it is in the cities where the great architectural issues of the 1970s (and probably the 1980s) are really on stage — the issues of public concern and interest in architecture, issues of preserving existing character of neighborhoods, issues of design theory, is-

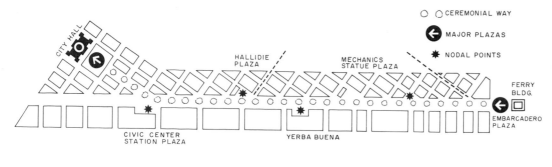

Market Street Rehabilitation,
San Francisco, California
Urban Design Consultants: Mario J.
Ciampi and Associates and John Carl
Warnecke and Associates;
Landscape Architect:
Lawrence Halprin and Associates

Over the years, this once-proud street had become shabby and unfashionable. When the city's BART system was approved, it meant digging up Market Street; and this in turn made feasible the street rehabilitation shown here.

Three major plazas—two of them at BART stops—and numerous smaller parks were created by dead-ending streets leading into Market on the diagonal from the north. Sidewalks were widened to 35 feet, reducing traffic from six lanes to four, and two of those bus express lanes. All commercial establishments must respect new sign ordinances; all pedestrian paths are brick, with granite trim; hundreds of trees were planted; and bus stops and all street furniture, as well as all graphics, designed to a high standard.

sues of preservation, issues of context, issues of mixing old with new in a sensitive and meaningful way.

Two of the many interviews conducted by the author in the course of researching this book bear heavily on these issues and are quoted extensively here—one an interview with Jaquelin Robertson, one of the founders of the Urban Design Group, the first director of New York's office of midtown development, designer at Llewelyn-Davies Weekes, and now an architect in private practice, and the other

with Ieoh Ming Pei, one of the most influential designers of the decade whose suberb design was recognized by the AIA Gold Medal in 1979. Taken together, the two interviews present a broad and thoughtful discussion of architecture in the context of changing cities and changing attitudes about cities. Said Robertson, for example: "I think the most significant issue of the past 10 years has been the 'discovery' (and it almost amounts to a discovery) by architects that buildings don't sit alone; that they sit in a context which has already been

Paul Rudolph's design for the New Haven
Government Center is the most sophisticated kind
of urban in-fill: it creates new buildings
sympathetic to the old in color, massing and
character—and adds some fine new outdoor spaces

New Haven Government Center
New Haven, Connecticut
Architect: Paul Rudolph

Rudolph's job was to create a 240,000-
sq-ft City Hall and a new library, with
underground parking, on a site bounded by the New Haven Green and a
potpourri of existing buildings on the
block, including the existing 32,000-
sq-ft City Hall. His scheme would preserve part of the existing Victorian
Gothic building facing the green—and

use this section with its grand stair as
the entrance to the new city offices.
The library would be on the lower
floors of the building to the left of the
existing building in both photos above.
A ceremonial outdoor space would be
created between the City Hall and
library wings. The new buildings echo
the verticality of the old City Hall—
tall contemporary window slits echo-
ing the Gothic windows, slant-topped
stair and elevator wells suggesting
"towers" in a city of towers.

built and which will continue to change. They
also now realize that it is their responsibility to
design to that context rather than just to design
a building—that buildings ought to be seen
not as objects, but as urban neighbors. This is
a profound change in the way cities are
thought about. . . . I think this is the most important change in architecture—there haven't
been any technological breakthroughs, and the
designers are not any better at pure design than
they have ever been; it's just that they are more
responsible. The evidence is everywhere: in

hundreds of small renovations and small in-fill
buildings. Open any of the magazines and you
will see buildings that—in terms of scale and
materials and character—are in keeping with
the buildings on both sides. This carries up
from the small buildings to the new skyscrapers. Most of those new buildings in New York,
for example (see pages 242–249) are attempting to relate to the surrounding city, to
the appearance of the surrounding buildings,
and to the needs of the people. Citicorp
(pictured in the previous chapter) is an ob-

vious example. It is a building which connects to the subway and provides a host of activities on the lower floors that relate to the city, to the people. That is a sharp change from, say the Seagram Building, where the requirements of the city and the passersby were swept away to create that classical, clean, beautiful plaza. Seagram is a much more beautiful building; Citicorp is a much more responsive building. That makes it a very important prototype of what has and will be happening to buildings in the city."

Ieoh Ming Pei spoke not only of urban-community needs—but demands: "Today, community groups are very vocal. In some ways, that makes architecture harder to do. But it is entirely fair that what we architects do be scrutinized in relation to the community in which the buildings will be placed. That puts tremendous constraints on us—but they are not necessarily bad constraints. Our buildings would seem less free, more involved with non-architectural issues—but these are nevertheless very important.

"Consider what it takes to get a building built in New York. First of all, you have a whole set of rules (building codes) to look at, and you have to be a lawyer to understand them. . . . After you have a fairly good idea about what the rules are, then you have to learn how to play the game of getting the variances you want—not for profit, but for the sake of what is good for architecture and what is good for the city. To break the rules is not all bad—and sometimes the only way to get what is most important to achieve. . . . Then you go

This multi-purpose development in Seattle would create new retail vitality linked to existing department stores and a monorail terminus — and a new public museum

Westlake Park
Museum Retail Parking Complex
Seattle, Washington
Architects:
Mitchell/Giurgola Architects

This is a joint public and private development. The site — surrounded by three department stores — contains a terminal of the monorail to the Seattle Fairgrounds. Constructed on the site will be a 300-car underground public parking garage; a new monorail ter-

minal; four levels of shops, restaurants, and theaters with access bridges to the department stores and — on the upper two levels — new facilities for the Seattle Art Museum. The plan would save two worthwhile buildings (one a hotel) on the site, and create an elevated pedestrian plaza and a huge public plaza developed as a sculpture garden. The developers — Mondev International Limited — would bear about two-thirds of the projected construction cost of about $50 million.

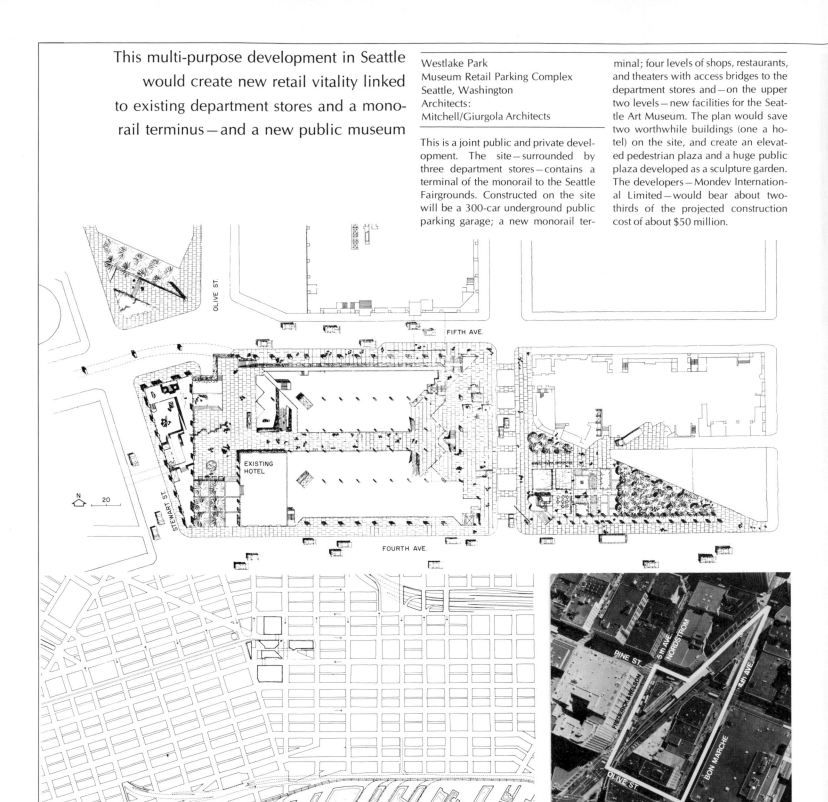

through a series of community-board approvals — and those people are thinking in very different terms of 'How is this going to affect my neighborhood?', and so on through agencies galore. Today, we are a long way from the architect sitting in his drafting room thinking up the best way to create form and space.

"Those constraints are very real. They determine to a great extent what our buildings are like, and therefore what our cities are like. They cut both ways: sometimes they are just plain bureaucratic headaches, but sometimes

they are opportunities. Political trade-offs can't be good; but being required to think of a building as part of its urban context is a very good constraint."

Jaquelin Robertson was asked to what extent he thought the skyscrapers were being shaped by the constraints and incentives of the now-famous Urban Design Group begun under Mayor Lindsay: "I would have to say that nearly all of the projects being designed in the city today show the imprint of that work. What we said to developers in the earliest days was:

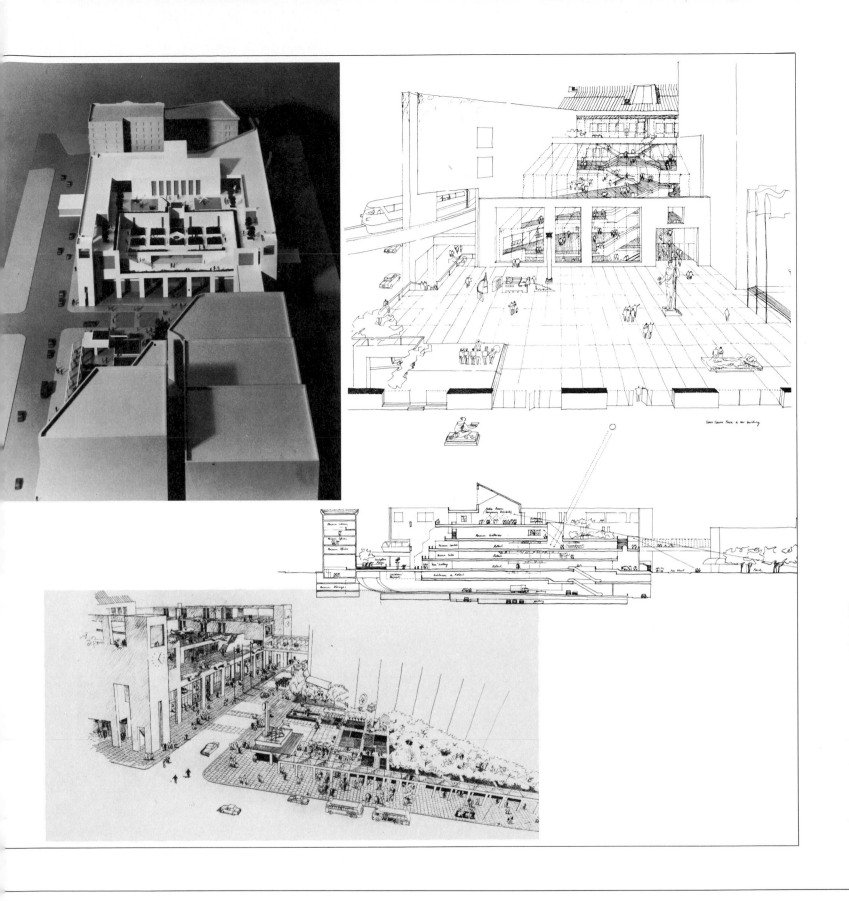

'Look, what you do up in the air is, within reason, your affair; what you do when you bring your building to the ground is the public concern. And since each ground condition, each site, is slightly different, the design of buildings reflects that. Maybe the design does something to let the sun into a public space. Or make a connection to the subway. Or create some new shopping frontage, or a view, or an enclosed public park that can be used in the winter as well as the summer. There is now a twist, as it were, to the bottom of almost every major building not just in New York but in most cities. You can't treat the bottom of a building as you treat the top; you can't just bring buildings to the ground and call it a day. All the good new buildings concern themselves with the requirements of the people in the neighborhood and the passersby; concern themselves with the design of the street. To put it the other way around, the design of the street—the architecture of the street—imposes its requirements on the architecture of individual buildings. That is what Rockefeller Center (pages 238–241) was about. . . . It is what Citicorp is all about (pages 216–219); what IDS in Minneapolis is all about; it is what all those new Manhattan skyscrapers (see pages 242–249) are all about.''

And Robertson thinks that, given the rules of constraint and offsetting incentives, developers have no trouble at all with the new concepts: ''If you change the rules and get a few good examples (like Citicorp) built, the developer will have his lawyer and accountants and others who evaluate his plans look at these new

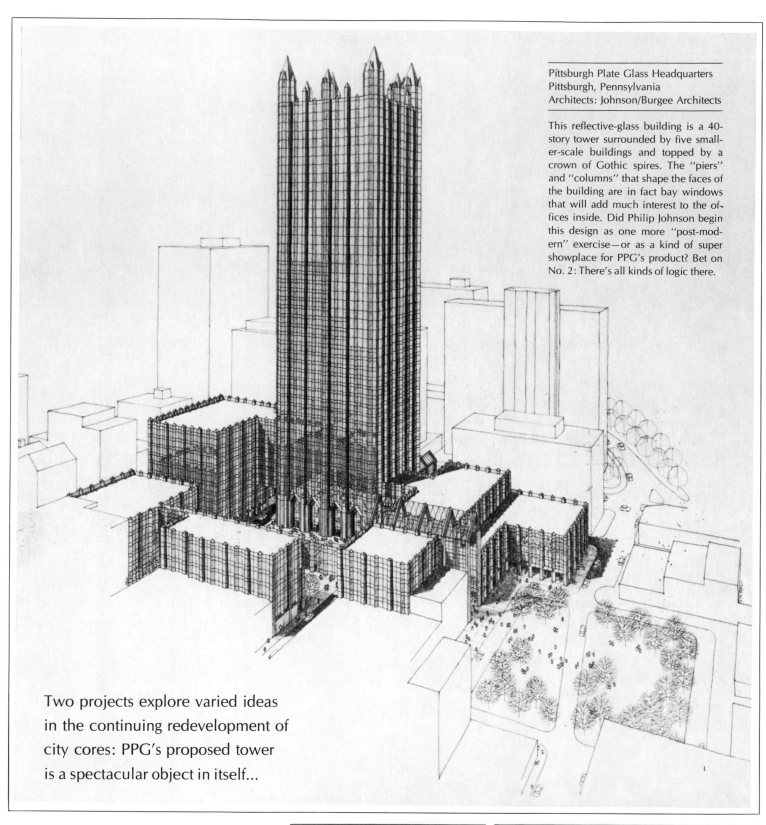

Pittsburgh Plate Glass Headquarters
Pittsburgh, Pennsylvania
Architects: Johnson/Burgee Architects

This reflective-glass building is a 40-story tower surrounded by five smaller-scale buildings and topped by a crown of Gothic spires. The "piers" and "columns" that shape the faces of the building are in fact bay windows that will add much interest to the offices inside. Did Philip Johnson begin this design as one more "post-modern" exercise—or as a kind of super showplace for PPG's product? Bet on No. 2: There's all kinds of logic there.

Two projects explore varied ideas in the continuing redevelopment of city cores: PPG's proposed tower is a spectacular object in itself...

designs with a different set of glasses. They're saying: 'If that's what the city or the neighborhood wants, that's what we'll give them.' And they're finding new opportunities in the new ground floor/street connections and they enjoy it. What's more, we're seeing a new kind of developer—a developer who has grown up a generation; a man to whom quality is important—indeed part of his lifestyle. Not so long ago Zeckendorf was considered a wild man to involve himself with Pei. But today developers like Gerry Hines and Dick Ravitch and James

Grant Street Plaza
Pittsburgh, Pennsylvania
Architects: Hellmuth, Obata
& Kassabaum

This six-block project for Oxford Development Company will provide 2 million square feet of office space, 180,000 feet of retail space along the circulation ways and varied recreational facilities—all linked by a major landscaped plaza along Grant Street.

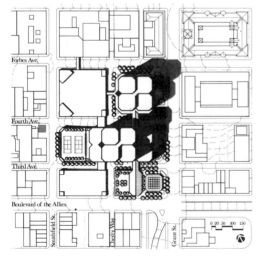

...while this cluster of towers—more ordered but in many ways more complex—hope to be a magnet attracting people to a center of varied activities

Rouse and Rocke Ransen see not just the desirability from a quality point of view, but the need from a competitive point of view, of retaining quality architects.

"The corporations set the pace: they are more of a model for developers than is generally recognized. And that began back in the fifties and sixties, with buildings like Pepsi Cola (page 246) and Lever House (page 247). As more and more high-quality corporate buildings are built, the developer realizes that those buildings set a standard against which his spec-

ulative building is measured when people come to look at a lease. The same developer who ten years ago said, 'I wouldn't build a building by Philip Johnson if you forced me at the point of a gun,' is now calling up Johnson to see if he might do a building for him—and probably being turned down."

I.M. Pei agrees generally that it is easier to get the client to accept quality today: "The reason: good modern architecture is thoroughly accepted. I remember clients asking, 'Why have you given me a modern building? Why not a

classical building?' Thirty years ago I couldn't get a mortgage on my house because they said a modern house wouldn't sell. But there are no such questions anymore. The style of architecture is no longer questioned—and of course today we see much more variety and experimentation accepted by clients—and in some cases demanded by clients .

"Think about the buildings by good architects that you are showing in this chapter—especially the New York ones. Why are the developers accepting—perhaps even asking

A proposal to save
Radio City Music Hall
has implications for
landmarks everywhere

Proposal for an income-producing
tower over Radio City Music Hall
New York, New York
Architects: Davis, Brody and
Associates

The Music Hall, one of the centerpieces of Rockefeller Center, has long
been troubled by operating deficits—
and its future remains clouded. Many
proposals have been put forth to protect the Hall's superb 1930s interiors;
not just as a landmark but as a badge
of the city's civic pride. One proposal—developed by Davis, Brody and
Associates under the auspices of the
Urban Development Corporation—
would use the air rights over the Hall
for a 900,000-square-foot tower that
would provide supporting revenues.

for—something new and different? Look at it
this way. There were literally millions of
square feet of office space built in the city at a
time when construction costs were very much
lower than they are today. Today, a developer's new space costs twice as much—but he
can't charge twice the rent. To get the premi-
um rents he needs he has to offer something
very much better, something unusual, something that will attract tenants and offer other
ways—like retail facilities—to generate profit
. . . . They're starting to build hotels again in
New York, after a long period of inactivity.
Why—because the new hotels can offer a kind
of comfort and convenience (and maybe excitement) that the old hotels just don't have
anymore.

"And maybe the higher costs of buildings
have something to do with the speculative
developer coming to the name architects. He
wants high rents, because he has very high
fixed costs. And unless he can offer the public
something it perceives as very special he can't
get those high rents . . . Another reason is that

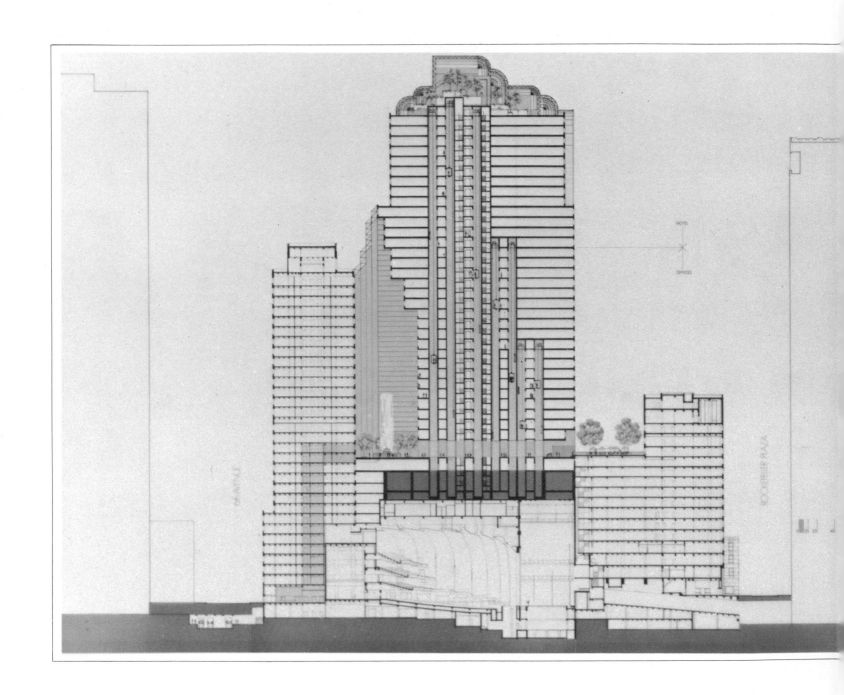

he wants the Community Boards and the Planning Commission and the Board of Standards and Appeals to accept the variances he wants—and he knows that using an architect with a reputation for quality and performance will make it easier for him to get those variances. I'm not really sure about that, but it's a possibility. . . ."

But Pei soon returned, in his interview, to broader questions of the environment: "I am still most concerned that architecture be concerned with the total environment. An urban building can no longer be thought of as an isolated object—indeed, few buildings can, wherever they are built. . . . In any great period of architectural history, eventually you have to reach a point where the whole environment is a good place to be. To build an environment that is unified, one that is pleasing as a whole, means that you have to—to a certain extent—suppress a certain amount of individuality of design and think of the total and larger concern. While we are all beginning to understand that, I don't think we are doing it yet. Think of

The difficult problem at Radio City would be, of course, how to bring the proposed 35-story office or mixed-use tower down on top of the existing stage house and 7500-seat auditorium. The architect's proposal is to erect two pairs of massive columns—each column 10 feet square—at either side of the stage and at the rear of the auditorium (plan below). These would support perimeter beams 35 feet deep—and this platform would in turn support a conventional steel tower. At the platform level, a "garden lobby" would be created with restaurants and retail space—reached by a series of external elevators linked to the south street entry by escalators.

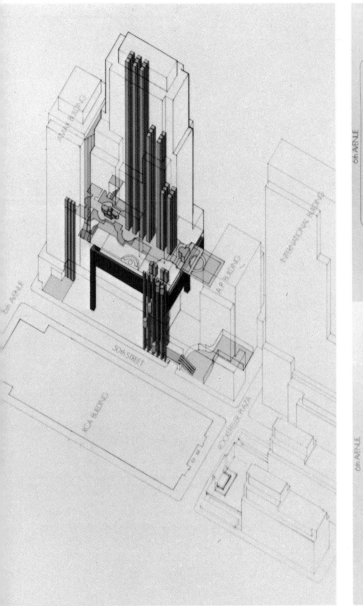

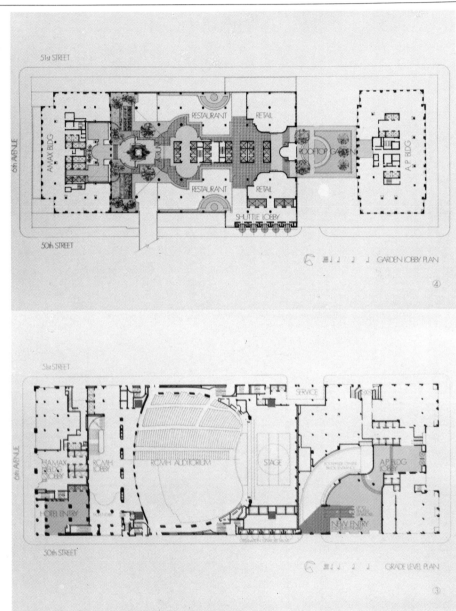

Georgian England. What a beautiful city London became. Look at its architecture: very few acrobatics. . . . Look at Paris. Is there really a first-rate building in Paris? But what a beautiful city!

"Is creating the beautiful city the province of the architect, or of some other profession? Who else? This is our proper province. You can talk all you want about architectural theory and beautiful design, but I think the ultimate measure of our profession is whether we are capable of building a physical environment for

life that is healthy, happy and humanistic. I feel that challenge has not been addressed sufficiently.

"There was more talk of it back in the 1950s than there is today. We made a lot of very serious mistakes with our attempts at urban renewal, but there was a lot of personal concern then. For the first time, architects had a chance to deal with whole sections of cities—but because we made too many mistakes, and very bad ones, we lost the opportunity. It is true that the mistakes were not all ours—typically

650 Fifth Avenue
New York, New York
Architects: John Carl Warnecke and Associates

To help fit into its Fifth Avenue context, this building is sheathed in granite—a clear gesture to its
Rockefeller Center neighbors. It is built to the
street line—with shops opening off the grand
boulevard. The building entrance is around the
corner on 52nd Street—but it is given importance
by a 30-foot arcade that opens to a multi-level
pedestrian space full of more shops. The setback maintains the prevailing cornice line along
the Avenue. This building makes good use of
New York's incentive zoning rules.

Real-estate arithmetic dictates
—most of the time—massive
scale, more and more
architects are clearly searching
for ways to "stay in context,"
be respectful to the streetscape
or give the passerby a treat

Wolfgang Hoyt © ESTO

the architect was brought in only after the site
was cleared and standing there vacant. And
that was the first and biggest mistake. Sometimes only a portion of the buildings should
have come down—but it didn't work that way.
Nonetheless, we were desperately searching
for a vocabulary that would apply, that would
enable us to weave that part of the city—that
is, the urban renewal section—back into the
fabric of the total city. We tried—I think of my
work at Society Hill in Philadelphia, which I
think was reasonably successful. There is nothing in that project—no individual building—
that is anything like an exciting work of architecture; but the concern there was a very different kind of concern. It was the concern for
an area, for a part of the city, with its own history and the continuity that goes with it. It was
part of a time sequence. That kind of concern
is important and healthy—and is not addressed
enough today. I really hope we are headed
back in that direction—not just in terms of
housing, but in terms of the total urban picture.
"Years ago, I remember arguing that if you

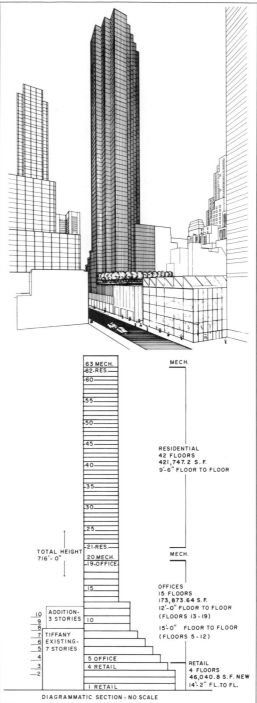

725 Fifth Avenue
New York, New York
Architects: Swanke Hayden Connell and Partners
Director of Design: Der Scutt

This 60-story, multi-use building was designed for the former Bonwit Teller site; and thus was a controversial proposal from the start. The architects configured the building in a number of ways to offer a suitable (if immensely larger) alternative. There are five levels of retail space—a total of 85,000 square feet—in a lively off-the-street atrium (drawing below) that will be connected with the galleria in the IBM building under construction on the same block (and shown opposite). Above are 13 floors—170,000 square feet—of office space; and some of these floors open to the cascading set of terraces which extend down and reduce scale at street level. Above the offices are 320 luxury condominium apartments on 40 stories. The 45-degree angling of the building relates to the adjacent IBM design and—above the terrace of set-backs—creates a strong new plane along the Avenue.

sprinkled twenty Seagram Buildings up and down Park Avenue, you wouldn't make a great avenue. There is something else needed—and that is the challenge. I don't see why buildings, at least most of our buildings, couldn't be designed and built so that they mix and work together and form a unity. What is architecture? Is it the individual building, or the neighborhood, or the whole city? What was the genius of our time? A single building? Pick one that is the most important as a single work of architecture. Is that the genius of our time? Obviously not.''

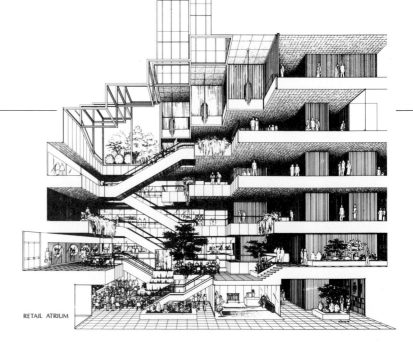

RETAIL ATRIUM

A triangular building creates a triangular greenhouse as a public plaza and park usable year-round

IBM Building
New York, New York
Architect: Edward Larrabee Barnes

This 43-story tower will share a major portion of its site with a public plaza. The triangle left by the building's shape will be a sawtooth-roofed greenhouse with trees up to 40 feet and protected access through the block to the building opposite.

Jaquelin Robertson emphasized in his interview the need to preserve—and indeed to generate—mixed use in downtowns, including residential. "What is happening on Fifth Avenue (in some of the towers shown in this section) reinforces what we hoped would happen when the Office of Midtown Planning wrote the Fifth Avenue Special District legislation. Putting aside comment on the design of some of the buildings, we are getting what we hoped for: All of the special-district zoning was essentially intended to reinforce mixed use. We wanted mixed use, responsiveness of buildings to the public-sector issues—the first five or six floors; the way the building relates to the transportation systems; the encouragement of residential development (which inevitably is upper or middle-income in these circumstances).

Robertson explained in more detail: "We felt from the beginning of planning that luxury residential was an essential component of luxury retail and hotel activity. Fifth Avenue, because of its location, its historic value, the investment already there, clearly needed to remain as a top retail street. The only way to do that was to encourage new buildings to incorporate luxury retailing. The only way to do *that* was to make it more difficult to incorporate other things on the ground floor that would have been financially more attractive—such as banks and airline ticket offices. The best reinforcement for luxury retailing is luxury residential. To stem that flow of retail away from the core to the residential neighborhoods—which is a natural flow in any city—we had to re-establish the Fifth Avenue area as a top dollar res-

Pei on Park Avenue:
Is simplicity and
quiet color the best
answer of all?

Park Tower
New York, New York
Architects: I.M. Pei and Partners

This office building—relatively
small at 25 stories of 10,000
square feet each—turns a quiet
gray glass face to Park Avenue.
Around the corner is a 60-foot-
high sculpture garden and running diagonally through the
building to house shops.

Across Park Avenue from the
Park Tower is the Olivetti
Building (formerly the Pepsi
Cola Building, Skidmore Owings & Merrill, 1959), the "context" to which Pei chose to
relate his building.

Ezra Stoller © ESTO

idential address and force the developers to
put luxury retail into ground floors—and that
is just what happened. If you ask the people of
the Fifth Avenue Association what the best
thing in the last ten years was for them—they
will say the building of the Olympic Tower
(which combines retail on the ground level,
offices and residential above). Since then, the
other projects along Fifth Avenue that you are
showing in the book came along—people are
building retail and apartments to reinforce the
existing base in an area that ten years ago

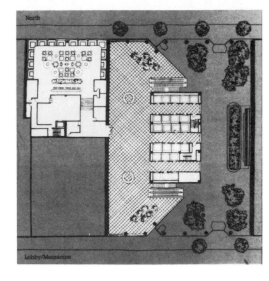

... and then there's the question of air rights: SOM's design for a site behind Stanford White's Racquet and Tennis Club

Park Avenue Plaza
New York, New York
Architects: Skidmore, Owings & Merrill

The club has long been a low-rise oasis among some of Park Avenue's best towers—Lever House (below) is across 53rd Street, Seagram across the avenue. Financial maneuvering lasting nearly 10 years finally resulted in the developer—who had assembled the mid-block site behind the club—assuring the future of the club by paying $5 million for its air rights. The developer also agreed to a mid-block retail arcade from 52nd to 53rd Streets. The new tower will be 44 stories, 15-sided, with a narrow, notched Park Avenue facade centered on the Racquet Club's elegant arched entrance.

everyone thought could never be residential again. And that's very healthy."

These days, of course, you cannot underestimate the importance of saving worthwhile older buildings as part of the rebuilding of our cities—and examples of re-use (or adaptive-use) projects are spotted throughout this book. But—to stay with New York City a while longer—there are few such projects more difficult to consider, few projects on such valuable land, few projects with as much potential for preserving the character of an area than the

Ezra Stoller © ESTO

Lever House (Skidmore Owings & Merrill's all-glass building of 1952) was a precursor of today's monochromatic glass towers—its green glass spandrels matched as closely to its green glass lights (Gordon Bunshaft says) as the technology of its time would allow.

Philip Morris Headquarters:
a design to relate to two very
different streets, to Grand
Central Station, and to the
public with a very special
amenity—a new museum

Philip Morris Incorporated
Headquarters
New York, New York
Architects: Ulrich Franzen
and Associates

A major feature of this new office tower is a 6000-square-foot, 42-foot-high pedestrian gallery which will house a new branch of the Whitney Museum of American Art. Architect Franzen designed the gallery in cooperation with the museum—and the design and operation of the museum will be funded by the building owners. The gallery will have entrances from both 42nd Street and Park Avenue—across the street from Grand Central. The two major elevations are very different—designed to relate to the very different characters of Park and 42nd Street, with emphasis on "not competing" with the Beaux Arts station.

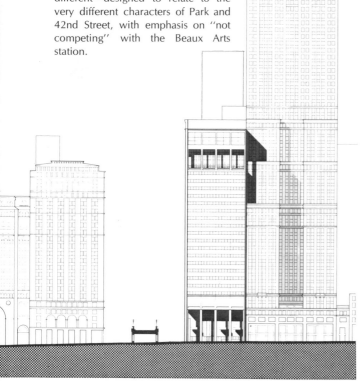

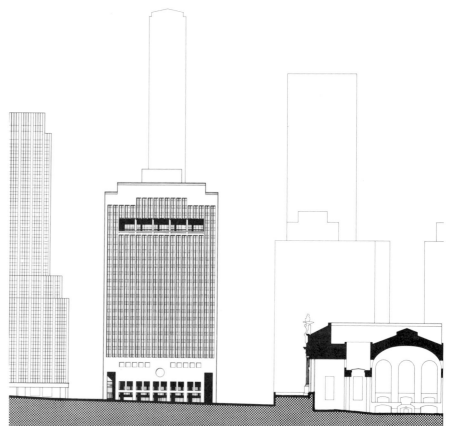

proposal (shown on pages 238–241) for saving the Radio City Music Hall, one of the centerpieces of New York's "core" public amenity, Rockefeller Center. As RECORD associate editor Barclay Gordon wrote in his thoughtful article: "The implications of (saving Radio City Music Hall) go far beyond a single landmark or even a single city or state."

He wrote: "Among the first problems that the Davis Brody proposal had to confront was how to bring a 35-story office or mixed-use tower down on top of an existing stage house

and auditorium. In order to deep the sightlines unobstructed and to leave the auditorium's landmark interior intact, the tower loads are designed to be distributed over two pairs of massive concrete columns. There 10- by 10-foot elements are carefully located at either side of the stage and at opposite sides of the promenade areas between the lobby and the auditorium. The columns will support post-tensioned perimeter beams that are 35 feet deep (see drawing page 241). Above the platform created by this arrangement, a tower of con-

ventional steel design rises to occupy the airspace between the adjoining AMAX and Associated Press buildings to the west and east respectively. The connection to the Associated Press Building is comparatively uncomplicated since the A.P. Building rises only four floors above the roof of the Music Hall. However, the new tower's relationship with the AMAX Building, a much taller structure, is somewhat more problematic.

"Davis Brody's proposal envisions a slender, 22-story atrium space between the two struc-

Georgia-Pacific Center
Atlanta, Georgia
Architects: Skidmore,
Owings & Merrill

On the Peachtree Street side, this 52-story tower rises a sheer 730 feet from the entrance plaza. On the other side, the vertical and horizontal setbacks create office floors ranging from 40,000 to 17,000 square feet. The setbacks of the tower are echoed in the design of the attached low-rise building (photo left) that will house the computer center above ground-floor retail space.

In smaller cities, zoning and economics seem to permit more flexible design—like this stepped-back tower in Atlanta...

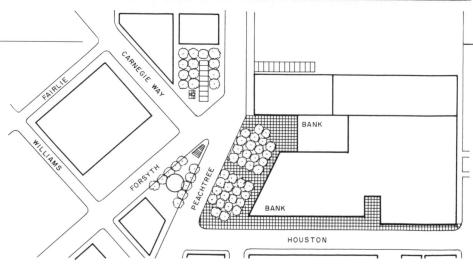

tures, an atrium with a garden and a fountain at its base. Though the atrium will appear from outside as no more than a vertical ribbon of glass spacing the two buildings apart, the proposed tower's lower floors would be stepped back to give the atrium space some horizontal dimension.

"The base of the atrium is, of course, part of the transfer floor or 'garden lobby' with connections to both adjoining buildings and access to the tower above. Raymond Hood's original conception had visualized an aerial

State Compensation Insurance Fund
Headquarters
San Francisco, California
Architects: John Carl Warnecke
and Associates

The stepped-back design of this 17-story office building provides numerous "sky gardens" for the occupants, with changing foliage visible from the street. An open landscaped plaza covering nearly half the site has a two-tiered pool, a redwood grove, seating spaces—and an open stair leading directly from the plaza to a public cafeteria on the second floor.

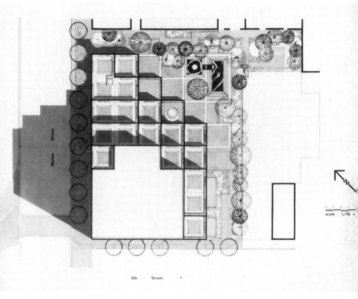

... and this "building block" design in San Francisco that creates terraces for occupants and passersby

garden on the roof of the A.P. Building. Davis Brody propose to realize this earlier plan and make the new garden an outdoor extension of the 'garden lobby.' Restaurants and retail space will add further enrichment, making this lobby a remarkable and decidedly spectacular public space.

"The remaining problem—and in some ways the most vexing problem—was how to provide access to a structure set back from the street with a lobby that is fourteen floors over the sidewalk. A vertical discontinuity is, for

251

For all of the interest
in large-scale projects,
individual buildings
are still dominant....

McDonnell Douglas Tract III Office Complex
St. Louis, Missouri
Architects: Hellmuth, Obata & Kassabaum

This 870,000-square-foot office/computer center
is highly energy-efficient: the huge bank of computers heats the entire complex and energy required for cooling will be used at off-peak hours
and stored as cold water. Only 14 per cent of the
building is glazed; the walls are heavily insulated
aluminum panels.

all practical purposes, unavoidable. Several
schemes were examined. None was ideal. The
preferred solution proposes a series of external
elevators reached from 50th Street by escalators and carrying passengers to the 'garden
lobby' where they transfer to a conventional
elevator system that serves the tower. These
'observation elevators' would doubtless offer
an entrancing ride, but beyond that they would
offer high visibility and identification to a project so far removed from the street, a street
which makes many competing claims on the

attention of the passerby.

"If built as proposed, the new tower would
be sheathed in limestone and would be executed in finishes that so far as possible repli-
cate the materials used in Rockefeller Center.
In short, the materials would be those that
Hood himself would have selected.

"Landmark designation was bestowed on
the Music Hall during the period this proposal
was being developed, but many questions still
linger about how the Music Hall should be
'saved.' Not everyone is agreed, of course,

that a tall, revenue-generating tower can be
justified considering the heavy additional bur-
den it will inevitably place on services in the
Rockefeller Center district, services that are
already strained. But if such a structure is to be
built and if the necessary variances are forth-
coming to make the proposal attractive to developers, then the Davis Brody proposal is
worth close study. It approaches a difficult site
and task with exceptional sensitivity and the
kinds of spaces it envisions are exciting and
full of promise."

These buildings are all handsome, all appropriate to their function, all energy-conserving, all built to budget. This is still the bread and butter

Biochemical Sciences Building
Princeton University
Princeton, New Jersey
Architects: Davis, Brody and Associates

This laboratory building is simple in concept and an appropriate addition to the University's handsome campus. The plan very simply puts the general laboratory spaces, which will be most heavily used, around the periphery. A core of communal research spaces are massed in the center. All of the laboratory spaces are designed on a modular grid so that teams of two, four, six or twelve researchers can set up a team space of appropriate size with all of the required services easily tapped in.

Corning Glass Works Engineering Building
Corning, New York
Architects: Davis, Brody and Associates

This building, very different in form from the one above, has a similar appropriateness for its function—crisp, organized, giving importance to the work inside. Located adjacent to the company headquarters, it will house 800 people from six departments of the Manufacturing and Engineering Division in one place for improved communication and idea exchange. The 250,000 square feet of space, divided on three floors, is 20 per cent lab space, 80 per cent office. All spaces are lit not only by exterior windows but also by a skylit atrium central to the building and opening at either end as entrances.

This seminary building—on a site large enough that it can be handled as an "object" without special attention to context—is complex but clearly organized, totally contemporary but related to its New England surroundings

Hartford Seminary Foundation,
Hartford, Connecticut
Architect: Richard Meier and Associates

This building draws its complexity from a complex program—visitors and students enter through a small semi-protected courtyard that begins the separation of the spaces within from the pastoral site. The circulation leads to the chapel and beyond to the meeting room and library; there the building turns and the spaces change to private study rooms—almost like monastic cells. Yet from all of the spaces—through window panels large and small—there are glimpses of the outside. The building is of white porcelain enamel steel panels—a reflection of the generally white-painted New England surroundings.

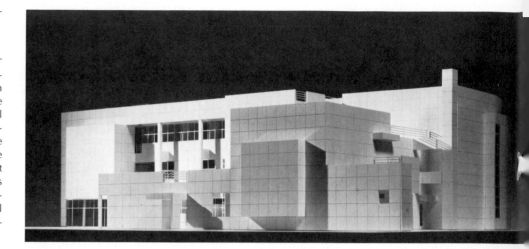

This final image of this book on the architecture of the 1970s serves well as a "closer"—it is a very beautiful building, and unlike many of the urban buildings shown on the preceding pages, it is an "object building"—designed without the constraints of close surroundings or limitations of site. This is the kind of building and scale that architects work with most often—and it sets a standard of quality that other architects, the client, its users, and the public can all admire. The building is the Hartford Seminary Foundation in Connecticut, set on a 20-acre pastoral suburban site. On a larger scale, it expresses many of the architectural concepts of Meier's houses (see also the caption above): A hierarchy of elements, a separation of public spaces and private spaces, and a kind of very rational and understandable complexity that grows out of the expression of those separate elements.

Of architecture (including his) as it has evolved through the 1970s, Meier says: "One of the basic things that has happened is a movement away from monumentality, toward concern with scale and relationship with human scale. Symbolism is becoming more important as we learn that a building has to signify more than simply a sense of its function. Hartford is therefore very complex in some ways, yet fairly simple in others. Its organization and circulation scheme are simple; yet it is articulated to try to convey a sense of varied spaces that respond to the varied ways people use the building. It is a deliberate attempt to communicate to users, to the client, to the public, and to architecture as an art form. It is intended to have

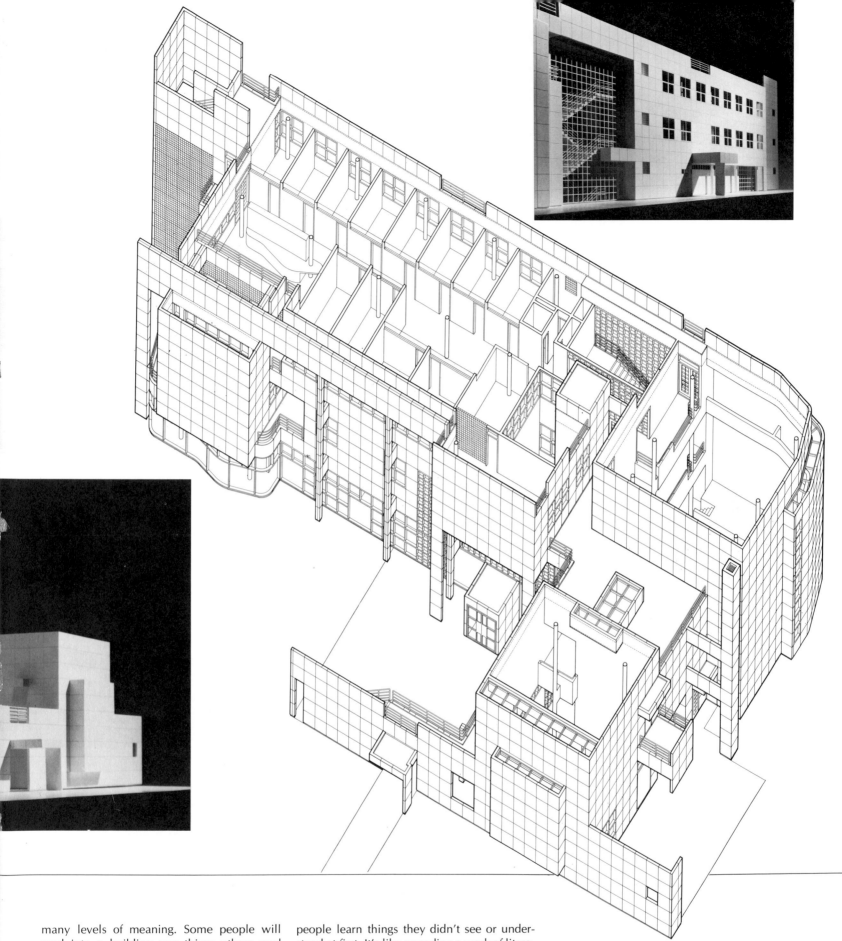

many levels of meaning. Some people will read into a building one thing; others read something else. What is important is for a building to communicate. Indeed, it is the impulse to broaden the ability of architecture to communicate to its audiences that is such a major issue today. One of the problems any architect is faced with is that his ideas and intentions as expressed in his design may not be communicated instantly—sometimes ideas take longer to be perceived. Perception is a constant reawakening—in a good building,

people learn things they didn't see or understand at first. It's like rereading a work of literature; you keep finding things, finding meanings, you hadn't found the first time.

"All this is complicated by increased public and client awareness of architecture. In some ways that helps; in other ways it forces you to fight more to reach a quality level that meets *your* standards as an architect. Some clients don't want the fight—don't want to make the effort to get quality.

"But I think there's no doubt that during the

1970s a much greater public awareness of architecture, and of the character of buildings and neighborhoods, emerged. And we architects have changed too—our historic perceptions are still there, but we are constantly seeing more and broadening our perceptions.

"I am very, very hopeful about architecture. The complexity and the problems are all part of it—part of our learning and part of our art. I wouldn't do anything else . . ."

INDEX

H

I

N

O

S

T

U

V

W

Y

Z